"In *An Introduction to Practical Theology*, one finds a vigorous presentation of the international scope of practical theology today, its grounding of the practice of communicating the gospel, and its relationship to a fast-changing and secularized social context. Students, practical theologians, pastors, and church leaders working in the field will benefit greatly from Grethlein's excellent work."

—CHRISTIAN B. SCHAREN, Vice President for Applied Research,
The Center for Theological Education, Auburn Theological Seminary

"English readers have good reason to welcome this book, translated and abridged from its original edition, for giving us a wonderful grasp of a German perspective on practical theology and an approach that is exceptional even in its own context, turning the discipline's attention from generic study of religion to a more focused exploration of how the 'gospel' is conveyed through teaching, celebrating, and instruction on living, modeled after Jesus' ministry."

—BONNIE J. MILLER-McLEMORE, E. Rhodes and Leona B. Carpenter
Professor of Religion, Psychology, and Culture, Vanderbilt University

"Keenly aware of the precariousness of the church today, Grethlein creatively urges practical theologians to focus on 'communicating the gospel'—exploring interactive encounters that can engage a wider range of participants through core, evocative practices of Christian faith. Such a proposal stretches us outward. From his German grounding of theology and praxis, Grethlein offers contemporary proposals that move beyond the conventional, ones that ought to stimulate our own thinking regardless of the location of our ministry and scholarship."

—JAMES NIEMAN, President, Lutheran School of Theology at Chicago

"Grethlein's *An Introduction to Practical Theology* is an important review and updating of the crucial topic of 'practical theology' for the theological world. His work expands the subject of practical theology by complexifying its longstanding attention to the contextual and practice-focused character of faith. Theological attention to the complexity of communication itself is a real gift, and while this practical theology is written from a German perspective, its insights are widely applicable."

—MARY McCLINTOCK FULKERSON, Professor of Theology,
Duke Divinity School

An Introduction to Practical Theology

*History, Theory, and the Communication
of the Gospel in the Present*

Christian Grethlein

Uwe Rasch, translator

BAYLOR UNIVERSITY PRESS

© 2016 by Baylor University Press
Waco, Texas 76798

Cover Design by Alyssa Stepien

Library of Congress Cataloging-in-Publication Data

Names: Grethlein, Christian, 1954– author. | Rasch, Uwe, translator.
Title: An introduction to practical theology : history, theory, and the
    communication of the gospel in the present / Christian Grethlein ; Uwe
    Rasch, translator.
Other titles: Praktische Theologie. English
Description: Waco, Texas : Baylor University Press, 2016. | Includes
    bibliographical references and index.
Identifiers: LCCN 2016003892 | ISBN 9781481305174 (pbk. : alk. paper) | ISBN
    9781481305198 (ebook-mobi/kindle) | ISBN 9781481305204 (web pdf)
Subjects: LCSH: Theology, Practical. | Communication—Religious
    aspects—Christianity. | Missions. | Evangelistic work.
Classification: LCC BV3.G6913 2016 | DDC 230—dc23
LC record available at http://lccn.loc.gov/2016003892

Printed in the United States of America on acid-free paper with a minimum of
30 percent post-consumer waste recycled content.

CONTENTS

PART 3
Methods for Communication of the Gospel

FOREWORD

This book is based on the textbook *Praktische Theologie* (de Gruyter: Berlin, Boston 2012; second, improved edition 2016).[1] This present version has been abridged to about half its original length and presents the fundamental principles of this discipline that is informed by the—hitherto only adumbrated—concept of the communication of the gospel while at the same time elaborating it. The reader who wishes to be informed in greater detail about the historical backdrop of Practical Theology or the specific ecclesial backgrounds in Germany is advised to consult the German version of this book, which also provides more detailed references to the German literature. In comparison, this version proposes a systematic and condensed conceptual groundwork for an internationally oriented Practical Theology, which would have to be elaborated to integrate regional ecclesial aspects. The reader is nonetheless advised to keep in mind that this book has been written from a German perspective, and that the pertinent issues are first and foremost discussed with reference to the German context. This not only reflects the formative background of

---

[1] First reactions to the first edition have been collected in Michael Domsgen and Bernd Schröder, eds., *Kommunikation des Evangeliums: Leitbegriff der Praktischen Theologie* (APrTh 57) (Leipzig, 2014).

the author, but also pays tribute to the fact that Practical Theology emerged in the German-speaking world and has been developed here for the past two hundred years.

My arguments are based on the observation that practical-theological theorizing and, in consequence, ecclesial praxis are encumbered with an imprecise terminology that impedes an accurate and theologically reflected perception of present-day reality. Therefore, considerable emphasis will here be placed on the exact definition of terms. Particularly the context from which a term originates needs to be heeded to avoid "zombie categories" (Ulrich Beck).[2] Such an approach at the same time offers new possibilities for the integration of biblical perspectives into practical-theological work more than has hitherto been the case. A context-sensitive, communication-theory-oriented analysis shows that particularly the example of Jesus' appearance, ministry, and destiny still contains high innovation potential for Practical Theology.

To encourage closer study, I have placed basic literature at the beginning of each section. In the subsequent pages it is then cited only parenthetically within the text, not in separate footnotes. All abbreviations for cited publications follow the encyclopedia *Religion Past and Present*.[3] As a rule, all quotations from German sources have been rendered into English. Italics or spaced lettering appearing in the original have not been adopted.

The German version of Practical Theology was enabled by a two-year opus magnum grant of the Volkswagen Foundation. The foundation also graciously provided the funds for the English translation, kindly undertaken by Uwe Rasch, M.A.

My thanks also go to Marcell Saß, who took over my teaching obligations for the duration of the opus magnum grant, and who provided the decisive impetus for the English translation; Michael Domsgen, Lutz Friedrichs, Jan Hermelink, Erhard Holze, Christhard Lück, Claudia Rüdiger, and Bernd Schröder, with each of whom I have been privileged to work in close collaboration for a number of years, and who are important dialog partners; my colleagues Martin Rothgangel and Robert Schelander from Vienna, my colleagues Wolfgang Drechsel, Johannes Eurich, Fritz Lienhard, and Helmut Schwier from Heidelberg, and my Catholic colleagues Reinhard Feiter and

[2] Approvingly quoted by John Reader, *Reconstructing Practical Theology: The Impact of Globalization* (Hampshire, 2008), 1.

[3] Hans Dieter Betz et al., eds., *Religion Past and Present: Encyclopedia of Theology and Religion*, 14 vols. (Leiden, 2007–2013), hereafter *RPP*.

Norbert Mette for illuminating discussions during the preparation of the book; my son Jonas Grethlein, whose literary and cultural-hermeneutical expertise provided invaluable insights.

Beate Hannig-Grethlein also supported me in the writing of this book. Through her admirable work in integrative and inclusive education she provided me with many relevant suggestions. The fact that she also shares my life never ceases to fill me with wonder and deep gratitude.

Münster, Westphalia, summer 2015
Christian Grethlein

INTRODUCTION

Practical Theology is facing two major new challenges:

First of all, the number of church members is declining. The facts of baptism and church membership are drifting apart. A growing number of people, partly church members, partly members of other religious communities, to a certain extent lead non-Christian lives informed by non-Christian values. In this situation, the conflation of church, Christianity, and religion, hitherto customary in Practical Theology, stands in the way of a discerning perception of present-day reality.

And second, the triumph of the new electronic media cannot be overlooked. The forms of communication that have thereby become possible alter our perceptions of reality, the way we live, and our forms of social interaction. Assumptions that have so far been taken for granted in Practical Theology need reviewing.

In these circumstances, the ecumenical phrase of the "communication of the gospel" offers the theoretical framework capable of a differentiated empirical analysis and theologically sound orientation for praxis. In keeping with its ecumenical origin, it does not presuppose any specific ecclesial conditions. It was Ernst Lange who introduced this phrase in the context of his program of German church reform.[1] In doing so, he pointed to the dialogic quality of what had thus far been referred to as "proclamation."

At the same time, the "communication of the gospel" incorporates the insights of theories that face up to the challenges posed by the processes of individualization and the resultant fragility of institutions. "Communication" is the key term here.[2] Advances in defining communication now allow a more sophisticated approach than Lange's. Furthermore, the related question of the social forms in which communication takes place has gathered momentum due to the recent development of media technology.

Empirically, the "communication of the gospel" goes further than "the church," which becomes less and less important due to its marginalization as an institution or organization. In this sense, the phrase responds to Dietrich Rössler's concept of contemporary forms of Christianity.[3] In a new context, it will however be formulated differently, that is, in terms of communication theory. The instituting question of the communication sciences is: "How is communication possible?"[4] To answer this question, all communication theories offered from diverse disciplinary perspectives concentrate on the observable. They zero in on observable interactions—as opposed to the customary focus on subject and belief with their empirically nonvalidatable introspection.

Theologically, the "communication of the gospel" designates, more precisely than the term "religion," the subject of practical-theological reflection; clearly, the "gospel" forms the center of Christian belief. Non-Christian religious praxis will be taken into consideration insofar as it contributes to the understanding of present forms of communicating the gospel. Moreover, the "communication of the gospel" easily connects with contemporary theology. In an advanced encyclopedic reflection, Ingolf Dalferth defines Protestant

---

[1] See Ernst Lange, "Versuch einer Bilanz," in *Kirche für die Welt: Aufsätze zur Theorie kirchlichen Handelns*, ed. Rüdiger Schloz (Munich, 1981), 101–29.

[2] See Horst Firsching, "Warum 'Kommunikation'? Auf welche Problemstellungen reagieren kommunikationstheoretische Ansätze in der Soziologie—insbesondere in der Religionssoziologie?," in *Religion als Kommunikation*, Religion in der Gesellschaft 4, ed. Hartmann Tyrell, Volkhard Krech, and Hubert Knoblauch (Würzburg, 1998), 187–240.

[3] See Dietrich Rössler, *Grundriß der Praktischen Theologie* (Berlin, 1986), 79–83.

[4] Klaus Beck, *Kommunikationswissenschaft* (Konstanz, 2007), 150. All translations of German quoted material are by the translator unless otherwise noted.

Theology as an "interpretational praxis of communicating the gospel."[5] The gospel as the center of Christian faith reveals itself to people through communication. Similarly, traditional dogmatic terms such as "doctrine," "word of God," or "proclamation" indicate forms of communication. They are, however, oriented along the lines of a scientifically outmoded one-track sender-receiver model, thus impeding accurate perception and consequently appropriate action. At the same time, the concept of "communicating the gospel" establishes the connections between Practical Theology and all other theological disciplines.

To understand what "gospel" means one has to refer back to the Bible. This biblical term is connected in a variety of ways with other biblical themes and concepts. Moreover, the Christian history of (partly erroneous) interpretations of the Gospels need to be called to mind to make the insights and findings thus gained in the scholarly investigation of the Bible productive for present-day challenges. Also, the doctrinal and practical interpretations in dogmatics and ethics need to be considered to the extent in which they critically reflect and assist the ongoing process of interpretation.

With regard to Practical Theology, recourse to "communication" helps integrate the traditional perspective of Pastoral Theology, now, however, considering the changed situation of the pastoral profession. On the one hand, it should be quite clear that ministry today essentially means interaction (as opposed to one-way instruction). On the other hand, it remains in view that communicating the gospel is not the sole prerogative of ministry.

Combining theology with communication science, the concept of communication opens up a wide range of opportunities for multiperspectival approaches to the issues and tasks of Practical Theology. In this sense, Practical Theology is "fundamental"[6] for Protestant Theology if it wishes to accomplish the Reformers' mission of mediation.[7]

To summarize, Practical Theology elaborates theories for the understanding of communicating the gospel. It is not the praxis itself, but critical

[5] Ingolf Dalferth, *Evangelische Theologie als Interpretationspraxis: Eine systematische Orientierung* (ThLZ.F 11/12) (Leipzig, 2004), 53–128.

[6] Here I build on the practical-theological concept of Don Browning, *A Fundamental Practical Theology: Descriptive and Strategic Proposals* (Minneapolis, 1996 [1991]).

[7] See Christian Grethlein, "Theologie und Didaktik: Einige grundsätzliche Verhältnisbestimmungen," *ZThK* 104 (2007), 503–25.

reflection on praxis.[8] This characteristic of Practical Theology is cogently expressed in the theoretical concept of communication. Practical Theology is—as the etymology of the term "theory" (Gr. *observation*) indicates—constitutionally concerned with concrete praxis.

[8] See Friedrich Schleiermacher, *Die praktische Theologie nach den Grundsätzen der evangelischen Kirche im Zusammenhange dargestellt*, ed. Jacob Frerichs (Berlin, 1850), 12.

PART 1

Historical Introduction to Practical Theology

With regard to its genesis, Practical Theology is a "regional science."[1] Its development had for a long time been (largely) confined to the German-speaking world. Similar problems were of course addressed in other parts of the world, but it was only in German theology that a proper theory was elaborated seeking to integrate all the different ecclesial fields of praxis conceptually. There are several likely reasons for this development: the secure position of theology at German universities, and its diversification of disciplines at the turn of the nineteenth century to the twentieth; the particular relationship of church and state in Germany; the German two-church system, which allowed both churches the development of state-like structures.

It was only in the second half of the twentieth century that a homegrown variety of Practical Theology was developed in the United States.[2] Some of

---

[1] Friedrich Schweitzer, "Praktische Theologie in Nordamerika," in *Geschichte der Praktischen Theologie—Dargestellt anhand ihrer Klassiker* (APrTh 12), ed. Christian Grethlein and Michael Meyer-Blanck (Leipzig, 1999), 565–96, 565.

[2] See, for an overview, Bonnie Miller-McLemore, "The Contributions of Practical Theology," in *The Wiley-Blackwell Companion to Practical Theology*, ed. Miller-McLemore (Chichester, 2012), 1–20.

these pastoral or ecclesial fields of praxis underwent in part rather tempestuous changes, particularly in the area of hospital chaplaincy. The overall practical-theological perspective, however, was not able to attract much attention. Praxis-oriented theology, on the other hand, could stake out greater claims than in Germany.

Furthermore, for a long time it was primarily in Protestant Theology that the discipline of Practical Theology found a home. In the first half of the nineteenth century, under the auspices of the Enlightenment, there were only some forays into similar approaches in Catholic Theology. They were, by the token of a papal renunciation of the general cultural developments as expressed in the *Syllabus* (1864), the dogma of papal infallibility (1870), and the supremacy of neo-Scholastic Theology, pragmatically reduced to canon law and liturgy. Only with opening up in the course of the Second Vatican Council did an independent Practical Theology within the Catholic Church start to emerge.

Owing to the significantly different origins of Practical Theology in the United States and its slower emergence in Catholic Theology, I will treat these developments separately in chapter 2, focusing on the comparative aspects pertinent to the development of an international Practical Theology.

A budding interdenominational internationalization of Practical Theology seems to take form in new projects such as the International Academy of Theology[3] and the *Journal of Practical Theology*.[4] Both emerged in the 1990s, thus belonging to the more recent developments of the discipline.

For the time being, however, it still seems difficult to push forward to a concerted formation of a comprehensive theoretical basis that would integrate practical-theological work in different countries and across different denominations. This can for example be studied in the "international reports" of the *International Journal of Practical Theology*, which give insight into the practical-theological work in different countries and regions. These reports primarily reveal the differences. Transnational or cross-cultural projects, on the other hand, are generally missing. In terms of science theory, the reason for this is to be found in the contextuality of practical-theological reflection.

---

[3] For their objectives, see Don Browning, "The Idea of the International Academy of Practical Theology," in *Practical Theology—International Perspectives*, ed. Friedrich Schweitzer and Johannes van der Ven (Erfahrung und Theologie. Schriften zur Praktischen Theologie 34) (Frankfurt, 1999), 157–64.

[4] For their objectives, see *IJPT* 1 (1997), 1–5.

Thus, the historical development of Practical Theology reveals the essential insight of the theory of communicating the gospel, which will be elaborated in the second part of this book: the gospel is communicated in concrete contexts. For this very reason, all pertinent theorizing is regionally determined. General terms such as "religion" or "society" seem to imply a more comprehensive theoretical claim, but they obscure this basic characteristic of communication. At the same time, the obvious tendencies toward globalization warrant the internationalization of the present practices of practical-theological theory.

1

PRACTICAL THEOLOGY
IN GERMANY

The development of Practical Theology as an independent theological discipline in the nineteenth century happened along convoluted paths. It is not
possible to give an exact date for the emergence of this late theological discipline. Its concerns reach back to the early Christian era and have been treated
in a wide stream of pastoral theological writings.[1] Only at the beginning of
the nineteenth century did an independent theological discipline emerge from
this, establishing itself within two important contexts: first, within the encyclopedic definition of theology, resulting from the general differentiation of
the sciences; and, second, within the reform of academic theological studies
and of the formal training of pastors that seemed necessary to bridge the distance between everyday life and doctrine-based pastoral practice.

The emergence of Practical Theology was closely linked with major political, social, and cultural changes challenging churches and theology. Ecclesial
traditions, institutions, and practices were no longer in sync with the times.
Practical Theology is a theological attempt to deal with this critical situation

---

[1] Compare the list of the most important works in Uta Pohl-Patalong, "Pastoraltheologie," in *Praktische Theologie: Eine Theorie- und Problemgeschichte*, ed. Christian Grethlein and
Helmut Schwier (APrTh 33) (Leipzig, 2007), 515–74, 519–24.

constructively. A similar process could be observed with regard to society as a new sizeable factor, and the subsequent emergence sociology as a new discipline.[2]

To this day, the crisis concept has been the driving force of Practical Theology. It defines its concerns from the perspective of crises, that is, problematic situations that require innovative action. In concrete terms, three such "crises" mark the stages of practical-theological theory formation: first of all, the political, social, and cultural changes since the beginning of the nineteenth century; next, the challenges of "modernity" at the turn of the nineteenth century to the twentieth; and finally, the diverse reform efforts since the end of the 1960s.

In this manner, practical-theological work is constantly informed by the present situation, principally turning its attention to difficulties and social injustices. When reading practical-theological literature, this lopsided focus must be kept in mind to avoid adopting a distorted, negatively biased view of the circumstances.

1. Challenges in the History of German Practical Theology

Literature: Volker Drehsen, *Neuzeitliche Konstitutionsbedingungen der Praktischen Theologie: Aspekte der theologischen Wende zur soziokulturellen Lebenswelt christlicher Religion*, 2 vols. (Gütersloh, 1988); Christian Grethlein and Michael Meyer-Blanck, eds., *Geschichte der Praktischen Theologie: Dargestellt anhand ihrer Klassiker* (APrTh 12) (Leipzig, 1999); Christian Grethlein and Helmut Schwier, eds., *Praktische Theologie: Eine Theorie- und Problemgeschichte* (APrTh 33) (Leipzig, 2007)

The Beginnings in the Nineteenth Century

Looking back today, the expansion of theology by a practical discipline seems only consequential. Its task was to integrate lifeworld changes into theological discourse. At the same time, the alignment of changing ecclesial praxis and theological bodies of knowledge and thus their Christian identity had to be

---

[2] See the overview in Bernhard Schäfers, "Sociology: II. History," *RPP* 12 (2012), 117–18.

ensured. However, it took nearly a hundred years to establish the independence and singularity of this task.

In this context, the emergence of Practical Theology in Germany during the first half of the nineteenth century can be appreciated only by recalling the major political, social, and cultural as well as the ecclesial and theological upheavals of that period:

First, in 1806, after a period of nearly a thousand years, the Roman Empire of the German Nation came to an end. From the hundreds of princedoms, dukedoms, and so on, a confederation of at first thirty-nine, then forty-one states emerged. Whereas before Catholics and Protestants had lived in different states, for the first time denominational plurality made itself felt in everyday life.

Second, the demographics during that period changed dramatically. The old empire contained roughly thirty million people at the end of the eighteenth century, in 1865 there were already fifty-two million.[3] This required a new social order, also in the church.

Third, traditional estate-based society was transformed into a civil society. Accomplishment and profession replaced status based on lineage.[4]

Fourth, and connected with these developments, the process of individualization emerged as another important factor transforming religious life and the church. Beginning in the upper strata of the social order, it continued its way into other social groups.

In addition, further major cultural changes exerted their impacts: since the beginning of the nineteenth century, church and Christianity had been drifting apart. Scientific discoveries were putting pressure on theology. The philosophical demolition of metaphysics called for new rationales for Christianity and religious praxis. A second major wave of change was produced by the triumph of historicism at German universities, casting doubt on the hitherto unquestioned implicitness of traditions. In the wake, basic religious assumptions were also put into perspective.

To take up these and further challenges, time-honored dogmatics proved inadequate. A new field of theology opened up that would respond to these challenges: Practical Theology. Important catalysts of this movement were

---

[3] Thomas Nipperdey, *Deutsche Geschichte 1800–1866: Bürgerwelt und starker Staat*, 5th ed. (Munich, 1991 [1983]), 102.

[4] See Nipperdey, *Deutsche Geschichte*, 255.

Friedrich Schleiermacher's encyclopedic work,[5] which defined theology as a positive science with a constitutive function regarding the governing body of the church; the Practical Theology of Carl Immanuel Nitzsch,[6] which developed the church as starting point and subject of Practical Theology; and, finally, the ethics-based Pastoral Theology of Christian Palmer.[7]

However, the oft-cited characterization of Schleiermacher as the "founding father of practical theology as a science"[8] is only partly true. Indeed, based on his idea of a theology integrated by its practical task (of church leadership), Schleiermacher arrived at the necessity of a practical discipline. His idea, however, was to consign it merely to the application of the knowledge that would be furnished by the other theological disciplines.

Thus, Practical Theology emerged during the nineteenth century. It set out to deal academically and theologically with the challenges posed by the political, social, cultural, and religious changes. Even in Nitzsch it became clear that this was not only a methodological challenge but one that requires a specifically theological, a practical-theological, effort. Right from the start, the chief concerns of Practical Theology were the church and its praxis. Here, it follows in the footsteps of traditional Pastoral Theology, if pastoral praxis is seen as an important expression of ecclesial praxis. At the same time, it reaches beyond pastoral care since ecclesial praxis clearly is not exhausted by pastoral duties. Two alternatives offer themselves in the approaches to the concrete relation with the church: Nitzsch's dogmatic and Palmer's ethical orientation. Nitzsch's solution, which asserted itself first, put the life and praxis orientation of practical-theological work second to dogmatic regulations and, later, historical elaborations. This historical accent helped Practical Theology underscore its academic rigor when historicism had gained a foothold. The price was a removal from the reality of practice.

---

[5]   See Friedrich Schleiermacher, *Kurze Darstellung des theologischen Studiums zum Behuf einleitender Vorlesungen*, ed. Hans Scholz (Darmstadt, 1973).

[6]   See Carl Immanuel Nitzsch, *Praktische Theologie*, vol. 1 (Bonn, 1847).

[7]   See Christian Palmer, "Zur praktischen Theologie," *JDTh* 1 (1856), 317–61.

[8]   Ernst Christian Achelis, *Lehrbuch der Praktischen Theologie*, vol. 1 (Leipzig, [3]1911), 14.

Empirical Incentives—At the Beginning
of the Twentieth Century

In the course of the reform efforts concerning church and (the study of) theology at the threshold of the nineteenth and twentieth centuries, Practical Theology developed a distinct profile.[9] In view of the social and cultural changes and the pastoral duties under changed ecclesial conditions, the empirical approach proved to be the most efficient.

Holistic concepts of life, as in the form of guild laws, receded. The concomitant process of individualization, which started to reach lower social classes, caused widespread insecurity with regard to proper conduct of life. At the same time, new empirical sciences began to establish themselves: psychology, sociology, and ethnology. In the natural sciences, disciplines diversified. In the medical field, for example, different medical disciplines emerged, and in each of these different chairs each pursued increasingly differentiated research goals. Also, the relevance of theology in universities decreased. The year 1914 saw the first foundation of a German university without a theological faculty (Frankfurt; 1919 Hamburg). And finally, at the cultural level, the youth movement at the end of the German Empire began to establish a critical stance toward civilization, which has accompanied social development ever since. Particularly the sons and daughters of the protestant-liberal bourgeoisie set the agenda. Equally, in the field of religion, the search for viable forms of experience was on.

Practical Theology reacted to these and other challenges by expanding its repertoire. New practical-theological disciplines, religious ethnology, church studies, and religious psychology, broadened its horizon and scope. Research in these fields required cooperation with other disciplines, such as ethnology, psychology, and sociology. However, for an interdisciplinary Practical Theology of this kind, no methodological toolkit has yet been created.

The disaster of the First World War led to a reappraisal within Protestant Theology, which was fundamentally opposed to the fresh start envisioned by Practical Theology. The (aimed-for) exclusive focus on the word of God allowed no room for an independent, empirical Practical Theology interested in culture and successful communication. As a result, between 1930 and 1965, the discipline largely fell into a deep sleep. In the context of the more recent

---

[9]   A seminal read: Paul Drews, *Das Problem der Praktischen Theologie: Zugleich ein Beitrag zur Reform des theologischen Studiums* (Tübingen, 1910).

liturgical movement, a sideline of Practical Theology attempted to adopt an aesthetical approach. However, it failed to assert itself against the prevailing dogmatic word-of-God theology. Other practical theologians were beguiled by national socialist ideology.

Overall, the further development and the increasing emigration of the church from society clearly show the price to be paid by a theology that eclipses the empirical approach of Practical Theology: remoteness from life and, therefore, insignificance.

Nontheological Impulses—In the Last Third of the Twentieth Century

After the interlude of the word-of-God theology, the (second) empirical turn of the 1960s and 1970s reconnected Practical Theology again with the developments in nontheological studies. As before, radical changes in state, society, and culture now affected the church and the religious outlook of people,[10] and required practical-theological reflection. There were the horrors of the Vietnam War, which had been escalating since 1963, and which television brought right into people's living rooms. This fueled people's fears, also fanned by the arms race between the United States and Soviet Union. In 1973 the unprecedented rise of oil prices marked a major watershed. The limitedness of natural resources and the concomitant ecological challenges have been a central issue of social discourse ever since. Simultaneously, beginning in the 1960s, a growing pluriformity became evident with regard to individual lifestyle choices. It was not least the influence of the foreign workers who had been recruited by German industry since 1955 who helped put the customary predominant middle-class lifestyle into perspective. With the influx of Turkish migrants, Islam took root in Germany. Religion, hitherto clearly synonymous with Christianity, became a problematic term. And finally, beginning at the end of the 1960s, churches were faced with a constant loss of membership, which, among other things, weakened them financially. Theologically, the word-of-God theology failed to persuade because it opposed a differentiated perception of people's needs. The churches, however, increasingly resorted to empirical instruments to capture their members' attitudes and criticisms.

[10] See Thomas Grossbölting, *Der verlorene Himmel: Glaube in Deutschland seit 1945* (Göttingen, 2013).

In this context practical-theological research earned new recognition. The reception of socioempirical methods helped individual research projects in Practical Theology gain independence, particularly in the fields of pastoral-psychological counseling and religious education at school. Various influences from the United States amplified this tendency because the U.S. clergyman's training focuses on individual assignment-specific forms of praxis as opposed to general practical-theological theory formation.

Three important textbooks managed to pool practical-theological research while at the same time integrating the diverging individual studies. In the first of these, following the paradigm of sciences of action, Karl-Fritz Daiber[11] focused on the practical requirements of the theological and clerical professions. He recommended conceiving Practical Theology as the theory of its own practice. In addition, he wished to limit the scope of Practical Theology for reasons of methodology. The second, by Dietrich Rössler,[12] is such a theory for the pastoral profession. However, Rössler solved the problem of describing the subject area by drawing on the differentiations from the theory of Christianity. In this way, he could, on the one hand, integrate extant practical-theological forms of theory with their ecclesial connections and the requirements of the pastor. On the other hand, he also broadened the view to include the processes of pluralization and individualization. His concrete suggestions, however, remained restricted to the pastoral-theological outlook. In his textbook, Gert Otto[13] took a conceptually more radical approach. He left the previous ecclesial paradigm of Practical Theology behind and drafted a Critical Theory between the poles of society and religion. Rejecting the commonly accepted sectoral architecture of Practical Theology, he recommended a perspectival approach. Similar to Rössler, he did however not attempt to answer the methodological questions that his suggestions begged.

A closer look at these concepts reveals that the weaknesses of one mark the strengths of the other. First, opening up for fresh perspectives (Otto) broadens the scope for Practical Theology, but at the same time threatens to destroy its systematic coherence (Rössler). Second, clear job orientation (Daiber) allows methodological precision, but narrows the scope. And finally, as

---

[11] See Karl-Fritz Daiber, *Grundriß der Praktischen Theologie als Handlungswissenschaft* (GT.P 23) (Munich, 1977).

[12] See Dietrich Rössler, *Grundriß der Praktischen Theologie* (Berlin, ²1994 [1986]).

[13] See Gert Otto, *Praktische Theologie*, 2 vols. (Munich, 1986–1988).

the (exclusive) point of reference for Practical Theology, the church seems to be too limited (Otto), society, on the other hand, too broad (Rössler). And yet, Daiber, Rössler, and Otto were trying to come to grips with the very same problem: how to describe the subject matter of Practical Theology within the context of a pluralistic society.

2. The Current Situation of Practical Theology in Germany: Struggling for Its Subject

Literature: Wilfried Engemann, *Personen, Zeichen und das Evangelium: Argumentationsmuster der Praktischen Theologie* (APrTh 23) (Leipzig, 2003); Wolf-Eckart Failing and Hans-Günter Heimbrock, "Von der Handlungs-theorie zur Wahrnehmungstheorie und zurück," in *Gelebte Religion wahrneh-men: Lebenswelt–Alltagskultur–Religionspraxis*, ed. Wolf-Eckart Failing and Hans-Günter Heimbrock (Stuttgart, 1998), 275–94; Wilhelm Gräb, *Lebensgeschichten–Lebensentwürfe–Sinndeutungen: Eine praktische Theologie gelebter Religion* (Gütersloh, 1998); Albrecht Grözinger, *Praktische Theologie und Ästhetik: Ein Beitrag zur Grundlegung der Praktischen Theologie* (Munich, 1987); Manfred Josuttis, *Religion als Handwerk: Zur Handlungslogik spirituel-ler Methoden* (Gütersloh, 2002)

The current state of the debate in German Practical Theology can be under-stood only in its context. All of its practical-theological concepts are united in their effort to face up to the changes, however, in fairly different ways.

Context

Political and social: The dissolution of the Eastern Bloc only briefly gave rise to the hope for a peaceful global community. As early as 1993, political scientist Samuel Huntington had caused a stir with his *Foreign Affairs* article "The Clash of Civilizations," a thesis that he extended to book length in 1996: "In the post–Cold War world, the most important distinctions among people are not ideological, political, or economic. They are cultural."[14] And: "The rivalry of the superpowers is replaced by the clash of civilizations."[15] This brought

---

[14] Samuel Huntington, *The Clash of Civilizations and the Remaking of World Order* (New York, 1996), 21, quoted from the paperback edition of 2003.

[15] Huntington, *Clash*, 28.

religion into the sphere of political debate. Indeed, at the very latest with the media attention paid to the Twin Towers and Pentagon attacks on September 11, 2001, a new conflict began to dominate the headlines, which, in the general discussion, still today boils down to the controversial question: is Islam a threat to Western civilization? This debate became dramatically heated when the United States and its allies invaded Iraq. The equally controversial American military intervention in Afghanistan is also fraught with problems of Islamic fundamentalism.

Since then, the dialog between the religions is top of the political agenda, particularly since the local Islamic populations—to the surprise of many Europeans—identify the Western troops as "Christians." The programmatic use of the term "crusade" in the speeches of then–U.S. president George W. Bush only helped to reinforce this impression.

A few years after the al-Qaeda attacks, the financial breakdown of major banks—and states—shook the economic world and led to a global financial crisis. The hitherto unchallenged economic prosperity of the wealthy nations seems to be fundamentally at stake, entailing disastrous consequences for the poor countries. Thinking about the future can no longer be shelved. In the days after the collapse of the Lehman Brothers investment bank, a *New York Times* front-page headline implored: "Confidence."

This is equally true for ecological issues. Reputable scientists agree that climate change is largely caused by human action. In some regions, these changes have already begun to imperil the lives of people: the increase of adverse weather and floods, droughts, and prolonged spells of heat are among them, just as changes to vegetation and the extinction of animal species. In connection with the global economic problems sketched above, we here witness incalculable conflict potential for future generations in the making. This is particularly true of the issue of energy production. The Japanese nuclear disaster of Fukushima in March 2011 again—twenty-five years after Chernobyl—brought drastically home how fragile modern civilization is.

Cultural: The political and social changes sketched above are necessarily accompanied by cultural changes. Overall, received notions have become rather brittle. Quests reflecting this situation are particularly evident in contemporary *art*. Styles are blended, the past quoted and recontextualized, and so on. Electronic data processing engenders new forms and effects, ranging from installations through music and sound to theater and performance through to feature films. Overall, an intimate connection between art and economics can be observed. The aesthetics of advertising photography, for instance, have a palpable influence in other fields. Religious themes feature regularly. The complex and rich, and sometimes competitive, relationship between art and religion also feeds into this phenomenon.[16]

At the same time, the discussion about the social impact of cultural diversity is gathering momentum. For some time, the German government tried to address this problem in their integration policies for immigrants by ignoring the religious factor, for example, in education by introducing intercultural education. In view of the fact that integration seems particularly difficult for immigrants with an Islamic background, this approach proved to be inadequate. Accordingly, religious issues now feature more prominently in the public debates on integration or inclusion.

Finally, computers are increasingly ruling everyday life. Initiated by the U.S. Department of Defense in 1969 as a tool to connect different research sites, transformed in 1993 by the launch of the first publicly accessible browser into the World Wide Web, the Internet ("interconnected networks") created new communication possibilities. Access to a mushrooming wealth of information as well as the emerging new forms of interaction have fundamentally change everyday life, science, and politics. New social forms have emerged, also in the field of religion.

Theological: The marginalization of the great Christian churches in the public sphere and the individual lives of people and, simultaneously, the media-fueled debate on the question of religion have their repercussions on theology as an academic discipline: on the one hand, future pastors and religious instructors need to have a good knowledge about non-Christian life plans and values. Accordingly, theological faculties establish chairs for religious studies; in other instances, denomination is combined with Intercultural Theology. On the other hand, nondenominational religious studies[17] is establishing itself as a third discipline next to the denominational theologies. This new discipline receives a tremendous boost from the new issues globalization has given rise to. Furthermore, departments and chairs for Islamic Theology are instituted to train teachers for Islamic instruction in German schools and imams for Muslim communities in Germany. Interreligious

---

[16] See Christian Albrecht, "Kunst und Religion: Ein Forschungsüberblick," *IJPT* 8 (2004), 251–87.

[17] See Sigurd Hjelde, *Die Religionswissenschaft und das Christentum: Eine historische Untersuchung über das Verhältnis von Religionswissenschaft und Theologie* (Leiden, 1994).

perspectives are thus institutionalized at German universities and pose a challenge to Practical Theology.

Practical Theology: Establishing a Profile

The two textbooks by Gert Otto and Dietrich Rössler were two 1980s landmark blueprints for German Practical Theology, and they remain valid today. The past twenty-five years, however, have seen some new foci and points of departure, although none have as yet yielded such elaborate and commanding concepts. The most important of these concepts are discussed in the following.

Manfred Josuttis (b. 1936): Josuttis opened up new, if controversial, horizons for the whole field of Practical Theology. Only five years into his teaching post, he published the much used "Introduction to the Basic Questions of Present-Day Practical Theology."[18] In this, he singled out three "crucial shortcomings" of Practical Theology: pastoral-theological reductionism, a deficiency in empirical research, and the lack of a conclusive theoretical framework for Practical Theology.[19]

Following the phenomenological design of philosopher Hermann Schmitz from the University of Kiel, Josuttis criticizes the hermeneutical approaches common to Practical Theology. His point of departure is "the reality of the holy" (Josuttis, *Religion als Handwerk*, 31) in the present. If this is the case, religion—according to Schmitz—is "acting from being affected with the Divine" (79).[20] Since this reality is dangerous, it is in need of an expert guide to "the hidden, and latterly also forbidden, zone of the holy," that is, the pastor.[21] For this expedition, specific expedients are necessary (see 21–31). For their development, Josuttis opens up the horizon toward religious studies. In concrete terms, the Divine, or God, expresses itself in the form of "energies"—a concept[22] already familiar from medieval orthodox theology. Referring to the

---

[18] Manfred Josuttis, *Praxis des Evangeliums zwischen Politik und Religion: Grundprobleme der Praktischen Theologie* (Munich, 1974), 11.

[19] See Josuttis, *Praxis*, 11.

[20] With reference to Hermann Schmitz, *Das Göttliche und der Raum: System der Philosophie* III/4 (Bonn, 1977), 11.

[21] Manfred Josuttis, *Die Einführung in das Leben* (Gütersloh, 1996), 18 (similarly reiterated on 34, 50, 67, 85, 102, 119, 135, 152).

[22] Referring to the Athos monk and later patriarch Gregorios Palamas (1296–1359); see Manfred Josuttis, *Segenskräfte: Potentiale einer energetischen Seelsorge* (Gütersloh, 2000), 40, 60, 215–16.

Divine in this manner produces a particular kind of religious methodology (see 81). The practices implemented here follow the logic of physical exercise, structuring Josuttis' argument:

> It begins with preparing the body through ascetic exercise. This is followed by the invocation of the Godhead through prayer. In this way, people, places and objects will receive the kind of consecration that will allow for religious acts of sacrifice. The vital energy resulting from this can be spent in blessing in such a manner that, through a specific kind of concentration, even physical healing processes can be induced. (17)

Josuttis insistently poses the question of the understanding of reality and of religion guiding Practical Theology. Emphatically, he argues the case for the reality of Divine Power. It does not exist in the interpretation of interpersonal and inner-worldly events, but has an autonomous quality, which, for instance, reveals itself in visions. His religio-phenomenological approach integrates many traditions from Christian history and the present longing for immediate experience. Pithily summed up, however, Josuttis' is an elitist theory in pastoral-theological guise. Only painstaking spiritual work full of privation will provide access to the Divine Mystery. The Enlightenment's critical objections to a separate world remain unheeded.

Wilhelm Gräb (b. 1948): The fundamental cultural changes and modern man's quest for meaning they have brought about are Gräb's points of departure. He radically opposes the idea of a wholly other world. His guiding key term for practical theology is "interpretation." The purpose of religion and church is to assist a reading of reality for meaning. Reflecting on this, Practical Theology will come across other modes of interpretation and meaning, which it should try to integrate. Modernity itself develops "religion-productive tendencies" (Gräb, *Lebensgeschichten–Lebensentwürfe–Sinndeutungen*, 32), which Practical Theology needs to absorb on a theoretical level, the church and pastors on a practical level. In this manner, Gräb opens Practical Theology wide for aesthetical questions, not least the media landscape.[23]

---

[23] Elaborated in Wilhelm Gräb, *Sinn fürs Unendliche: Religion in der Mediengesellschaft* (Gütersloh, 2002); also see the dissertation supervised by Gräb: Jörg Herrmann, *Sinnmaschine Kino: Sinndeutung und Religion im populären Film* (PThK 4) (Gütersloh, 2001).

Gräb defines Practical Theology as "a practical theory of Protestant culture."[24] Within the "cultural studies of Christianity,"[25] it functions as the practical discipline, while simultaneously also being a "systematic discipline." With this culture theoretical approach owing to Schleiermacher,[26] Gräb intends to reconnect theology and church with contemporary experience. "Lived religion"—a term Rössler introduces into the current debate—is the catchphrase he opposes to ossified orthodoxy. Gräb extols the fundamental communicative nature of religion. It is the duty of theology to join in the universal communication about this fact. The price for this proximity to everyday life is a radical "desubstantialization" (214) of the imaginative contents of Christian religion. Furthermore, the diaconal dimension remains eclipsed; material needs are integrated into and subsumed under the quest for meaning (see 15–16). In the end, Gräb's concept of religion is fraught with problems that cannot be overlooked.

Hans-Günter Heimbrock (b. 1948) (Frankfurt concept): Hans-Günter Heimbrock and Wolf-Eckart Failing conceptualize a Practical Religion between the postulate of the holy as a separate reality (Josuttis) and the understanding of religion as interpretation (Gräb). The point of departure for the two practical theologians, teaching together in Frankfurt between 1994 and 2001, is the following question:

> What are the qualities of a Practical Theology that is both theoretically and theologically articulate with regard to phenomena and at the same time able to perceive and interpret changes in religion and the lifeworld? (Failing and Heimbrock, "Von der Handlungstheorie," 275)

The authors build on the insight—shared by Josuttis and Gräb—that religious practice is going through a phase of renewal, which not least also affects the church. This is happening in the context of changes in other institutions whose regulatory function is shrinking or can be dispensed with (see 277).

---

[24] Wilhelm Gräb, *Sinnfragen: Transformationen des Religiösen in der modernen Welt* (Gütersloh, 2006), 53.

[25] Gräb, *Sinnfragen*, 75.

[26] See Wilhelm Gräb, "Praktische Theologie als Theorie der Kirchenleitung: Friedrich Schleiermacher," in Grethlein and Meyer-Blanck, *Geschichte der Praktischen Theologie*, 67–110.

Instead of focusing on the church or the pastoral profession, Failing and Heimbrock start with the subject. Based on an understanding of theology as a cultural science (see 283), their reflections center on the phenomenological concept of the "lifeworld" in the sense of Edmund Husserl and later Maurice Merleau-Ponty and Bernhard Waldenfels. Lifeworld here means the general horizon of meaning, within which perception and concept are not yet separated. It forms the incomplete horizon of every perception—compared to which daily routine is stable and reliable.

In the meantime, Heimbrock and colleagues (most of whom also studied or work in Frankfurt) are working on a pertinent methodology under the name of "Empirical Theology." Contrary to other approaches, this is no functional or statistical method, but priority is here given to the stance of the phenomenologist, who with a "defamiliarizing sideglance"[27] discloses the usually hidden. The phenomenological position has a threefold orientation: insofar as it offers an alternative to methods hitherto applied in Practical Theology, it serves a heuristic function; it is critical of functional reductionism; and it opens the perception for new phenomena (see 294).

Doubtless, this practical-theological approach provides ample scope for research, as the studies of Heimbrock's students show.[28] Yet even in the principal reflections, theological positioning takes a backseat. Programmatically, only the concern of the "pathic" is adopted, that is, the (christologically substantiated) suffering from reality (see 281–82).[29]

Albrecht Grözinger (b. 1949): This practical theologian teaching in Basel (Switzerland) is a pupil of Otto's and thus interested in a critical expansion of the horizon. At the same time, however, he is engaging in the issue of positioning Practical Theology, in which he singles out "the fundamental problem of practical-theological theory formation": "How can transcendence in limited

[27] Bernhard Waldenfels, "Phänomenologie unter eidetischen, transzendentalen und strukturalen Gesichtspunkten," in *Sinn und Erfahrung: Phänomenologische Methoden in den Humanwissenschaften*, ed. Max Herzog and Carl Graumann (Heidelberg, 1991), 65–85, 83.

[28] See, e.g., Inken Mädler, *Transfigurationen: Materielle Kultur in praktisch-theologischer Perspektive* (PThK 17) (Gütersloh, 2006); Christopher Scholtz, *Alltag mit künstlichen Wesen: Theologische Implikationen mit subjektsimulierenden Maschinen am Beispiel des Unterhaltungsroboters Aibo* (Research in Contemporary Religion 3) (Göttingen, 2008); and—at least inspired by Heimbrock—Ilona Nord, *Realitäten des Glaubens: Zur virtuellen Dimension christlicher Religiosität* (PThW 5) (Berlin, 2008).

[29] Also see Hans-Günter Heimbrock, "Empirie, Methode und Theologie," in *Einführung in die Empirische Theologie*, ed. Astrid Dinter et al. (Göttingen, 2007), 42–59, 58.

communication be thought, spoken and carried out without being swallowed up by immanence?" (Grözinger 1). To approach this specifically theological endeavor, Grözinger turns to aesthetics.[30] In his explorations of literature and philosophical reflections he gains fundamental insights that merit theological attention. Thus, revelation becomes accessible as an "act of communication between God revealing Himself and the listening and perceiving human being" (92). This is illustrated in the story of Moses' appointment (see 92–96) and in the Emmaus pericope (see 99–102).

Theologically, Grözinger follows the basic idea of Walter Benjamin's aesthetics about the "dialectics of presentation and withdrawal in the course of esthetic perception" (150). Fundamentally, aesthetics, as much as Practical Theology, is about keeping up the tension, not only in theory but also in practice (see 183). This recourse to aesthetic debates enables Grözinger to capture the tensions better that define Practical Theology: because one of its central issues, ecclesial action, always has an aesthetic dimension (see 216). In this understanding of Practical Theology, the "model" as a mediator between theory and praxis attains supreme importance in practical-theological work (see 221). It provides the space for individual perspective without imposing system constraints.

In his further research, Grözinger repeatedly turns to individual forms of artistic expression.[31] In doing so, he interpolates biblical and/or systematic-theological and aesthetic perspectives, thus demonstrating that the extension of the practical-theological horizon need not necessarily entail theological reduction. Scientific theoretical reflection is pushed into the background. Practical Theology is located "exactly at the interface between art and science."[32]

Wilfried Engemann (b. 1959): Similar to Grözinger, Engemann, now teaching in Vienna (Austria), contributes an important perspective to practical-theological work. With reference to Umberto Eco's semiotics, he emphasizes the communicative nature of what lies at the heart of Practical Theology. In a nutshell, it is about the "communication of the gospel by individuals in different situations on the basis of signs" (Engemann, *Personen, Zeichen und das Evangelium,* 15–16). Being so comprehensive, this ideology-critical approach

[30] See Albrecht Grözinger, *Erzählen und Handeln: Studien zu einer Grundlegung der Praktischen Theologie* (Munich, 1989).

[31] See Albrecht Grözinger, *Praktische Theologie als Kunst der Wahrnehmung* (Gütersloh, 1995).

[32] Grözinger, *Praktische Theologie,* 158.

overcomes all previous restrictions of Practical Theology, making it abundantly clear that the gospel is a communication process involving several people. As one consequence, higher demands are placed on the pastor. It is, after all, the pastor's task to transform the ambiguity inherent in communication into a successful communicative process. Extraneous circumstances here carry considerable weight, since they can facilitate or obstruct the desired decoding.

In later publications, Engemann adds to his definition of the communication of the gospel the goal "to shape the Church . . . for the dedication and appropriation of liberty."[33] Here, ideas from Practical Philosophy[34] and the debate on the art of living come into play.[35] There is no doubt that Engemann's emphasis on the communicative structure of the gospel compels Practical Theology to communication-theoretical reflections.

Common Denominator: Perception

For all their positional differences, these contributions to practical-theological theory formation share one thing in common: they all strive for a better and more comprehensive kind of perception. The associated widening of the horizon is a reaction to the diverse changes in society, culture, and church. The traditional subject area of parochial pastoral praxis becomes less important. The resulting change of the discipline becomes clear in the following three examples. The first two represent thematic expansions, the third names a general methodological change.

The generation perspective: Fresh attention to age enhances practical-theological research in the two following regards. First is Child Theology[36] (and, more recently, Youth Theology[37]), an educational approach from the 1990s that

---

[33] Wilfried Engemann, "Kommunikation des Evangeliums als interdisziplinäres Projekt: Praktische Theologie im Dialog mit außertheologischen Wissenschaften," in Grethlein and Schwier, *Praktische Theologie,* 137–232, 140, 142.

[34] See Peter Bieri, *Das Handwerk der Freiheit: Über die Entdeckung des eigenen Willens* (Munich, 2001).

[35] See Wilfried Engemann, "Die Lebenskunst und das Evangelium," *ThLZ* 129 (2004), 875–96.

[36] See Gerhard Büttner, Petra Freudenberger-Lötz, Christina Kalloch, and Martin Schreiner, eds., *Theologisieren mit Kindern: Einführung–Schlüsselthemen–Methoden* (Stuttgart, 2014).

[37] See Thomas Schlag and Friedrich Schweitzer, eds., *Jugendtheologie: Grundlagen–Beispiele–kritische Diskussion* (Neukirchen-Vluyn, 2012).

feeds on various ideas. Although he did not consider the development of religion in children, Jean-Jacques Rousseau already claimed that the child's perspective be taken seriously in its own right.[38] Specifically, Child Theology owes its existence to a movement in philosophy. In 1970 Matthew Lipman founded the Institute for the Advancement of Philosophy for Children (IAPC) at Montclair State University in New Jersey. While Lipman still focused on a philosophy for children, the adaptation of his ideas in Germany revealed the philosophy of children. This is the cue religious educators in Germany have been taking since the 1990s, being particularly interested in theological interpretations children produce autonomously and in pertinent approaches.

At the other end of human life, old age, observations are made in pastoral care and diaconal work,[39] which in some ways reflect those made in Child Theology. Manifestly, in both life phases, fundamental human problems condense. Skills and abilities necessary for an autonomous adult life are still missing or start to become fragile. These issues come, as it were, to a head in elderly patients suffering from dementia. Traditional theologoumena are of little or no help for the communicative needs in these cases. Instead, forms of religious praxis that have been known for years create opportunities for marvelously creative adaptations of traditional forms.[40] These two age-related perspectives are not confined to the spheres of religious education, pastoral care, or diaconal work. They are, in fact, important for every field of action that requires practical-theological deliberation. Pertinent research must pay meticulous attention to the concrete communication situation.

Performance: Increasingly, practical theologians turn to questions of structure and form and the challenges and problems connected with them. One part of this is the decline of traditional praxis pietatis. On the other hand, important impulses come from developments in contemporary art, often in connection with the concept of "performance."[41] In religious didac-

---

[38] See Friedrich Schweitzer, *Die Religion des Kindes: Zur Problemgeschichte einer religionspädagogischen Grundfrage* (Gütersloh, 1992), 117–33.

[39] See Ralph Kunz, ed., *Religiöse Begleitung im Alter: Religion als Thema der Gerontologie* (Zürich, 2007).

[40] See Andrea Fröchtling, *"Und dann habe ich auch noch den Kopf verloren . . .": Menschen mit Demenz in Theologie, Seelsorge und Gottesdienst wahrnehmen* (APrTh 38) (Leipzig, 2008), 350.

[41] For an introduction, see Marvin Carlson, *Performance: A Critical Introduction* (London, 1996).

tics, a didactic approach has developed that—drawing on gestalt pedagogics and theater sciences—calls itself "performative."[42] In (so-called) mock performances, young people gain experience in the religious field, which they then—in accordance with the concept of school as a place of learning—critically discuss.

In liturgics, theater theoretical insights are absorbed to come to a better understanding of the particular character of liturgical praxis and to improve liturgical training.[43] References to the corporeal dimension in this context prove fundamental for religious communication, particularly with regard to the gender perspective. These efforts entail heightened aesthetical demands on the liturgical community.

Finally, the performance concept is also adapted in homiletics. In his "Dramaturgical Homiletics," Martin Nicol, for instance, promotes preaching "as an art in its own right."[44] Employing the programmatic notion of "preaching within" borrowed from U.S. practice, he sketches a theory of preaching as a "living performance."[45]

Multiperspectivity: Further differentiations relating to daily life shape practical-theological work. As a result, distinct typologies are replaced by perspectives and their relativities, that is, their necessary relationships with other perspectives. Multiperspectivity thus becomes a methodological prerequisite. It must, however, not be confused with arbitrariness. Clearly, multiperspectivity opens up perception, but requires, for that very reason, a precise definition of its subject.

Summary

Since the publication of the fundamental textbooks of Practical Theology in the 1980s (by Dietrich Rössler and Gerd Otto), deeper perception has become the central concern of the discipline. Changes in politics, society, and culture have made it necessary to have a solid understanding of the starting situation.

---

[42] See Thomas Klie and Silke Leonhard, eds., *Performative Religionsdidaktik: Religionsästhetik–Lernorte–Unterrichtspraxis* (PTHe 97) (Stuttgart, 2008).

[43] See Ursula Roth, *Die Theatralität des Gottesdienstes* (PThK 18) (Gütersloh, 2006).

[44] Martin Nicol, *Einander ins Bild setzen: Dramaturgische Homiletik* (Göttingen, 2002), 16.

[45] Nicol, *Einander ins Bild setzen*, 55–64.

To this end, a rich repertoire of empirical methods has been developed, which allows discerning insights into our present lifeworld.

In contrast, the theological framework theories receive only limited attention. Apparently, the grand theological designs by Schleiermacher and Barth are incapable of guiding, particularly in a praxis-oriented manner, a discerning analysis of the present situation. Their positionality, most pronounced in the concepts of Josuttis and Gräb, misses the required differentiations. The Frankfurt research, however, notwithstanding its useful outcomes, displays a palpable deficit in the contentual clarity of their concept of religion.

The introduction and elaboration of a communication-scientific approach such as Engemann's has more reach. In terms of science theory, it provides broad access to a number of sciences; its connection with the gospel preserves a precise theological context.

Finally, it is apparent that only part of the changes enumerated at the beginning of this chapter has remained in view. In terms of contents, the following desiderata can be observed, which are clearly in opposition to the, in part comprehensive, objectives of Practical Theology: The challenges posed by religious plurality, not least in church members, are largely ignored. A generic concept of religion masks the processes of pluralization and differentiation. Furthermore, issues related to material needs are neglected. Diaconal care remains an academic side issue (and is still missing almost completely in the denomination of practical-theological professorships). The big ecological questions also do not feature in academic Practical Theology. Practical-theological theory formation—at least in the region of German Protestant Theology—centers around people with a lifestyle distinguished by higher education and the absence of material cares. The latter problems are thrown into relief when one leaves the province of German Protestant Practical Theology.

2

PRACTICAL THEOLOGY IN CATHOLICISM AND THE UNITED STATES

For a long time, Practical Theology used to be primarily at home in German-speaking Protestant Theology. However, in the last few decades, an expansion both across borders and across denominations could be observed. One reason for this seems to be the process of globalization, which, by simultaneously strengthening tendencies toward regionalization, creates interesting tensions. Consequently, international contacts in the field of Practical Theology are increasing. In this process, the shared challenges as well as the specific features of the different countries and regions become more apparent. At the same time, denominational homogeneity dissolves in regions, relationships and families. This is why Protestant practical theology must be mindful of the Roman Catholic Church, its pastoral praxis and the resultant theories. In brief: to involve Roman Catholic Christians (and increasingly non-Christians) is part and parcel of the praxis of Protestant churches (and their theologies).

To compare different forms of praxis and their related theories requires methodological clarity. Borrowing from and in intense debate with Comparative Educational Science (and Comparative Religion) Bernd Schröder presented a convincing proposal for a Comparative Study of Religious Education, which can be easily transferred to the field of Practical Theology.[1] Schröder proposes four methodical steps of comparison: first, the ideographic comparison seeks to identify the particular and unique within specific contexts; next, generalization aims at the common features of the compared theories or fields of action; the purpose of the elenctic approach then is to gain insights for one's own praxis; and, in the end, the final purpose of the comparison is to establish a dialog. However, in adapting this program for Jewish religious education in Israel (as compared to Christian school education in Germany) the generalizing step proved awkward since the particular contexts were difficult to integrate.

As opposed to Schröder, I do not compare concrete fields of action but theories, albeit practical-theological theories referring to religious praxis. Schröder's (tried and tested) methodological approach can however be applied in a Comparative Practical Theology. In a first step, the differences need to be established in their contexts (ideographic). The main purpose of this is a critical review of one's own theory (elenctic). Whether or not this will result in dialogic corollaries, remains to be seen. For a first comparison, Catholic Practical (or Pastoral) Theology[2] suggests itself, which is also particularly advanced in the German-speaking world.

Internationally, I will reconstruct important strands of development and discussion in the United States, which has the greatest number of researchers in the field of Practical Theology. Factually, the immigration-induced cultural diversity of American society deserves particular attention, as it quintessentially reflects the process of globalization.

It would of course be interesting to have a look at Practical Theology in the French and Spanish speaking countries. However, the hermeneutic necessity of an at least rudimentary reconstruction of the concrete context of theory formation is barred by the mere listing of so-called facts.

Finally, it needs to be pointed out that Practical Theology is limited to the domain of Western churches. It is (largely) missing in Orthodoxy as well as in more recent movements of Pentecostal communities or Holiness churches.

---

[1] Bernd Schröder, *Jüdische Erziehung im modernen Israel: Eine Studie zur Grundlegung vergleichender Religionspädagogik* (APrTh 18) (Leipzig, 2000), 22–43, 37–39.

[2] In this book, "Catholic" always refers to Roman Catholic theology.

1. Catholic Pastoral Theology and Practical Theology

Literature: Daniel Bourgeois, *Die Pastoral der Kirche* (AMATECA 11) (Paderborn, 2004); Rainer Bucher, *Theologie im Risiko der Gegenwart: Studien zur kenotischen Existenz der Pastoraltheologie zwischen Universität, Kirche und Gesellschaft* (PTHe 105) (Stuttgart, 2010); Walter Fürst, "Die Geschichte der 'Praktischen Theologie' und der kulturelle Wandlungsprozeß in Deutschland vor dem II: Vatikanum," in *Die katholisch-theologischen Disziplinen in Deutschland 1870–1962: Ihre Geschichte, ihr Zeitbezug,* ed. Hubert Wolf (Paderborn, 1999), 263–89; Anton Graf, *Kritische Darstellung des gegenwärtigen Zustandes der Praktischen Theologie* (Tübingen, 1841); Norbert Mette, *Einführung in die katholische Praktische Theologie* (Darmstadt, 2005); Thomas Nipperdey, *Deutsche Geschichte 1866–1918,* vol. 1: *Arbeitswelt und Bürgergeist* (Munich, ²1991), 428–68; Wolfgang Steck, "Friedrich Schleiermacher und Anton Graf—eine ökumenische Konstellation Praktischer Theologie?," in *Praktische Theologie heute,* ed. Ferdinand Klostermann and Rolf Zerfaß (Munich, 1974), 27–41

At the beginning, we will focus on contextual particularities that are important to the understanding of the development of Practical Theology in the Catholic Church. More concretely, this refers to the specific ecclesial conditions.

In a second step, three important contributions for the foundation of the discipline in its present shape will be introduced. Here, a basic conflict surfaces—exemplified by the two opposing positions held by Daniel Bourgeois and Norbert Mette in their respective textbooks. These two views are complemented by the concept of Rainer Bucher, which as yet, instead of a textbook, exists only in the form of a collection of essays.

The comparative angle of this chapter justifies the selectivity of the process. This unfortunately precludes a summary such as in chapter 1, which would incorrectly suggest completeness. Instead, this and the next part of chapter 2 will result in a set of "suggestions" systematically bundling the main points.

One could question whether it is at all necessary to take a separate look at Catholic Practical Theology. Would it not make more sense to focus on an ecumenical version of Practical Theology? This is, of course, generally true. In fact, Catholic contributions will be included in the second and third parts of this book. Recent attempts have however shown that reference to a separate Catholic Practical Theology is not obsolete yet (see Mette, *Einführung*, 9).

Context

First and principally it must be stressed that Catholicism is pluriform, with regard to both organization and contents—starting with its system of religious orders, through its many national variants to the variegated forms of popular devotion and different theological concepts. The Vatican's centralization efforts of the past 150 years have not managed to change anything fundamentally about this.

Nevertheless, Roman policy has a palpable impact on the development of Practical Theology. Notably, the decisions of the recent council form a common basis for the current state of Catholic Practical Theology. However, differences can be observed with regard to the selection of conciliar passages as well as their interpretations.

State-church: Indeed, the Roman Catholic Church has a long history of being critical of the state. The Middle Ages were caught up in a struggle of imperium versus sacerdotium. Particularly because of its community spanning countries and nations, the Catholic Church always, at least up until 1914, showed some reserve toward nationalism.

The so-called Kulturkampf (culture struggle) marked an open conflict between Church and state.[3] In a failed effort, Bismarck's state system tried to subdue the Church by forceful interventions, such as arrests of bishops. The principal gap between Church and state that so clearly displays itself in these conflicts can be observed in the German Catholic Church and elsewhere to date.

Society-church: During the period of the Enlightenment, Protestant and Catholic clerics alike thought of themselves as teachers of the people. The pastoral theologies of the day, such as the three volumes by Johann Michael Seiler (1751–1832),[4] to a certain extent testified to an interdenominational consensus. This changed, at the latest, with First Vatican Council

---

[3] For a brief outline of the course of events and specific issues, see Hans-Ulrich Wehler, *Deutsche Gesellschaftsgeschichte*, vol. 3: *Von der "Deutschen Doppelrevolution" bis zum Beginn des Ersten Weltkrieges 1849–1914* (Munich, 1995), 892–902.

[4] See Norbert Mette, "Praktische Theologie in der katholischen Theologie," in Grethlein and Meyer-Blanck, *Geschichte der Praktischen Theologie*, 531–63, 535–37.

(1869–1870). During the preceding two decades, the papacy had already extended its supremacy under the flag of ultramontanism. In this manner, it prepared for the dogmatization of papal infallibility in ex cathedra decisions, put into effect in First Vatican Council. In Germany, this dogma was controversial—with the episcopate and even more so with theological scholars (see Nipperdey, *Deutsche Geschichte*, 429–31). The innovations following and based on the council (Antimodernist Oath, juridification of the Church) only widened the gap between the socially dominant Protestant majority and the Catholic population. Organizationally, this resulted in the foundation of many Catholic associations, producing a "subculture" in the form of a "club and society Catholicism" (*Vereins- und Verbandskatholizismus*) (Nipperdey, *Deutsche Geschichte*, 439).

After a great many preliminary reform efforts—in liturgy, catechism, and pastoral care—it was only Second Vatican Council (1963–1965) under John XXIII that tried to develop a fresh and positive relationship with modernity. It began with the goal of "instauratio" (renewal), thus the invitation by the pope, and went on to issue a number of documents that would change the Catholic Church profoundly. However, there was considerable room for interpretation, which has caused disputes since.

This brief outline already singles out one particular feature of Catholic Practical Theology: the outstanding importance of conciliar decisions. Particularly, the pastoral constitution *Gaudium et Spes*, which will require closer examination later, has posed many problems to Catholic practical theologists over the years. Conversely, this text has not attracted any attention in Protestant Practical Theology.

Theology: In accordance with the Roman Catholic centralization tendencies, the general conditions and the contents of Catholic theological studies today are standardized worldwide. For this purpose, John Paul II published the apostolic constitution *Sapienta Christiana* in 1979, which was substantiated by the valid Congregation for Catholic Education.

According to these, with regard to teaching and state-church law, Practical Theology is nonexistent. Pastoral Theology, liturgics, and Church law are independent subjects. It is presumably the strong connection of theology as a whole to the magisterium that makes the integration of these subjects superfluous.

Foundations

The current practical-theological efforts in Catholic Theology are marked by three points of departure. The first two develop basic themes, which will be further discussed in the following: the pastor and the church. This, however, is not possible without disruptions, since the surge of neo-Scholasticism in the mid-1800s halted experience-based theory formation. Only as part of the reform movements at the beginning of the nineteenth century—first with regard to specific fields of practice, particularly catechetics—could a renewed interest in actual practice of faith gain a foothold. Third, the pastoral constitution of the Second Vatican Council needs to be analyzed. It is the currently valid fundamental text for Catholic pastoral care.

Pastoral Theology: In the course of academic reform during the Enlightenment—at the behest of Marie Theresa and her successor, Joseph II—Franz Stephan Rautenstrauch (1734–1785) had introduced into the study of theology a final year devoted to Pastoral Theology, his primary goal being the formation of personality.

In devising the course program, Rautenstrauch followed the Calvin-based three-office doctrine of Christ (teacher, priest, shepherd). He split up these tasks into the duties of instruction, (ad)ministration, and edification. He had encountered this division elsewhere: it dominates Catholic pastoral-theological writing until Second Vatican Council. This connection of Christology and pastoral praxis integrated Pastoral Theology into theology as a whole.

The Church: The Tübingen School[5] critically turned its back on the Enlightenment emphasis on reason and Natural Religion. Against it they set the affirmative and the historical aspects of revelation. This brought the dimension of praxis into view, which made the Church with its inner mission and outer form the dominant theme. Anton Graf (1811–1867)[6] focused in this context on Pastoral Theology as "the science of ecclesiastical, divine-human activities through the agency of instituted persons, preferably clerics, for the edification of the Church" (Graf, *Kritische Darstellung*, 149),

---

[5] For a basic overview, see Johann Sebastian Drey, *Kurze Einleitung in das Studium der Theologie mit Rücksicht auf den wissenschaftlichen Standpunkt und das katholische System* (Tübingen, 1819).

[6] See Franz Xaver Arnold, *Seelsorge aus der Mitte der Heilsgeschichte: Pastoraltheologische Durchblicke* (Freiburg, 1956), 178–94.

emphasizing its theological-scholarly character. In his detailed comments he referred to works from Protestant Practical Theology.

However, he distanced himself from Schleiermacher (see Graf, *Kritische Darstellung*, 138–39; see Steck, "Friedrich Schleiermacher"), whose rooting of theology as a positive science in the duties of the church leadership struck him as misguided. Instead, Graf aimed at explaining the necessity of Practical Theology from the term itself. The proximity to the Practical Theology of Carl Immanuel Nitzsch with its focus on the Church as subject is evident; in his programmatic deliberations on the Church, however, Graf emphasized the contrast between clergy and laity.

By emphasizing its scientificity and by explaining its place in the Church, Graf highlighted two points that are essential to Practical Theology to date. Despite their thematic similarities, however, his remarks on the Church display denominational differences from those of Protestant theologists.

Pastoral constitution: It seems the pastoral constitution was not the instigator but rather a result of the work of (German-speaking) Catholic theologians at the time, which achieved overall impact thanks to the council text. Work on the five-volume *Handbuch der Pastoraltheologie* (Handbook of pastoral theology, 1964–1972) had begun before the council text was written. Furthermore, several new pastoral-theological treatises had been published at the beginning of the 1960s.[7] In spite of this, *Gaudium et Spes* is the text to which Catholic Theology will furthermore multifariously refer.

A groundbreaking feat was achieved in the fresh conceptualization of the term "pastoral." Contrary to its previous reference to the dogmatically defined professional conduct of clerics, it now comprehensively designates the ecclesiastical mission as such. The Church needs "to be and to act where God is and acts, namely, where the people are and be there for them, and this manner give God the glory."[8] Even the introductory sentences of the pastoral constitution illustrate this new beginning:

> The joys and the hopes, the griefs and the anxieties of the men of this age, especially those who are poor or in any way afflicted, these are the joys and

---

[7] See Mette, "Praktische Theologie," in Grethlein and Meyer-Blanck, *Geschichte der Praktischen Theologie*, 547–48.

[8] Norbert Mette, "Gaudium et spes—Die Pastoralkonstitution und das Pastoralkonzil," *MThZ* 54 (2003), 114–25, 115, Engl. by the translator.

hopes, the griefs and anxieties of the followers of Christ. Indeed, nothing genuinely human fails to raise an echo in their hearts. (*Gaudium et Spes* 1)

The goal is to overcome the chasm between "the world" and the Church, which has so far marked statements of the teaching office. This fundamentally changes the way in which the Church is understood: away from a self-sufficient institution of salvation to one actively engaging with the challenges of the times. To read the "scrutinize the signs of the times" (*Gaudium et Spes* 4) becomes an important theological task. Thus the council reaffirms the significance of the Church for theology, while at the same time emphasizing the importance of cultural-hermeneutical analysis for pastoral care (in its broadest sense).

Developing a Profile

As already indicated, questions of Practical Religion are dealt with in different ways within Catholic Theology:

The first example, from France, presents a sacramental-theologically grounded theory of the church, which, at first, seems interested only in dogmatic repristination. The fact, however, that this book has been included in the international textbook collection AMATECA[9] shows that it, with regard to the Church as a whole, evidently does not represent an outsider position, notwithstanding that it is barely adapted in German-speaking pastoral care.

A quite different approach is presented by Norbert Mette, who conceives Practical Theology in terms of a science of action. Mette is clearly indebted to the practical-theological theory formation in Protestant Theology, but his considerations implicate further perspectives.

This section ends with the presentation of Rainer Bucher's concerns, who in the first place elaborates Mette's approach while, under the impression of many changes, shifting the emphasis.

Daniel Bourgeois (b. 1946): The dogmatic-conciliar orientation of his *La pastorale de l'Eglise* deserves attention. It is not the pastoral constitution *Gaudium et Spes*—which the French monk of the Apostolic Brotherhood of the Order of Malta naturally quotes as well—that is at the center of his argument, but the Second Vatican Council's ecclesial constitution *Lumen Gentium*. His

---

[9] The textbook series "Assoziazione Manuali di Teologia Cattolica" is edited by an international board of bishops and professors.

understanding of the Church as sacrament is essential for his concept of "pastoral care":

> The Church is in Christ like a sacrament or as a sign and instrument both of a very closely knit union with God and of the unity of the whole human race. (*Lumen Gentium* 1 [adapted from the official Engl. version]; quoted in Bourgeois, *Die Pastoral der Kirche*, 194).

The subject of Pastoral Theology, therefore, is "the whole living web of the economy of salvation as the personal relationship of God with his people" (Bourgeois, *Die Pastoral der Kirche*, 39). Bourgeois here clearly distances his approach from dogmatic and moral theology. In contrast to these disciplines, "pastoral care" focuses not on conceptual definitions, but on "the mystery within the multiplicity of authoritative meaning" (Bourgeois, *Die Pastoral der Kirche*, 39). Theologically, Bourgeois insists that "the Church" in its "sacramentality" is worthy of particular theological reflection. Accordingly, Bourgeois deduces the basic structures of pastoral care from church doctrine. He rejects empirical analyses as being inappropriate, since they only take recourse to individual capabilities. Disregarding Bourgeois' strictly denominational deliberations, which display no sign of interest in ecumenical exchange, one point still remains remarkable: the subject of practical-theological reflection, the church, is essentially impervious to human activity since it owes its existence to God's grace alone.

Norbert Mette (b. 1946): A rather different approach, now proposing an explicitly Practical Theology, was submitted by Norbert Mette in 2005, in which the lay theologian takes recourse to two fundamental approaches or elaborations that have been decisive for the development of Practical Theology in the Catholic Church: Mette bases his systematic considerations on Karl Rahner's (and Edward Schillebeeckx's) "anthropological turn" (Mette, *Einführung*, 63), according to which every statement about God implicates statements about mankind. This understanding was crucial for the five-volume *Handbuch der Pastoraltheologie* (1964), which, as mentioned above, was conceived during the Second Vatican Council and which, at the suggestion of coeditor Rahner, addressed the "Selbstvollzug der Kirche in der Gegenwart," the self-actuation of the church in the present (13).[10] This still essen-

---

[10] See August Laumer, *Karl Rahner und die Praktische Theologie* (STPS 79) (Würzburg, 2010).

tially Church-oriented approach was further developed in the two volumes of the *Handbuch Praktische Theologie*, published in 1999–2000, to which Mette contributed an article, and which expanded the scope of Practical Theology to include the "praxis of people." In part, Mette substantiates this program in close reference to magisterial pronouncements, especially the above mentioned passages from *Gaudium et Spes* (see 65). In addition, he draws on suggestions from Protestant practical theologians; particularly Henning Luther's theory of the fragmented subject meets with Mette's approval (63–64).

The concept of "communicating the gospel" is central to his thought, since it connects different domains such as the empirical and the normative (15). For him the idea of the gospel fairly globally describes "the total of God's manifestation in his love for and allegiance to mankind, as witnessed, most of all, in the Bible, but also in other religions as well as in creation as a whole" (20). In reference to material matters, he displays a socioethically accentuated concept of faith: faith can be understood only as something that seizes the individual "neck and crop" (45) and can therefore not be limited to the private sphere (46). As a consequence, the congregation can be understood only as a community in which the "unity of mysticism and politics" is practiced (108). He takes his concrete examples primarily from France, from the worker priests to current reform movements in the form of base communities. These instances also evidence Mette's critical interest in the socio- or politico-economic sphere, as it is represented in Liberation Theology, and which informs his approach to Practical Theology.

Rainer Bucher (b. 1956): The German Rainer Bucher has held the Chair for Pastoral Theology and Pastoral Psychology at the Catholic Theological Faculty of Graz (Austria) since 2000. Bucher deeply engages in questions of understanding and explaining the rationale of Pastoral or Practical Theology, two terms he thinks are "strictly coextensive" (Bucher, *Theologie im Risiko*, 11).

His approach starts from the observation that Catholic Pastoral Theology has for a considerable time been under pressure to defend its legitimacy. Bucher contraposes this finding by defining Pastoral Theology as a "cultural science of God's people." He criticizes the "Empirical Theology" primarily of Dutch origin[11] for confining itself to religious aspects and losing sight of the nonreligious "signs of the times" (192). He criticizes the action-theoretical

---

[11] See Johannes van der Ven, "Practical Theology: From Applied to Empirical Theology," *JET* 1 (1988), 7–27.

approach pursued by both Mette and the *Handbuch Praktische Theologie* for being normatively overfraught. He doubts that Habermas' notion of praxis appropriately reflects the fragmented experience of people living today, and he prefers to shift to focus to "the other, the alien, the new" (194). Drawing productively on the Church theoretical insights of *Gaudium et Spes*, he tries to explain the main point of the pastoral constitution in terms of the "kenotic." Just like the Church that needs to relinquish its claims to power in order to become worthy of belief, Pastoral Theology must lose all safeguards—be they academic, institutional, or ecclesial. By virtue of this, and following ideas of philosopher Gianni Vattimo, the incarnation of God, his kenosis, becomes the central concept of Pastoral Theology (see 231n88).

Overall, Bucher manages to analyze the present state of affairs while at the same time firmly anchoring Pastoral Theology in the Church—not, however, in traditional hierarchy, but in "God's people." Similar to the *Handbuch Praktische Theologie*, a Pastoral Theology based on these precepts involves "all phenomena of human existence" (223). Its strong cultural reference provides unrestricted access to the pluralistic realm of contemporary experience; its firm footing in "God's people" prevents ignoring the political dimension—something Protestant Practical Theology has been accused of.

Valuable Ideas for Protestant Practical Theology

The following definitions and findings of the concepts sketched above are of particular interest for Protestant Practical Theology:

Rationale: All three authors present a genuinely theological rationale for Pastoral/Practical Theology. Their foundational norms, it is true, are in part derived from different contexts or varying readings of the documents of the Second Vatican Council; what they share in common, however, is the prevalence of the normative over the descriptive.

Grace: Despite all differences in rationale—informed by a denominationally dogmatic concept of the sacrament on the one and ideas regarding identity ("from gratuity"; Mette, *Einführung*, 70–73) on the other hand—both Bourgeois and Mette (and in a certain sense also Bucher) emphasize that Pastoral/Practical Theology deals with issues that elude human disposability. The grace of God, which precedes all human action, forms the basis for Pastoral/Practical Theology, that is, sacramental praxis, the praxis of people, or the pastoral care of God's people.

The Church: For Catholic theologians the Church always remains a central concern. While the material considerations in terms of both topical focus and treatment differ significantly, Bourgeois and Mette clearly agree on the central role they assign to the praxis of the faithful. The insignificant role the Church plays in the lives of most Catholics today is for both only a tendency that needs to be overcome.

While Bourgeois bases his approach on the intrinsic difference between baptismal and ordained priesthood (derived from *Lumen Gentium*, art. 10; see Bourgeois, *Die Pastoral der Kirche*, 176–78), Mette models his ideas on concrete forms of community such as Christian base communities. Bucher, on the other hand, opens up new avenues by taking stock of the discontinuities and contradictions of contemporary experience, without yet making exactly clear where they might lead.

Politics: The importance of Mette's and Bucher's emphatic case for the socio- or politico-economic in Practical Theology cannot be stressed enough. Both point to the global significance of this dimension and censure the Protestant reduction of Practical Theology to the merely cultural. This is where the broad horizon of a world Church weighs in, a Church that—at least to a certain extent—is committed to the causes of the poor and disenfranchised in Asia, Africa, and Latin America (even if sometimes incurring papal disapproval).

2. Input from the United States

Literature: Don Browning, *A Fundamental Practical Theology: Descriptive and Strategic Proposals* (Minneapolis, 1991); Kathleen Cahalan and Gordon Mikoski, eds., *Opening the Field of Practical Theology: An Introduction* (Lanham, Md., 2014); Seward Hiltner, *Preface to Pastoral Theology* (New York, 1958); William James, *Die Vielfalt der religiösen Erfahrung: Eine Studie über die menschliche Natur*, trans. Eilert Herms and Christian Stahlhut (Frankfurt, 1997) (*The Varieties of Religious Experience. A Study in Human Nature* [New York, 1902]); Tony Jones, *The New Christians: Dispatches from the Emergent Frontier* (San Francisco, 2008); Bonnie J. Miller-McLemore, ed., *The Wiley-Blackwell Companion to Practical Theology* (Chichester, 2012); Mark Noll, *Das Christentum in Nordamerika* (Kirchengeschichte in Einzeldarstellungen IV/5) (Leipzig, 2000); Richard Osmer, *Practical Theology: An Introduction* (Grand Rapids, 2008); Robert Putnam and David Campbell, *American Grace: How Religion Divides and Unites Us* (New York, 2010); Friedrich Schweitzer,

"Praktische Theologie in Nordamerika," in *Geschichte der Praktischen Theologie: Dargestellt anhand ihrer Klassiker* (APrTh 12), ed. Christian Grethlein and Michael Meyer-Blanck (Leipzig, 1999), 565–96; James Woodward and Stephen Pattison, eds., *The Blackwell Reader in Pastoral Practical Theology* (Oxford, 2000); Dana Wright, "The Contemporary Renaissance in Practical Theology in the United States: The Past, Present, and Future of a Discipline in Creative Ferment," *IJPT* 6 (2002), 288–319

This section gives an overview of the fundamental framework of ecclesial life and theological work in the United States. The second passage presents important stimuli for the genesis of the particular brand of Practical Theology to which the United States is home. The third section deals with the emergence of Practical Theology in the country as an academic discipline. This will be done by looking at two quintessential textbooks,[12] whose authors, Don Browning and Richard Osmer, represent two institutions crucial to U.S. Practical Theology research: the Divinity School of the University of Chicago,[13] at which Browning taught until 2002, and the Princeton Theological Seminary. Apart from these schools, there are further important pragmatist concepts reflecting on the ways in which social and cultural change impacts the organization of Christian religion. As an example of these, the concept of "emergent Christianity" will be cited. The section concludes with a comparative summary of the ideas that might prove most productive for German (Protestant) Pragmatic Theology theory formation.

[12] A different approach has been chosen by Kathleen Cahalan, following Paul Lakeland's theory of modernity: Cahalan, "Three Approaches to Practical Theology, Theological Education and Church's Ministry," *IJPT* 9 (2005), 63–94. She classifies Don Browning as a late modernist and Craig Dykstra and Dorothy Bass as protagonists of a virtue-oriented position critical of modernity. Moreover, she cites so-called postmodern approaches, represented by Rebecca Chopp's feminist take, among which, however, Cahalan primarily counts the many varieties of Liberation Theology. The latter two concepts have however not been systematically developed with a view to Practical Theology as a global subject.

[13] The University of Chicago played a major role in building the theoretical foundations for a "modern" liberal Christianity in the United States in the twentieth century; see, e.g., Shailer Mathews, *The Faith of Modernism* (New York, 1924).

Context

State and churches: Due to the different kinds of relationship between the state and religions in the United States, church organizational forms and theological education differ fundamentally from those customary in Germany. In the United States, different formational strands continue to exert overlapping forms of influence (for more detail, see Noll, *Das Christentum*, 64–181). At the beginning, the immigrants imported their native denomination into the New World. Denominational differences were therefore defined by national origin (e.g., Swedish Lutherans, Dutch Reformed Christians). The great Puritan influence made itself felt in public and private lives deeply infused with moral principles (see Noll, *Das Christentum*, 72–75). From the multitude of different denominations emerged—unlike the generally denominationally homogeneous European countries—something referred to as "denominationalism."

The denominations are organized in different fashions, as some of their names indicate (e.g., Congregational, Episcopal, Presbyterian). Doctrine differs accordingly, such as regarding baptism (e.g., Baptist vs. Catholic) or the Trinity (e.g., Unitarian vs. Lutheran). The general notion of a uniform U.S. Protestantism thus does not hold (see Noll, *Das Christentum*, 147).

The constitutional foundation of all ecclesial praxis and theology lies in the First Amendment to the Constitution, added in 1789: "Congress shall make no law respecting an establishment of religion, or prohibiting the free exercise thereof."

Civil religion: The strict separation of organized forms of religion and state did not incur a laicist expulsion of the religious dimension from politics and public debate, but helped instead consolidate a interdenominational and independent—if clearly Christian-Protestant—basic consensus underpinning political and social organization, a consensus that has been, on the basis of the inaugural presidential speeches, reconstructed by sociologist Robert Bellah as "civil religion."[14] It is this civil religion that, with recourse to biblical motifs and symbols, has played a pivotal role in the integration of the pluralistic American society. Civil religion is

> this ensemble of beliefs, symbols, and rituals which binds the citizen to the political body, and which makes this commonwealth ultimately appear to be transcendentally legitimized in its institutions and representatives. It

[14] Robert Bellah, "Civil Religion in America," *Daedalus* 96 (1967), 1–21.

defines the values which should, fundamentally, not be at the individual's discretion while placing the history and the destiny of the nation in a publicly mediated context of meaning.... It is a "faith of order," joining the ranks of the diverse "faiths of salvation" of the different denominations.[15]

The fact that the American flag is displayed in most American churches indicates this basic national consensus, which also now includes synagogues and has begun to include mosques. It was writ large during the commemorative service for the victims of the 9/11 attacks held on September 12, 2001, in New York.[16]

Pluralization: The necessity of independent organization at the same time promoted religious pluralization. At least since the Great Depression a decline of the old and wealthy mainline churches, that is, the earlier Protestantism, has been noticeable. Membership in Holiness, Pentecostal, and African American churches is however constantly on the rise (see Noll, *Das Christentum,* 176–82), partly also due to the higher birth rates in these communities. Questions of appropriate approaches to the Bible (e.g., the understanding of the creation stories) and the relationship with modernity (e.g., sexual ethics, currently the appraisal of homosexuality) quickly emerge as problematic issues. The responses to these issues separate liberal and fundamentalist denominations. The sexual liberalization starting at the end of the 1960s led to a countermovement in which a number of churches and Republicans closed ranks, the upshot of which was an increasing withdrawal particularly of the younger generation from organized religion. So-called nones, people without denominational affiliation, now make up a significant group in the U.S. ideological spectrum (see Putnam and Campbell, *American Grace,* 120–32). Only a few, however, are atheists.

The dissolution of denominations: The most important long-term development in the United States is perhaps the looming loss of significance of denominational difference. Approximately a third of Americans change their denominational affiliation at least once in their lives. The self-presentation of

---

[15] Manfred Brocker, "Einleitung," in *God Bless America: Politik und Religion in den USA,* ed. Manfred Brocker (Darmstadt, 2005), 7–12, 9.

[16] See Peter Cornehl, "'A Prayer for America': Der interreligiöse Trauergottesdienst in New York am 12. September 2001 als Beispiel für Civil Religion nach dem 11. September," in *"Die Welt ist voll von Liturgie": Studien zu einer integrativen Gottesdienstpraxis* (PTHe 71), ed. Cornehl (Stuttgart, 2005), 116–31.

the two authors of an almost seven-hundred-page study vividly illustrates the motley diversity of this trend:

> One of us (Campbell) is a Mormon. He is the product of what was initially an interfaith marriage—as his Mormon mother married his mainline Protestant father. Eventually, his father converted to Mormonism. His mother too had been a convert years before. As a child she left Catholicism to become a Mormon. . . . The family tree of your other author (Putnam) also encapsulates the religious churn that is so common in America. He and his sister were raised as observant Methodists in the 1950s. He converted to Judaism at marriage; he and his wife raised their two children as Jews. One child married a practicing Catholic, who has since left the church and is now secular. The other child marries someone with no clear religious affiliation but who subsequently converted to Judaism. Meanwhile, Putnam's sister married a Catholic and converted to Catholicism. Her three children became devout, active evangelicals of several varieties. (Putnam and Campbell, *American Grace*, 36)

"Congregation shopping" (167–72), in which people—often in the context of relocating—choose a new community conveniently catering to their immediate needs, has become a descriptive catchphrase. Denominational considerations clearly play a minor, if any, part in these choices. The emergence of generally denominationally independent mega churches (see, e.g., Rick Warren's Saddleback Church in Orange County, Calif.; Putnam and Campbell, *American Grace*, 54–69) can be seen as a reaction to this trend, as well as the emergence of the "Emergents" (see 177–79).

Theology and education: Theological education in the United States is also organized in different ways. On the one hand, one finds seminaries in which individual denominations educate their junior staff; on the other hand, there are institutions like Harvard Divinity School ("non-sectarian") and the above-mentioned Divinity School at Chicago University which are nondenominational and only subjected to the academic standards of their university. In addition, there are nondenominational institutions like the Union Theological Seminary in New York ("independent, multi-denominational").

In keeping with most theological institutions' orientation toward professional practice, the most common form is still that of "clergyman's training" (Schweitzer, "Praktische Theologie in Nordamerika," 567), that is, a concentration on individual fields of pastoral praxis. Correspondingly, the designation of the first chair of this kind was "Pulpit Eloquence and Pastoral

Theology" (est. in Harvard in 1819). Only since the mid-1900s have there been some systematically oriented forays into "Practical Theology," while "pastoral" and "practical" are interchangeably used today (see Woodward and Pattison, *Blackwell Reader*, 1–3). Effectively, most of the more recent practical-theological publications in the United States are pastoral-theological.

Foundations

Practical Theology, in the sense established in the German-speaking field, began to emerge in the United States only in the mid-1900s, although the pertinent questions had been part of American theology for much longer (see Wright 295–304). In his elementary outline of the development of Practical Theology in the United States, John Patton, professor of Pastoral Theology at Columbia Theological Seminary, lists three important origins:

William James (1842–1910): Thinking in terms of Practical Theology starts with the theory of religion of philosopher and psychologist William James. Three of his findings, or tenets, are particularly important for Practical Theology in the United States:

First and foremost, he was interested in individual experience. He therefore focused on individual religious experience and consciously disregarded questions of religious dogma (see, e.g., James, *Die Vielfalt der religiösen Erfahrung*, 59).[17] He expected particularly deep insights from the analysis of religious "geniuses," by which he hoped to gain access to what he thought were "original experiences" (42). James was fully aware that this particularly intense kind of experience was very often connected with what appeared to pathological or at least abnormal types of behavior. Second, this approach led to a method that Clifford Geertz later referred to as "thick description": a most fine-grained record of utterances and observations, the systematization of which remains of secondary importance. James often used this technique interpreting literary works. And third, putting the individual center stage also has philosophical consequences. Truth, in James, also turns out to be pragmatic: truth is not, as traditional concepts would have it, that which corresponds to reality but that which enables us to cope (see his example of happiness, 110). True therefore is that which I can live by. Religion thus becomes strictly pragmatic.

---

[17] James assumes a twofold concept of religion: institutional and personal. He is interested only in the personal variety (see *Die Vielfalt der religiösen Erfahrung*, 61).

Anton Boisen (1876–1965): Influenced by James, Edwin Starbuck, and other religious psychologists, the theologian Anton Boisen took up this psychological—and therefore above all single-case—interest in religion. For many the "father" of clinical pastoral care, Boisen himself suffered from a psychological disorder with severe fits. He trained pastoral students at the bedside and developed the concept of "living human documents"[18] for theological work. Charles Gerkin (1922–2004) extended this interest in individual suffering to a hermeneutical concept. The tension between psychology and Pastoral Theology on the one hand and pastor (spiritual caregiver) and the individual seeking help on the other is seen as a hermeneutical process of mutual interpretation. One motivation for this move is to prevent psychotherapeutic methodology from obscuring the Christian theological roots of the care of souls. Apart from Schleiermacher and Dilthey, Gerkin in particular draws on Gadamer's hermeneutical concepts of the "horizon of understanding" and the "fusion of horizons."[19]

In attending to the sick, Boisen transformed the hitherto indisputably asymmetric relationship between pastor and patient into a relationship of mutual learners. The crises offered him a unique opportunity to learn more about himself and the other person. By extending this method into a pastoral training program (Clinical Pastoral Education), Boisen prepared the ground for the pragmatic orientation of a Practical/Pastoral Theology that starts from the single person: the concrete communication with the sick individual. The close connection between theoretical reflection on Practical Theology and pastoral training is the common thread that runs through the further theological development in the United States—similar to the development of German Practical Theology as outlined earlier. In Germany, however, the organizational form of Clinical Pastoral Training made itself felt only in the second phase of pastoral training in preacher seminaries.

Seward Hiltner (1909–1984): Aside from translated works,[20] Seward Hiltner's 1958 *Preface to Pastoral Theology* probably marks the decisive advance into

[18] James already speaks of "documents humains" (*Die Vielfalt der religiösen Erfahrung*, 39).

[19] See Charles Gerkin, *The Living Human Document: Re-visioning Pastoral Counseling in a Hermeneutical Mode* (Nashville, 1984), 37–54 (esp. 45–48 on Gadamer).

[20] First, Johannes Jacobus van Oosterzee, *Practische Theologie: Een Handboek voor Jeugdige Godgeleerten*, 2 vols. (Utrecht, 1877–1878) (*Practical Theology: A Manual for Theological Students* [London, 1878]); the English translation omits important passages dealing with the development of Practical Theology (see Schweitzer, "Praktische Theologie in

a genuinely American Practical Theology, even though this "preface" never saw a followup. However, Hiltner's book goes well beyond discussing Pastoral Theology, which for him is defined in terms of the "shepherding perspective":

> Pastoral theology... is an operation-focused branch of theology, which begins with theological questions and concludes with theological answers, in the interim examining all acts and operations of pastor and church to the degree that they involve the perspective of Christian shepherding. (Hiltner, *Preface*, 24)

Hiltner sets "logic-centered fields"—such as Biblical Theology, Historical Theology, Dogmatics, Ethics, Psychological Theology, Aesthetic Theology, Comparative Theology—against "operation-centered fields,"[21] which again are divided into three scientific approaches: "Pastoral Theology" is characterized by the "shepherding" perspective and expresses itself in the communicative forms of "healing," "sustaining," and "guiding";[22] "Educational and Evangelistic Theology" is characterized by the dimension of "communicating," which finds expression in "learning," "realizing," and "celebrating";[23] and finally, "Ecclesiastical Theology" is characterized by the dimension of "organizing," which is expressed in "nourishing," "protecting," and "relating." Hiltner recognized the similarity of the latter theological fields with the German "Practical Theology" of the nineteenth century. However, he criticized that the Germans added only Practical Theology to the four disciplines of Old and New Testament studies, Church History, and Systematic Theology (see Hiltner, *Preface*, 24), while his model proposed only two categories. More pointedly, Practical Theology in German represented only a fifth, while study in the field of "operation-centered areas" made up half of all theology. Moreover, Hiltner, at a further remove from the German discussion, could not identify a generic term that would appropriately summarize the three areas mentioned. Contrary to the then current concentration on the methods of pastoral praxis in the United States, Hiltner emphasized the importance of theory: "The work

---

Nordamerika," 568).

[21] Compare the graphic illustration in Hiltner, *Preface to Pastoral Theology*, 28.

[22] The biblical connection is provided by the story of the Good Samaritan (see Hiltner, *Preface to Pastoral Theology*, 147).

[23] With great precision, Hiltner elaborates this dimension also with regard to observing the (four) basic requirements (*Preface to Pastoral Theology*, 192–94).

of the minister must have a theory, a general structure; it is not just doing, nor variation, nor skill, but in some sense the capture of a structure and an order."[24] However, he still cleaved to individual practices, which is illustrated by his criticism of a concept that would integrate research on and in individual fields of pastoral activity.

For his theoretical stance, Hiltner drew heavily on Paul Tillich's systematic-theological correlation theory while taking an even more radical approach: for him, "culture" can give answers to theological questions just as much as theology can propose answers to cultural questions (see Hiltner, *Preface*, 222–23n19). Hiltner illustrated his approach by showing how psychiatric interventions, for example, may support faith, and introduced terms like "interconnected theological method," "interpenetrating," "interrelated," "intervolve," or "amphidectic" (Hiltner, *Preface*, 223), even though they did not fully correspond to his objective of perfect mutual permeation of theological and nontheological study in Pastoral Theology. On occasion, he would also refer to Kurt Lewin's field theory (Hiltner, *Preface*, 188–89, 214–15)

Overall, Hiltner's main concern was a conceptually elaborated communicative approach. He emphasized that the first two of his basic perspectives of pastoral and ecclesial action, "shepherding" and "communicating," were inextricably linked. The third perspective, "organizing," had been a late addition to church practice, owing to its expansion. But it, too, needs a communicative design.

Hiltner's main interest clearly is to correlate theory and praxis—one fundamental concern of Practical Theology in the United States ever since. What happens is that practical-theological work is set "in motion": "Individual experience–comparison of individual experiences–generalization–development of a frame of reference–formation of a theory–testing of theory in practice–adaptation on the grounds of fresh experience."[25] In this process, it is the theological problem underlying the experience that guarantees the theologicity of Pastoral Theology. Hiltner's concept of "eductive counseling"[26] had, with a certain delay, a direct impact on German pastoral care, in which the mere adaptation of a dogmatically posited "word of God" seemed rapidly

[24] Seward Hiltner, "What We Get and Give in Pastoral Care. What We Get: Theological Understanding," *Pastoral Psychology* 5 (1954), 14–25, 15.

[25] Richard Riess, *Seelsorge: Orientierung, Analysen, Alternativen* (Göttingen, 1973), 202–3.

[26] See Riess, *Seelsorge*, 201–44.

dysfunctional. Hiltner's "principle of two-way communicating" (196) promised to bridge the divide between theological notions and concerns of the
lifeworld.

Developing a Profile

In keeping with its pastoral-theological orientation, theological study in the
United States focuses on specific fields of theological practice. A first impression of its breadth and diverse array of viewpoints is offered by the fifty-six
articles in the recently published practical-theological textbook edited by Bonnie J. Miller-McLemore. "Practical Theology" here acts more as "an umbrella
term comprising concrete religious praxis just as individual theological disciplines"[27] than as the name of a scientific theoretically elaborated discipline.[28]

In contrast, there are very few publications forming and systematically
describing the whole field of Practical Theology (see, for the literature up to
1998, Schweitzer, "Praktische Theologie in Nordamerika," 594–96). The two
books presented in the following, however, are two examples of approaches
that conceptually go beyond the German discussion. In addition, Tony Jones'
contribution opens up a perspective toward an appropriate organizational,
and therefore social form of communicating the gospel, which hitherto has
been absent from the German practical-theological discussion.

Don Browning (1934–2010): In his much-noticed book *A Fundamental
Practical Theology*, Don Browning conflated all practical-theological research
undertaken in the United States until the end of the 1980s integrating it in
his systematic outline. He also presented his work in Europe,[29] without, however, making much impact there. His starting point alone is highly interesting.
Browning places Practical Theology in the context of the beginnings of Practical Philosophy:

---

[27] From my review in *ThLZ* 137 (2012), 993–95, 994.

[28] In a similar direction points the new textbook edited by Kathleen Cahalan and Gordon Mikoski. They put "an emphasis on race, ethnicity, gender, class, and sexual orientation
arising from the situated and embodied character of human life" (Cahalan and Mikoski,
Opening the Field of Practical Theology, 3).

[29] See, e.g., Don Browning, "Auf dem Wege zu einer Fundamentalen und Strategischen
Praktischen Theologie," in *Praktische Theologie und Kultur der Gegenwart: Ein internationaler
Dialog*, ed. Karl Ernst Nipkow, Dietrich Rössler, and Friedrich Schweitzer (Gütersloh, 1991),
21–42.

> The rebirth of practical philosophy signals a wish to question the domi-
> nance of theoretical and technical reason, to secure in our culture and in the
> university a strong role for practical reason, and to demonstrate that crit-
> ical reflection about the goals of human action is both possible and neces-
> sary. Further, the rise of the practical philosophies, especially as influenced
> by Gadamer, has brought into closer relation historical thinking, herme-
> neutics or interpretation theory, and practical reason or ethics. This has
> brought a recognition that our present concerns shape the way we interpret
> the past. The reverse is also true. . . . These philosophical currents empha-
> size the importance of situations and how the situations of our inquiries
> inevitably color not only our practical thinking but all pursuit of knowledge
> and understanding. (Browning, *Fundamental Practical Theology*, 34–35)

The hermeneutically reflected starting point of (practical) theology is praxis,
not theory. This corresponds to Browning's triad—consciously opposing, for
example, Schleiermacher's "practice–theory–practice" (Browning, *Fundamental Practical Theology*, 7).

This resolute profiling of Practical Theology within a philosophical
framework reflects Browning's endeavor to place it in a context beyond the
confines of theology. At least for Western culture it is true that "there is a
quasi-theological component to social science description" (Browning, *Fundamental Practical Theology*, 90). Using examples from the field of psychology
(Sigmund Freud, Carl Rogers, William James) he traces the influence of each
scientist's religious background on their theories (see Browning, *Fundamental
Practical Theology*, 90). In this regard, Practical Theology makes essential contributions to understanding the present and is indispensable for self-reflective
social science.

This, however, necessitates a specific understanding of Practical Theology. Browning distinguishes between "fundamental" and "strategic" practical
theologies. "Fundamental practical theology" represents theology as a whole,
as long as it focuses on praxis. Browning defines this "as critical reflection
on the church's dialogue with Christian sources and other communities of
experience and interpretation with the aim of guiding its action toward social
and individual transformation" (36). This refers to the correlation theoretical
ideas of his Chicago faculty colleague David Tracy. Tracy defines Practical
Theology as "the mutually critical correlation of the interpreted theory and

praxis of the Christian fact and the interpreted theory and praxis of the contemporary situation."[30]

Embedded into this overarching concept of Practical Theology are the next theological work stages, that is, the "four submovements of descriptive theology, historical theology, systematic theology, and strategic practical theology" (Browning, *Fundamental Practical Theology*, 8). The most fundamental importance for practical-theological (and consequently theological) work is assigned to "descriptive theology," which focuses on the hermeneutical appreciation of the issue at hand ("horizon analysis"; Browning, *Fundamental Practical Theology*, 47). The following questions here guide theological reflection:

> What, within a particular area of practice, are we actually doing? What reasons, ideals, and symbols do we use to interpret what we are doing? What do we consider to be the sources of authority and legitimation for what we do? (Browning, *Fundamental Practical Theology*, 48)

Hans-Georg Gadamer's philosophy[31] here provides the hermeneutical foundation (see Browning, *Fundamental Practical Theology*, 39–40) that permits one to "understand the present situation in such a manner that an interpretative connection with Christian theology becomes possible" (Schweitzer, "Praktische Theologie in Nordamerika," 585) because it does not subordinate praxis to understanding. By employing Aristotle's concept of *phronesis*, Gadamer introduces a new understanding of practical reason. The aforementioned questions immediately lead to a historical view. Because only by assessing the past can the present be reasonably understood. At this point, the normative texts of the tradition offer themselves to Browning.

In the third step, that of systematic theology, something that Gadamer calls the fusion of horizons takes place. Browning raises some fundamental questions: "What new horizon of meaning is fused when questions from present practices are brought to the central Christian witness?" and "What reasons can be advanced to support the validity claims of this new fusion of meaning?" (Browning, *Fundamental Practical Theology*, 51–52). Only after

---

[30] David Tracy, "The Foundations of Practical Theology," in *Practical Theology: The Emerging Field in Theology, Church, and World*, ed. Don Browning (San Francisco, 1983), 61–82, 76.

[31] See Hans-Georg Gadamer, *Truth and Method* (New York, 1982) (*Wahrheit und Methode: Grundzüge einer philosophischen Hermeneutik* [Tübingen, 1960] and elsewhere).

these questions have been answered can the communicative tasks in the disciplines of traditional Practical Theology (liturgics, homiletics, etc.) be tackled. Specifically, the following four questions should be answered:

> How do we understand this concrete situation in which we must act?
> . . . What should be our praxis in this concrete situation? . . . How do we
> critically defend the norms of our praxis in this concrete situation? . . . What
> means, strategies, and rhetorics should we use in this concrete situation?
> (Browning, *Fundamental Practical Theology*, 55–56)

Browning's interest in philosophical and, above all, hermeneutical questions—besides Gadamer there are frequent references to, for example, Aristotle, Immanuel Kant, William James, Richard Bernstein, Jürgen Habermas, Richard Rorty, and Alasdair MacIntyre—suggests an unambiguous orientation toward praxis. Throughout, the book is informed by two dimensions of practical relevance.

Right at the outset, Browning outlines three concrete parishes. As he proceeds, he demonstrates the practicability of his theory by discussing its concrete impacts on pastoral work at one of these parishes.

Browning captures the second dimension by outlining a foundational course for theological studies while emphasizing that both fundamental practical theology and theological training employ parallel methods (72–74). Browning thus succeeds in vividly demonstrating the didactic potential of a theology that does not academically start from theory, but from the experience-related interests and questions of its students. It is these interests and questions that will then be investigated by exact description, historical inquiry, and systematic clarification, thus achieving a deeper understanding.

Richard Osmer (b. 1950): Osmer's ideas share a lot in common with Browning's approach. The Princeton scholar dedicates his introduction to Practical Theology to Browning (and to Charles Gerkin and Johannes van der Ven). His ideas, however, are strongly informed by a denominational outlook, that is, with a view to reformed theology. Osmer moreover strives less for philosophical-theological clarification than Browning. Instead, the didactically well-made book (see the charts in Osmer, *Practical Theology*, 37, 82, 136, 193) favors the pastoral theological perspective.

In parallel with the inner structure of Browning's Practical Theology, Osmer recommends the following four-step procedure of practical-theological work:

The descriptive empirical task. Gathering information that helps us discern patterns and dynamics in particular episodes, situations, or contexts.

The interpretive task. Drawing on theories of the arts and sciences to better understand and explain why these patterns and dynamics are occurring.

The normative task. Using theological concepts to interpret particular episodes, situations, or contexts, constructing ethical norms to guide our responses, and learning from "good practice."

The pragmatic task. Determining strategies of action that will influence situations in ways that are desirable and entering into a reflective conversation with the "talk back" emerging when they are enacted. (Osmer, *Practical Theology*, 4)

Epistemologically, Osmer strives for a hermeneutic understanding of Practical Theology, which draws heavily on Gadamer's philosophy (see 22–23). Accordingly, he follows Browning's "practice–theory–practice model" (148).

In sum, Osmer characterizes practical-theological work as a "bridge concept" that is meant to build bridges between the different practical-theological disciplines as well as the academic world and the church. By this token, Osmer aims at creating a new perspective for "congregational leadership" (17–18). He eschews the term "pastor," since others can also fulfill the role of "interpretive guides" within the congregation. The main task of such an "interpretive leader" is communication.

In elaborating this pastoral-theological goal, Osmer develops a clear profile, which also sets his approach off against Browning's. He acknowledges the strong influence of Charles Gerkin, for whom he worked as a research assistant when Gerkin was writing *The Living Human Document* (see Osmer, *Practical Theology*, 18). Clearly, Osmer joins ranks with the pastoral-theological Practical Theology initiated by Boisen that is interested in "living human documents." Normative insights are thus gained not only by recourse to the Bible, reformed tradition, and ethical reflection, but also by considering current practice, that is, concrete communicative actions:

Good practice provides normative guidance in two ways: (1) it offers a model of good practice from the past or present with which to reform a congregation's present actions; (2) it can generate new understandings of God, the Christian life, and social values beyond those provided by the received tradition. (152)

Osmer places the spirituality of the parish leader at the center of his consid-erations. By this, he understands a "leader's openness to the guidance of the Holy Spirit as she forms und transforms them toward the image of Christ in his body and his service of the church's mission" (27). His concept of "lead-ership" specifically refers to the reformed teaching of Christ's threefold office (priest, king, prophet) coupling it with the four steps of Practical Theology:

> [T]he descriptive-empirical task is a form of priestly listening, grounded in a spirituality of presence: attending to others in their particularity within the presence of God. The interpretive task is a form of wise judgement, grounded in a spirituality of sagely wisdom: guiding others in how to live within God's royal rule. The normative task is a form of prophetic discern-ment, grounded in a spirituality of discernment: helping others hear and heed God's Word in the particular circumstances of their lives and world. The pragmatic task is a form of transformation leadership, grounded in a spirituality of servant leadership: taking risks on behalf of the congregation to help it better embody its mission as a sign and witness of God's self-giving love. (28–29)

This kind of christological anchoring emphasizes virtues like "humility" as a fundamental pastoral quality. In the following of Christ, it becomes "the virtue of a contrast society" (193). This profile acquires particular significance in view of Osmer's unsparing assessment of the mainline churches' margin-alization in recent years (for exact numbers, see 175). He therefore calls for a "deep change," with regard to the identity, mission, culture, and practices of congregations. Viewed from the angle of "servanthood," fresh light is shed on these issues. The question cannot simply be one of mere preservation; the point is to be faithful to God's covenant.

Similar to Browning, Osmer makes some suggestions for the reformation of theological training. Just like Browning, he warns against the pillarization of theological disciplines, which he calls the "'silo mentality' in schools of the-ology" (234). He also recommends learning processes that start from concrete situations, allowing students to practice the four steps of practical-theological work in real-life examples.

Tony Jones (b. 1968): Browning and Osmer are both affiliated with main-line churches; Browning was ordained as a priest of the Christian Church (Disciples of Christ), and Osmer is an ordained pastor of the Presbyterian Church. Tony Jones is ordained member of the National Association of

Congregational Christian Churches, an association of over four hundred single congregations. He has many years of experience, also in leading positions, in the field of youth ministry, and, among other things, he graduated with a master's degree from the evangelical Fuller Theological Seminary in Pasadena and with a doctor's degree from the Princeton Theological Seminary.[32] Meanwhile, he is engaged in various pursuits. On his homepage (TonyJ. net), he describes himself as an "ecclesiologist—that's like a proctologist for the church."[33]

His book, *The New Christians: Dispatches from the Emergent Frontier*, was not, unlike the two books discussed above, written for academic teaching, but aims at contributing to concrete church reform. However, it implicitly contains some interesting theses about the development of Practical Theology in the United States. Most of all, Jones marks out some important trouble spots with regard to the communication of the gospel, which from his point of view from outside the mainland churches and their need for orderly administration seem to stand out more clearly.

Provocatively, the first subsection of his first chapter already proclaims, "Church is Dead" (Jones, *New Christians*, 4). In more concrete terms: "In the twenty-first century, it's not God who's dead. It's the church" (4). With this, Jones considers time-honored denominational differences to be obsolete— they simply are no longer of interest: "[D]enominations are an outmoded form of organized Christianity" (9). Particularly the bureaucratic form of organization of the mainline churches has outrun its function: "[B]ureaucracies also do two other things well: grow more bureaucratic tentacles and attract bureaucrats" (9).

The evangelical movement seems not to be fit for the future either. Proselytizing individuals neglects systemic problems like racism or poverty (see 13). In the final analysis, both the mainline churches and the evangelical movement reduce the complexity of the challenges posed by contemporary society.

As an alternative, Jones presents the "Emergents," that is, the proponents of an "emergent Christianity," as a model for a Christian community under postmodern conditions. This model quite literally emerged in the late 1990s from evangelical circles who were disappointed by the lack of vigor of their

---

[32] Tony Jones, *The Church Is Flat: The Relational Ecclesiology of the Emergent Church Movement* (Minneapolis, 2011).

[33] Retrieved May 1, 2013.

own movement and were looking for answers to the challenges of postmodernity, which was, for instance, expressed in Jacques Derrida's writings (see 47). Emergents forego affiliations or firm confessions of faith:

> Whereas traditional groupings of Christians are either bounded sets (for example, Roman Catholicism or Presbyterianism—you know whether you're in or out based on membership) or centered sets (for example, evangelicalism, which centers on certain core beliefs), emergent Christians do not have membership or doctrine to hold them together. The glue is relationship. (56)

As a result, a new understanding of being a Christian arises. It is now defined by "whether (and how thoroughly) one is woven into the fabric of global Christianity" (57). This is underpinned by the assertion that "Emergents see God's activity in all aspects of culture and reject the sacred-secular divide" (75).

This has consequences for (Practical) Theology. Conformable to the enculturation of the gospel (see 96), theological statements are contextual and situational: "Emergents believe that theology is local, conversational, and temporary. To be faithful to the theological giants of the past, Emergents endeavor to continue their theological dialogue" (111). This, of course, aims at reaffirming the limitations of human endeavors in the face of God's actions and finds expression in a very specific hermeneutics ("humble hermeneutic," 140). This "hermeneutic of humility" (141) translates the quest for "right" or "wrong" into one for a "better interpreter" (141). Emergents quite consciously refer to the Bible in its entirety, therefore including difficult passages that defy literal understanding (see Judg 11, 30–40; see Jones, *New Christians*, 144–47), thus leaving evangelical biblicism behind. In this context, interfaith dialogue (see Jones, *New Christians*, 155) takes on great significance, which Jones however fleshes out only with regard to the dialogue with the Jews.

This theological position has implications for church theory. Jones encourages the setting up of a "Wikichurch" (180), a nonhierarchical religious community, to which everyone can contribute. More specifically, he recommends organization in the form of an "open-source network." This moves communication into the focus of attention, in which the pastor becomes a "broker of conversation" (184). Jones admits that a structure like this is susceptible to error and mistake, much like Wikipedia, but a sclerotic church seems to him a much greater danger.

Most certainly, what merits particular attention in Jones' blueprint is the connection between the phenomenon of individualization and the individual's desire for community experience. Emphasizing concrete experience ultimately leads to a critique of traditional theological training (see 209–10). Jones deplores the missing connection between scholarship and spirituality.

On the whole, Jones poses the question of the correlation between the gospel and contemporary experience, which informs all Practical Theology in the United States, in a radically new fashion. His postmodern deconstruction lets the fragility of the human religious endeavor shine through. It opens up the horizon for the quest for a fresh understanding of the communication of the gospel, especially for its organization and the forms of community connected therewith.

Valuable Ideas for German Practical Theology

The pressure exerted on the mainline churches by the drastically declining membership has created an awareness in American Practical Theology that "deep change" is called for. This has led to a development that poses some particularly interesting challenges to German Practical Theology:

The Encyclopedic Position: Practical Theology—intended by Hiltner, systematically implemented by Browning—occupies a significantly larger space in American theology than in German theology. While Hiltner assumes two opposing, yet complementary, forms of theology—"logic-centered fields" and "operation-centered areas"—Browning integrates the whole of theological work. For him, theology becomes theology only in the form of "fundamental practical theology." Praxis, therefore, is constitutive of theology: it is nothing appended or added for practical purposes.

Hermeneutics: Practical Theology in the United States—above and beyond the approaches presented above—is fundamentally hermeneutic.[34] Social and cultural change need to be "understood." This kind of comprehension goes beyond a furtive look at statistics or the simple adoption of sociological analyses, as is attested by the importance that both Browning and Osmer assign to Gadamer's hermeneutics. Hermeneutics is the foundation on which the correlation between the gospel and the present can be tackled in all its complexity. This is in turn closely connected with the explicitly theological

[34] For an overview, see Sally Brown, "Hermeneutics in Protestant Practical Theology," in Cahalan and Mikoski, *Opening the Field of Practical Theology*, 115–32.

character of action-oriented considerations. Striking examples for this are Osmer's christologically substantiated importance of "humility" in pastoral care and Jones' extension of this virtue to comprise all church action. Finally, one cannot overlook the commitment of Practical Theology to understanding contemporary social developments. Based on this observation, Browning even goes so far as to postulate the indispensability of Practical Theology to the social sciences as a whole, since religious presuppositions are always implicit to sociological research, as well as to the researchers themselves.

Praxis orientation: All these practical-theological approaches share an emphatic grounding in concrete praxis. Browning and Osmer focus on the specific situations in congregations, while Jones concentrates on the biographical disruptions of individuals. In any case, the underlying thesis of "human living documents" deserves attention as a norm of theological reflection on an equal footing with Christian tradition. It is only at the price of reality that God's actions can be reduced to ancient scripture.

Theological training: As Browning has explained with regard to his concept of "fundamental practical theology," a resolute praxis focus has consequences for the understanding of theology as well as theological training. The study of theology is thus grounded in the hands-on experience of the students, which will be worked on in a practice–theory–practice mode.

This has some interesting consequences for theological programming. Instead of the so-called Stoffpläne ("subject-matter curricula"), which dominated the discussions on the reform of theological studies in Germany for a long time, the interest of the students comes into focus—not for pedagogical but for theological reasons ("living human documents").

The understanding of the church: Particularly Tony Jones draws attention to the problematic state of current church organization in both mainline and evangelical churches. Both fall short of meeting the exacting challenges of postmodernity. To be fit for the future, Jones insists, church organization must accommodate the complementary desires for individuality and community as well as the electronically changed forms of communication.

Summary of Part I

Practical Theology can only be understood in relation to its different contexts. Its development within German Protestant Theology can be reconstructed as the ups and downs of different approaches and interests—in the context of diverse changes.

Practical Theology thus suggests itself as a theory of balances. The following points need to be heeded:

First, the concentration on a well-defined subject of study necessary to research practice is in conflict with the breadth of religious and spiritual practices.

Second, the thematic restriction to theology is in conflict with the necessary inclusion of nontheological insights and research strategies.

Finally, the relevance of the practical-theological disciplines to theological praxis is in conflict with the multiperspectival approaches that lifeworldly complexity requires.

Comparing the profiles of Practical Theology in the Catholic Church and in the United States draws attention to the shortcomings of (German Protestant) Practical Theology:

First, compared to the wide horizon of the worldwide Catholic Church, as well as the less regulated social structure in the United States, German Practical Theology appears to be wanting with regard to political and socioeconomic questions.

Second, shortcomings also appear with regard to the theological definition of the discipline. Here an attention deficit can be observed with regard to more exact perception and general cultural discourses.

Third, and finally, attention needs to be paid to the emphasis of unavailability. The principal acts to which practical-theological theory formation takes recourse are due to—from the perspective of theological dogma—the grace of the Holy Spirit. In terms of communication theory, they escape, due to their complexity, all functional availability. As a consequence, one has to be mindful, for theological as well as communication-theoretical reasons, of the difference between God and human ideas of him or the church.

Against this backdrop, the "communication of the gospel" emerges from a variety of concepts as the leading category. First of all, it accurately defines the subject of the discipline. Second, it addresses the necessary connection with nontheological sciences. And third, it allows direct access to everyday living practice, which needs to be examined in its contexts of a democratic society and pluralistic cultures.

PART 2

Practical Theology as the Theory of the Communication of the Gospel

As shown in part 1, practical theologians of different provenance (Engemann, Mette, and Osmer)[1] suggest identifying the subject-matter of their discipline as the "communication of the gospel" (in the present day). This notion derived from the ecumenical discussion at the end of the 1950s and was meant to dynamize the theological understanding of Christian faith. In its substance it was critical of both the church and modern civilization:

> Today's Church exists in a secularized and extraordinarily dynamic mass society which is on the verge of disintegration. The Church, however, acts in many respects as though it still existed in the old, stable, confined world.[2]

With reference to his fellow countryman Johannes Hoeckendijk,[3] the Dutch ecumenist Hendrik Kraemer (1888–1965) pointed to the unity of

---

[1] Compare Fritz Lienhard, *La demarche de théologie pratique* (Brussels, 2006) with reference to the French discussion.

[2] Hendrik Kraemer, *Die Kommunikation des christlichen Glaubens* (Zürich, 1958) (Engl.: London, 1956), 91.

[3] See, in the first place, Johannes Hoekendijk, *Kirche und Volk in der deutschen Missionswissenschaft* (Munich, 1967) (Dutch: Amsterdam, 1948).

kerygma (sermon), *diakonia* (service), and *koinonia* (community)[4] for an appropriate understanding of the church. In doing so, he—having been a missionary in Indonesia for some years himself—widened the scope beyond the matter-of-course perpetuation of the conditions of a *Volkskirche* (people's church).

Theologically, his idea of communication still cleaved to the framework of an exclusively christocentric word-of-God theology. For him, the communication of the gospel was radically different from other forms of communication: it was a "category sui generis"[5] because apart from human beings it primarily involved the Holy Spirit, and its sole purpose was the conversion of individuals.

Ernst Lange (1927–1974) transferred this ecumenical impulse to German Practical Theology and the church reform discussions of the 1960s, thereby profoundly transforming the understanding of "communicating the gospel." He emphasized its dialogic character, which he thought essential for church action:

> We speak of the communication of the gospel and not of "propagation" or "preaching" because the concept accentuates the principally dialogic form of the act and furthermore renders visible the fact that all functions of the community which relate to the interpretation of the biblical testimony— from the sermon to pastoral care and confirmation instruction—as phases and aspects of one and the same process.[6]

Schooled on Dietrich Bonhoeffer's reformatory approach,[7] and due to his experience in youth work and his impressions from the United States, Lange aimed at dissolving the theological and organizational ossification of the German churches after the Second World War. Adopting incentives from, for example, Friedrich Gogarten, Lange recognized in modern reality the "impact history of promise." If nothing else, Lange thereby hoped to overcome the crisis in the pastoral profession diagnosed by him.

At the time, Lange's attempt at reform met with stiff resistance from the word-of-God theologians. In the meantime, the situation has changed. Social

---

4   Kraemer, *Die Kommunikation*, 93.

5   Kraemer, *Die Kommunikation*, 21.

6   Ernst Lange, "Aus der 'Bilanz 65,'" in Schloz, *Kirche für die Welt*, 63–160, 101.

7   See Ernst Lange, "Kirche für andere: Dietrich Bonhoeffers Beitrag zur Frage einer verantwortbaren Gestalt der Kirche in der Gegenwart," in Schloz, *Kirche für die Welt*, 19–62.

change, in particular processes of differentiation and pluralization, and technological innovations have made communication key in a variety of academic disciplines. In addition, academics from different fields have developed fresh and extended models of communication. Their multiperspectival models have created a sense of communicative complexity and proven the sender-receiver models—still dominant in the 1960s—to be too narrow and distorting.

This sophistication of communication models corresponds with the systematic-theological insight that earlier theological thought processes are incommensurate with the dynamics and pluriformity of contemporary developments. As a remedy, *Ingolf Dalferth (b. 1948)* convincingly proposes a form of "topical thinking in perspectives and horizons which is sensitive to multi-aspectivity and the recombinability of phenomena."[8]

For a differentiated—and expandable—analysis of the present, clear concepts and a qualified hermeneutical methodology are fundamental. Their clarification will therefore precede any content-related elaborations. In doing so, both the basic empirical conditions and the fundamental theological character of the communication of the gospel will be brought into play. In terms of content, the clarification of the concept of communication will be the organizing rationale informing all empirical investigations, for which, in accordance with the principle of multiperspectivity, I have drawn on studies deploying varying methods. It is on this basis that the modes of communication constitutive for the communication of the gospel in the New Testament will be analyzed. Materially, the historical reconstruction of Christianity is at the forefront of this investigation, since it is here that we find different context-dependent models for the communication of the gospel providing the stimulus for adapting the communication of the gospel for the present day.

---

[8] Ingolf Dalferth, *Evangelische Theologie als Interpretationspraxis: Eine systematische Orientierung* (ThLZ.F 11/12) (Leipzig, 2004), 12.

3

THE HERMENEUTICAL
FRAMEWORK

To begin with, the two fundamental concepts of Practical Theology, "communication" and "the gospel," need to be defined. It is advisable to begin with the concept of communication, since a complex understanding of communication will provide inroads into the understanding of the gospel insofar as it relates to communication processes. More precisely, Jesus' ministry suggests three connected modes of communication that alert to the beginning of the kingdom of God.

Next follows the analysis of the concept of religion. In the current German-speaking practical-theological discussion it generally designates the subject of Practical Theology. However, its origin as an intra-Protestant term of distinction defies this facile use. Only in due consideration of its history can "religion" contribute to the disclosure of contemporary value and life orientations. In this context, the concept of "spirituality" also warrants clarification, since in sociology of religion and in Practical Theology it sometimes replaces "religion."

This definition of terms is then followed by hermeneutical reflections. The first thing to remember here is the pluralism of the gospel, which has existed since the beginning of Christian history. Next, the internal structure of the communication of the gospel will be analyzed, in which the distinction between primary and secondary religious experiences, substantiated by religious history and, from a media-theoretical perspective, translated into a contemporary hermeneutical concept, is particularly useful.

The chapter concludes by proposing a differentiated understanding of the relationship between the communication of the gospel and its cultural context, drawing on distinctions established in liturgical contexts pointing out that the communication of the gospel includes the task of contextualization as well as that of cultural criticism.

All in all, these clarifications in many respects provide necessary precisions and differentiations owing to the basic insights of modern communication theory, the reconstruction of the three fundamental modes of communicating the gospel, the awareness of the internal tension of religious experiences, the definition of basic content-related tensions in the communication of the gospel, and, finally, a sophisticated awareness of the relationship between the communication of the gospel and its cultural context.

1. Clarification of Concepts: Communication–Gospel–Religion–Spirituality

Literature: Jürgen Becker, *Jesus von Nazaret* (Berlin, 1996); Corinna Dahlgrün, *Christliche Spiritualität: Formen und Traditionen der Suche nach Gott* (Berlin, 2009); Manfred Faßler, *Was ist Kommunikation?* (Munich, ²2003); Gerhard Friedrich, "Euangelizomai, euangelion, proeuangelizomai, euangelistes," *ThWNT* 2 (1935/1967), 705–35; Ferdinand Hahn, *Theologie des Neuen Testaments*, vol. 1: *Die Vielfalt des Neuen Testaments* (Tübingen, 2002), 180–322; Hubert Knoblauch, *Populäre Religion: Auf dem Weg in eine spirituelle Gesellschaft* (Frankfurt, 2009); Michael Meyer-Blanck, "Praktische Theologie und Religion," in *Praktische Theologie: Eine Theorie- und Problemgeschichte* (APrTh 33), ed. Christian Grethlein and Helmut Schwier (Leipzig, 2007), 353–97; Astrid Reglitz, *Erklären und Deuten: Glaubenspraxis in diskurstheoretisch-theologischer Perspektive* (Theologie–Kultur–Hermeneutik 12) (Leipzig, 2011); Jens Schröter, *Jesus von Nazaret: Jude aus Galiliäa—Retter der Welt* (Biblische Gestalten 15) (Leipzig, ²2009)

Communication

Communication is one of the central issues in contemporary social and cultural sciences. The decline of generally respected traditions and norms leads to an increasing interest in the phenomenon of communication (see Faßler, *Was ist Kommunikation?*, 27). Furthermore, due to the evolution of modern media, new social forms begin to emerge, which are best reconstructed from a communication-theoretical perspective. Surveying the most important communication-theoretical publications yields an array of different perspectives necessary for a sophisticated understanding of the phenomenon, already suggested by the etymological origins of the term:

> In the ancient world, the composite verb "communicare" had four different meanings: 1) to do jointly, to unite; 2) to let sb. know/participate, to impart/ to share (information); 3) to own jointly or to share; to help carry; 4) to get in touch, deliberate. In the final analysis, the core meaning of communication is "to share, to impart/(to let sb. know/participate/be part of)."[1]

In the following, I will first briefly consider the origins of modern communication science in telecommunications engineering, followed by a discussion of pertinent insights from psychology, semiotics, sociolinguistics, ritual, system, and action theories as well as poststructural approaches. They are all intimately interlinked in the current discussion and have been adopted thus in theological studies. In the current context, this multiperspectivity helps elucidate the fundamental multiplicity of factors at play in communication processes and the consequential open-endedness of all communication. What has previously been handed down as "teaching" is now translated into negotiation processes. Starting from the concept of communication, the focus now fundamentally shifts from the "subject" or "individual" to the "relationship" (which, of course, is that of individuals)—which is constitutive of communication.[2]

Impetus from communications engineering: An important impetus for the development of communication theories came from the mathematical-technological communication model of the two American mathematicians Claude Shannon (1916–2001) and Warren Weaver (1894–1978). This model describes the basic structure of signal transmission in the following

---

[1] Petra Korte, "Pädagogische Kommunikation oder Ein Plädoyer für alltägliche pädagogische Differenz- und Dissenskultur," in *Bildung und Bedingtheit: Pädagogische Kommunikation im Kontext individueller, institutioneller und gesellschaftlicher Muster*, ed. Renate Girmes and Petra Korte (Opladen, 2003), 141–52, 142.

[2] John Sullivan, "Communicating Faith and Relating in Love," in *Communicating Faith*, ed. John Sullivan (Washington, 2011), 359–68, 359–60.

way: Source of Information → Sender/Transmitter/Encoder → Channel → Receiver/Decoder → (Message) Destination.[3] This model was developed for the telephone company by which Shannon and Weaver were employed, and its aim was to facilitate a transmission of data with the lowest possible levels of noise. It clearly indicates the important factors for successful signal transmission. In the case of telecommunications technology, possible interferences in the channel (such as crackling noises or static) and their reduction are of major importance. To solve this problem, a probability calculus was employed: given the limited range of elements to be encoded, such as the letters of the alphabet, the interferences are reconstructed according to the statistical probability of their occurrence.

With respect to the transmitted messages, Shannon and Weaver introduced the concept of selection. According to this, the information content is constituted by the ratio of actual to possible messages, which again have a certain probability. Thus, already in this model, a larger context is implicated that extends significantly beyond the actually communicated messages but is critical for the decoding of these messages. However, this model deliberately ignores questions of the purpose and meaning of communication.

Insights from psychology: A fundamentally new dimension for the understanding of communication was introduced by psychoanalytical theory: Freud's insight into the psychological entities of the id and the superego draw attention to the problem that a mere concentration on the conscious actions and goals of the communicators, that is, on the ego level, unrealistically narrows the range of factors operating in communication.

This cue was then elaborated in action-oriented approaches like that of Friedemann Schulz von Thun (b. 1944), whose contributions received widespread attention. Adopting Karl Bühler's distinction of the descriptive, expressive, and appeal functions of language[4] and Paul Watzlawick's distinction of content and relationship level,[5] von Thun developed the so-called communication square, or four-sides model, which has become the staple of many

---

[3]   According to the graph in Beck, *Kommunikationswissenschaft*, 18 (with reference to Claude Shannon and Warren Weaver, *The Mathematical Theory of Communication* [Urbana, 1972]).

[4]   Karl Bühler, *Sprachtheorie: Die Darstellungsfunktion der Sprache* (Jena, 1934).

[5]   Paul Watzlawick, Janet Beavin, and Don Jackson, *Menschliche Kommunikation: Formen, Störungen, Paradoxien* (Bern, 1969).

communication trainings and counseling.[6] According to this, every communication contains four—principally equally important—messages: about the
matter being communicated (matter layer), about the speaker (self-revelation),
about the way the relationship is perceived by the speaker (relationship layer),
and the appeal, which contains the speakers wishes and desired effects. These
four levels apply to both the speaker ("tongues") and the receiver ("ears") in
each communication act. Both speaker and receiver are affected by internal
tensions—such as between a sense of duty and desire for idleness—which
increases the complexity and therefore the precariousness of communication.
It was its proximity to praxis that made this model approachable also for pastoral care.[7] In the meantime, it has been adapted for the study of intercultural
communication and proven useful as an analytical tool[8] for communication
impediments.

Insights from semiotics: Semiotics as the theory of signs, that is, of that
which carries meaning or may become a carrier of meaning, encompasses the
whole field of communication because it is always—also—concerned with
meaning. Particularly Umberto Eco's[9] theory of signs has had a profound
influence on Practical Theology.

Following Eco, Wilfried Engemann defines communication as a "process
of impartation and participation," reconstructing the communication of the
gospel as a process that can be analyzed in terms of semiotics.[10] Accordingly,
communication is carried out on the basis of signs by persons with specific
goals in specific situations. Communication processes refer to specific codes,
the mutual knowledge of which is critical for successful negotiations.[11] In each
concrete act, different codes overlap, increasing the complexity of the communication process. The semiotic approach clearly identifies the significance

---

[6] Friedemann Schulz von Thun, *Miteinander reden*, 3 vols.: vol. 1: *Störungen und
Klärungen: Allgemeine Psychologie der Kommunikation*; vol. 2: *Stile, Werte und Persönlichkeit-
sentwicklung: Differentielle Psychologie der Kommunikation*; vol. 3: *Das "Innere Team" und situ-
ationsgerechte Kommunikation* (Reinbek, 1981, 1989, 1998).

[7] See Christoph Morgenthaler, *Seelsorge* (Lehrbuch Praktische Theologie Bd. 3)
(Gütersloh, 2009), 242–43.

[8] Dagmar Kumbier and Friedemann Schulz von Thun, eds., *Interkulturelle Kommunikation: Methoden, Modelle, Beispiele* (Reinbek, ⁴2010).

[9] Seminal reading: Umberto Eco, *Einführung in die Semiotik* (Munich, 1972) (Ital.:
1968).

[10] Engemann, "Kommunikation des Evangeliums," 140–85.

[11] See, e.g., Karl-Heinrich Bieritz, *Liturgik* (Berlin, 2004), 44–46.

of the specific communication situation by analyzing the signs provided by it—for instance, the church interior during service or the doctor's consulting room. The situation forms communication expectations—on entering a church or a doctor's surgery.

Through these factors, communication theory connects with other fields of study and their findings and questions. The factor "person" leads to the field of psychology, "situations" to that of the social sciences. With regard to the explicit goals Engemann sets for Practical Theology, namely "shaping the church" and "giving and living freedom," economics, law, and philosophy must be added. In doing so, culture and society are placed at the heart of communication-theoretical analysis.

Engemann's approach at least principally allows one to consider the challenges posed by the electronic media and pinpoints the fundamentally distinctive feature of binary communication: it is, due to basic telecommunication needs, interested in the smooth, "noise-free" transmission of information, whereas in communication-theoretical terms, "noise," or disruptions, are constitutive of the communication of the gospel since it involves human processes of adaptation in which human beings "can be touched, moved, and changed."[12]

Sociolinguistic insights: The sociolinguist angle modifies the semiotic avenue to communication at a crucial point by drawing attention to the fact that participants in communication need a common code of communication to enable negotiation. Taking recourse to class theories, the British sociolinguist Basil Bernstein (1924–2000) distinguishes between "restricted and elaborated codes."[13] The former is marked by short, often incomplete sentences, heavily reliant on direct speech. It is emotional and situational, deliberations are concrete and graphic. The latter, however, is marked by the use of complex syntax and a propensity for generalizations, often without discernable situational reference. Its reasoning is abstract and conceptually compact. By this token, attention is drawn to the social contextuality of language and the resulting communication problems. As concerns Practical Theology, the distinction between restricted and elaborated codes attracted notice particularly

---

[12] Wilfried Engemann, "Kommunikation der Teilhabe: Die Herausforderung der Informationsmaschinen," in *Personen, Zeichen und das Evangelium: Argumentationsmuster der Praktischen Theologie* (APrTh 23), ed. Engemann (Leipzig, 2003), 255–69, 266 (no emphasis in original).

[13] See Basil Bernstein, *Theoretical Studies: Towards a Sociology of Language* (London, 1971).

in homiletics, as it helped clarify the communication problems between academically trained parish priests and formally less educated congregation members.

Insights from ritual theory: Speech act theory, which Schulz von Thun also incorporates, has been elaborated to accommodate ritual forms of communication. The basis for this is the English philosopher John Austin's (1911–1960) insight that utterances can be understood as acts.[14] This becomes quite plain if one considers legal acts like the contraction of marriage. The act of pronouncing "I do" has far-reaching consequences. Similarly, other speech acts—as, for instance, "I now declare this meeting open"—not only describe something, but also perform potent acts. In terms of exegesis, this has become particularly important for parable theory as the parables also offer access to fresh realities and have, among other things, an appellative character.[15]

Austin's speech act theory allowed ethnologists like Victor Turner (1920–1983) a deepened understanding of the communication acts in the tribes they studied.[16] They observed communications that were not designed merely to describe or interpret facts and circumstances. The performance of these "rituals" posited reality itself. In contrast, the importance of explicit statements in the sense of discursive language sometimes receded completely. Thus, ritual theory alerts to the particular potential of communication to posit reality.

Systems-theoretical insights: Sociologist Niklas Luhmann (1927–1998), in his turn, has opposed technical reductionism by drawing attention to the "improbability of communication,"[17] thereby opposing the generally accepted view that communication is identical sense making, which can be effected with a little goodwill. From a systems-theoretical point of view based on the theory of the autopoiesis of systems, communication occurs between two systems. In this approach, only the communication itself can be analyzed, not,

---

[14] Seminal reading: John Austin, *How to Do Things with Words* (Oxford, 1962).

[15] See Christoph Kähler, *Jesu Gleichnisse als Poesie und Therapie* (WUNT 78) (Tübingen, 1995), 17–41.

[16] Victor Turner, *The Forest of Symbols: Aspects of Ndembu Ritual* (Ithaca, N.Y., 1967). A brief outline of the fairly complex discussion is provided by Catherine Bell, *Ritual: Perspectives and Dimensions* (Oxford, 2009 [1997]), 61–92.

[17] Niklas Luhmann, "Die Unwahrscheinlichkeit der Kommunikation," in *Soziologische Aufklärung 3: Soziales System, Gesellschaft, Organisation*, ed. Luhmann (Opladen, 1981), 25–34.

however, the intentions, goals, denotations, and meaning that guide each system.[18] Communication itself is reconstructed as a system, in which the accent at times lies on "impartation," at other times on "information," or, eventually, on "understanding," and it is not reduced to the exchange between persons.[19] On the one hand, the systems-theoretical perspective alerts to the formidable difficulties underlying the communication process, which are based on the dissimilarity of the communicators. On the other hand, it emphasizes the internal dynamics of communication, which cannot be functionally understood by simply analyzing the underlying factors. By distinguishing between (inaccessible) consciousness and communication, Luhmann presents the difficulty of at all assessing the (improbable but) possible understanding in communication. Luhmann was criticized for disregarding the interactive character of communication resulting from the separation of the system communication from the communicators.

Dirk Baecker (b. 1955) develops Luhmann's approach further. According to him, redundancy and selection are the two forms in which communication occurs. Without redundancy communication cannot connect with the old, without selection it cannot access the new. Interpreting these insights in sociological terms, Baecker concludes that causality cannot capture communication: on the contrary, communication is marked by an "uncertainty index."[20]

Insights from action theory: It seems questionable whether uncertainty is true for every kind of communication.[21] By defining communication more clearly against other forms of action, Jürgen Habermas' (b. 1929) universal pragmatics offer an extended, action-theoretical understanding of communication processes. Habermas distinguishes between "instrumental," "strategic," and "communicative" forms of action.[22] Communicative action is distinguished by the fact that its outcome has not been established before, but will be determined only by the process itself. Such communication involves,

---

[18] Niklas Luhmann, *Soziale Systeme: Grundriß einer allgemeinen Theorie* (Frankfurt, 1984), 156.

[19] See Luhmann, *Soziale Systeme*, 226–27.

[20] Dirk Baecker, *Form und Formen der Kommunikation* (Frankfurt, 2007 [2005]), 48.

[21] Exceptions, as, for instance, with regard to military orders, need not be considered in the present context. The biblical understanding of belief/faith excludes such command structures for the communication of the gospel.

[22] Jürgen Habermas, *Theorie des kommunikativen Handelns*, vol. 1: *Handlungsrationalität und gesellschaftliche Rationalisierung* (Frankfurt, 1981), 385.

first, that "the uttered statement is true"; second, "that the speech act is correct with respect to an accepted normative context"; and third, "that the manifest speaker intention is meant the way it is uttered."[23] Hierarchies or other forms of dependency, clearly defined targets, and tactical behavior impede this kind of communication: it requires a domination-free public sphere. In the groundwork of his Practical Theology, Norbert Mette draws heavily on this Habermasian approach.[24]

However, in the final analysis the question remains whether this reductive concentration on language, which also disregards the possibility of communicative disruptions, unwarrantably distances the concept of communication from praxis. Habermas' concept of communicative action requires situations that normatively hide the precariousness of human identity under modern reflective conditions.

Poststructuralist insights: The problems in achieving successful communication have been accentuated in a novel fashion by authors like Michel Foucault (1926–1984). In his discourse theory, he emphasizes that communication is organized along the lines of power structures; discourses are the framework in which communication takes place.[25] Communicative disturbances are particularly interesting, and Habermas' guiding paradigm of symmetrical communication comes under ideology-critical analysis. Symmetrical communication implies role equity and a media structure enabling equitable mutuality. Functionally speaking, this symmetry is often impossible to achieve: the expert has expert knowledge his communication partners do not possess. This, however, does not mean that the whole communication process must unfold in an asymmetrical manner; on the contrary, it is only in phases of symmetrical communication that both sides win new insights.

New challenges: The technological innovations in the media and their significance for communication will be dealt with at a later point. At this stage, it is however important to mention two challenges that primarily impact sociality: First, there are the new media simultaneously expediting the two trends of standardization and individualization (see Faßler, *Was ist Kommunikation?*, 28). In the United States, first church-theoretically relevant repercussions

---

[23] Habermas, *Theorie des kommunikativen Handelns*, 149.

[24] See, e.g., Norbert Mette, *Einführung in die katholische Praktische Theologie* (Darmstadt, 2005), 19.

[25] Michel Foucault, *Die Ordnung des Diskurses* (Frankfurt, [10]2007 [French orig. 1972]), 10–11.

can be seen with the Emergents. They organize that which used to be called church and to them seems too inflexible in wiki format or as an open-source network. It is difficult to decide whether this constitutes an individualization of Christianity or a new form of congregation. In any case, it opens up new horizons for the organization of Christian life in which the transforming life-world is integrated by new media technologies.

Second, the distinction between "digital natives" and "digital immigrants" indicates a new, largely generation-specific hiatus, which is due to the different significance of electronic media use. The most striking distinction is the considerable amount of time "natives" spend on self-presentation in online communities and on keeping up-to-date. The time-consuming online participation of many young people may be explained by the relevance this form of communication has for (the development of) their sense of identity.[26] Other media, or other forms of social contact, become less important for time reasons alone. To depreciate this kind of change in terms of decadence theories, however, is not very helpful. The communication-theoretical implications of this development need first to be understood before practical-theological conclusions can be drawn.

Conclusion: Multiperspectival analyses reveal communication as a multiply complex process aiming at mutual understanding between people. First of all, in terms of communications engineering, communication processes are constituted by redundancy and selection. Psychological approaches discern different communication levels. In terms of semiotics, different codes emerge depending on specific situations, goals, and communicators. Sociolinguistics draws attention to class, milieu, or lifestyle-dependent uses of language that may pose obstacles to successful communication. Ritual theory emphasizes the action character of spoken communications and their capacity to posit new realities. The system-theoretical open-endedness and improbability of communication also imply its innovation potential. For truth-theoretical reasons, action theory emphasizes the significance of the open-endedness of communication. Discourse theory underlines the power structures informing communication processes. And, finally, technological innovation brings about both new opportunities and challenges.

---

[26] See Gerhard Franz, "Digital Natives und Digital Immigrants: Social Media als Treff-punkt von zwei Generationen," *Media Perspektiven* (2010), 399–409, 407–8.

All this has far-reaching consequences for a practical-theological theory of the communication of the gospel because it clearly implies that "the gospel" constitutes no content separate from the concrete act of communication. The proper meaning of the gospel is generated only in the communication act and therefore is, as a matter of principle, open-ended. Open-endedness of course does not entail arbitrariness, but quite on the contrary expresses the communication-theoretical prerequisite for the innovative and person-oriented character of the gospel. The gospel emerges afresh in each communication, in concrete situations, in the exchange between persons, and is open for discovery and a fresh view of reality. The precariousness of this interaction is implicated in the discourse-theoretical warning of the often hidden power structures inherent in communication processes. Communication of the gospel, however, categorically requires symmetrical constellations, which functionally include unavoidable asymmetries, as in the communication of theological insights. These insights therefore need to be contextualized in a manner that expresses the fundamental equality of people based on the creatureliness of every human being. Only thus can the gospel be communicated in an open-ended manner that will benefit everyone involved in the communication.

Gospel

The New Testament reports a variety of communicative situations in which people meet Jesus and find a new orientation. Jesus' message of the imminent kingdom of God proved to be a perspective that changed people's outlook on and orientation in life. His suffering, death, and the subsequent events leading to his new presence invested this change of perspective with credibility. The concept that summarizes this fundamental Christian impulse in the Greek New Testament is *euangelion*: "the good news—the gospel."[27] This concept needs to be examined further.

In a first step, I will outline its appearance in the New Testament. In this context, the ministry and destiny of Jesus of Nazareth take center stage, which, in accordance with our practical-theological inquiry, will be analyzed in terms of communication theory. From this analysis, three modes of

[27] Noun and verb are absent only in the Johannine corpus—with the exception of "the everlasting gospel" in Rev 14:6 (see the attempted explanation in Friedrich, "Euangelizomai, euangelion," 714–15).

communication emerge that acquire their specificity from the fact that they are united in the person of Jesus. To this day, they have shaped the structure of the communication of the gospel.

The gospel as a New Testament concept: The concept of the gospel (*euangelion*) plays a central part in the New Testament in two important ways: it is a theological key concept in Paul and it appears in the Jesus stories in the (synoptic) gospels.

For the meaning of the term "gospel" in Jesus' own time, two different semantic influences can be inferred without however any assertion as to their respective importance: On the one hand, the term "euangelion" appears in the LXX rendering and is translated from the Hebrew "bisar" (Piel: "to deliver a message"; for details, see Friedrich, "Euangelizomai, euangelion, proeuangelizomai, euangelistes," 710–11). In these instances—with one exception (1 Sam 4:17)—the term expresses a joyous message (705). It is of communication-theoretical importance that "euangelizesthai" requires a "euanglistes," a messenger, that is, that this act constitutes a personal interaction. It is interesting to note that the medium as grammatical voice of "euangelizesthai" here expresses an oscillation between active and passive voice. It thus models the tension of every communication as impartation, in which the participants alternately send and receive, that is, quite literally "im-part."

In the political arena, *euangelion* designated imperial messages (721–22). Adopting the term in the New Testament thus gave it a counterimperial twist. The acronym on Jesus' cross shows that Jesus' ministry was interpreted in this sense (see Becker, *Jesus von Nazaret*, 435–37).

Euangelion has the highest occurrence in Paul (forty-eight times; the verb *euangeliszesthai* occurs nineteen times).[28] In this context it is remarkable that *euangelion* (always in the singular) is combined with a variety of verbs: the communication of the gospel appears in a pleonasm (*euangelizesthai*: 1 Cor 15:1; 2 Cor 11:7; Gal 1:11), the gospel is proclaimed (by a herald: *keryssein*: Gal 2:2, 1 Thess 2:9), the gospel is revealed (*gnorizein*: 1 Cor 15:1), it is taught (*didaskein*: Gal 1:12), it is submitted for discussion (*anatithesthai*: Gal 2:2), it is received (*paralambanein*: 1 Cor 15:1; Gal 1:12), and it is accepted (2 Cor 11:4).[29] A conceptual grouping with regard to the personal medium apostle

---

[28] See Hahn, who reconstructs all of Pauline theology on the basis of all the facets of understanding the concept of "gospel."

[29] See Friedrich, "Euangelizomai, euangelion," 727.

communicating the gospel can be found in 2 Timothy 1:11: the apostle here calls himself "herald" (*keryx*), "emissary" (*apostolos*), and "teacher" (*didaskalos*) of the gospel.

Paul programmatically defines the contents of *euangelion* in his prescript of the Roman letter (Rom 1:1-4). He accurately drafts the basic structure of *euangelion* as a multilayered communicative procedure by referring to "the Holy Scriptures," that is, the Old Testament, which assume lasting significance by presaging the advent of Jesus Christ. The genealogical reference characterizes Christ as both (ordinary) human being and somebody who by his kinship with David is directly connected with prophetic promise. The central issue for Paul is the resurrection of Jesus underlining the significance of Jesus' ministry, including his death (1 Cor 15:3). It is by his destiny at the end of his life that his ministry appears in a new light, thus determining the contents of *euangelion*. It is precisely for this reason that the gospel books have taken on a fundamental significance for Christendom: because here "the gospel of Jesus Christ, the Son of God" (Mark 1:1) is transmitted. However, one cannot distinguish between the objective genitive, according to which Christ is the contents of the gospel, and the subjective genitive, according to which Jesus is the messenger: both blend into each other, or, in terms of communication theory, message and medium coincide. It is furthermore interesting to note that "euangelion" occurs as personal interaction in the Gospels (e.g., Mark 1:14; Matt 4:23). Accordingly—as will be shown in a moment—it takes shape in various ways.

The kingdom of God as Jesus' message: According to the Gospels, the central message of Jesus' ministry is "the kingdom of God," a concept with multiple connotations in early Judaism (see Becker, *Jesus von Nazaret*, 102). In a traditional-historical analysis, Jürgen Becker convincingly isolates Zion theology as the background Jews in Jesus' time were familiar with for the motif of "God's reign" (103). This initially inner-historically interpreted concept was built upon by Deutero-Isaiah, in a manner that was discussed above for the semantic field of *euangelizesthai*. According to this, a joyous message was delivered from Zion to the exiles, creating a hope that radiated into Jesus' time. God as creator and God as ruler were equally important, while over time creation-related statements faded into the background. Other hopeful beliefs were added to his, like that of an eschatological ruler (Messiah, Son of David, Son of Man). Initially it was thought that only the then-living generation would be able to enjoy the divine kingdom of peace, but this hope was expanded in the Isaiah apocalypse to include the resurrection of the dead (Isa 26:19) and the annihilation of death altogether (Isa 25:8).

The central idea of "God's reign" in Jesus' ministry (see 122) ties in with this line of tradition in three ways while at the same time transforming it:[30] First of all, Jesus did not regard the kingdom of God as a future event, but saw its beginnings in the present. According to Becker, the "punch line" of Jesus' message is "that God's reign takes place in this world as of now" (*Jesus von Nazaret*, 127), present and future forming a unified whole. Furthermore, Jesus updated traditional creation theology with respect to both wisdom and apocalyptic traditions for his message of the kingdom of God. In view of the forsakenness of Israel, as voiced so emphatically by John the Baptist in his penitential sermon, this dimension took on new significance for Jesus. It is the "totality of everyday creatureliness" (162) in which the kingdom of God can be experienced. In comparison, traditional salvation-historical motifs recede into the background. And the message of the nearness of God's kingdom begins to extend beyond the confines of Israel. Finally, "God's reign" is an expression of the salvation of the lost, as the pertinent parable in Luke 15 illustrates, thus challenging implicit cultic and ethical values. All in all, "the kingdom of God" thus means the loving and effective presence of God,[31] which made itself felt particularly in Jesus' ministry.

Communicating the immediacy of the kingdom of God:[32] Jesus employs three modes of communication to make the advent of the kingdom of God plausible to his fellow beings.

The first is that of teaching and learning in verbal communication. His preferred means of teaching consisted in the impartation of parables, similes, and metaphors. This was not an unusual procedure. However, Jesus' teaching is marked by two particularities: first, he used these literary forms extraordinarily frequently and, second, he preferred these utterances to speak for themselves and refrained from the customary lengthy explanations. His

---

[30] See, for the following, the detailed remarks in Becker, *Jesus von Nazaret*, 122–76.

[31] Compare Ingolf Dalferth, "Theologie und Gottes Gegenwart," in *Gedeutete Gegenwart: Zur Wahrnehmung Gottes in den Erfahrungen der Zeit*, ed. Dalferth (Tübingen, 1997), 269–85, 273.

[32] "Vermittlung der Nähe der Gottesherrschaft" is a chapter title in Becker, *Jesus von Nazaret*, 176; the following sketch is based on his detailed discussion on 176–233. His concentration on the idea of "communication" (impartation) on the one hand serves Jesus' concerns and on the other hand is fully compatible with the communication-theoretical approach.

aim is to "'hot-wire' the world of his contemporaries to the kingdom of God (Luke 11:20)" (Becker, *Jesus von Nazaret*, 183). He achieved this in a didactically admirable manner, which can be understood even today despite different social and cultural circumstances. Examining the contents of his parables, one can observe three significant elements: First, they all include strong imagery. The narrative mode opens up a larger interpretative field than that of mere visual impressions. Second, there is the frequent use of the meal motif, which, according to Jewish tradition, is connected with prayer and benedictions. Third, Jesus frequently reports acts of succor and relief, again implying the communion with God, whom he calls his Father. These three motifs are all but accidental, but indicate the interlocking of his three modes of communicating the gospel, each mode shaping the others.

However, the Gospels do not treat the understanding of parables and similes alone. In Mark there is even a reflection on their unintelligibility for the uninitiated and the disciples' need for further explication (Mark 4:10-12). In terms of communication theory, this passage addresses the pitfalls, the open-endedness, and even the improbability of communication.

As a further mode of verbal communication, Jesus' so-called disputations must not go unmentioned. In these brief exchanges, Jesus displays great sensitivity with regard to his interlocutors.

Functionally, this verbal mode of communication constitutes a teaching and learning process. In terms of communication theory, taking recourse to the known (redundancy), the attention is turned to the new (selection). The discovery of the new is intended to produce sustainability, that is, the transformation of life through profoundly affecting and ongoing teaching and learning processes. Accordingly, the Gospels call the closest followers of Jesus "disciples/students" (*mathetes*) and Jesus himself was addressed as *rabbi* (e.g., Matt 26:25, 49; John 1:38)

As the second mode central to Jesus' ministry, Becker singles out the meal communities. While talk naturally also accompanied the meals, the focus lay here on eating and drinking and the satiation of hunger and thirst. This connected with the traditional apocalyptic expectation of a feast at the end of days (Isa 25:6) as well as with the sapiential assertion that God is giver of all food (see Matt 6:11). As mentioned above, Jesus included the meal motif in his didactic tales, but the Gospels also report of his partaking in several banquets (see Becker, *Jesus von Nazaret*, 201). On each of these occasions, Jesus apparently extended the table because for him the kingdom of God necessarily included feeding the hungry (see, e.g., Matt 5:6). In the same manner, he encouraged his contemporaries to show solidarity with those excluded for ritual or moral reasons, the so-called sinners and publicans. So, extended table fellowships are to be expected.

For Jesus, these meals constituted the beginning of God's reign: hunger and thirst are assuaged, there is even festive abundance,[33] social outsiders are integrated into the community. In view of the small geographical area in which Jesus acted within the Galilean villages and the frequency with which these meals took place, the strong impact this form of communication must have had can easily be understood. The communal meals were accompanied by benedictions and prayers. They expressed the communion with God in daily life.

This communion became particularly evident in the Last Supper (see Schröter, *Jesus von Nazaret*, 293–94). It is historically unlikely that a repetition was on anybody's minds, but it suggested itself because of the significance Jesus assigned to these meal communities to assert the advent of the kingdom of God. Their connection with eating and drinking, two basic necessities for every human being, emphasized the basic character of these meals, which can be best expressed by the adjunct "communal."[34] In terms of communication theory, the significance of communal celebration as a means to understand the message of the beginning of God's kingdom was underscored by these meal communities. As in the verbal mode of communication, the pitfalls of communication also surface in this mode, as instanced in the vilifications of Jesus as a "glutton and winebibber" and "a friend of tax collectors and sinners" (Matt 11:19).

From a communication-theoretical point of view, these meals probably contained elements of both traditional ritual communication, particularly benedictions, and simple open conviviality. The written record of the Gospels however foregrounds the ritualistic side focusing on the benedictions and Jesus related interpretive words. The communication thus becomes less susceptible to disruptions but at the same time forfeits some of its innovative potential.

[33] See Peter-Ben Smit, *Fellowship and Food in the Kingdom: Eschatological Meals and Scenes of Utopian Abundance in the New Testament* (WUNT II, 234) (Tübingen, 2008).

[34] See Jürgen Roloff, "Heil als Gemeinschaft: Kommunikative Faktoren im urchristlichen Herrenmahl," in *Exegetische Verantwortung in der Kirche*, ed. Martin Karrer (Göttingen, 1990), 171–200.

The final communicative mode is the concrete help for living Jesus provided. Becker emphasizes the significance of faith healings in Jesus' ministry, which were, "analogously to his speaking in similes and the meals, the third realm in which God's reign, asserting itself in the salvific turn, could be experienced" (Becker, *Jesus von Nazaret*, 220). According to numerous reports in the Gospels, Jesus acted as therapist and exorcist. Similar activities have been reported of other of Jesus' contemporaries, not to the same extent however. These acts in any case meant further attention to the corporeal dimension expressing the kingdom of God. The usual punitive or self-help miracles are absent in Jesus (see 215). Instead he moved his healing acts—which was extraordinary for his time—into the horizon of God's dominion. His fundamental concern was the individual's relationship to God:[35] in the healing process, individuals are delivered from their sins—from that which separates them from God. Thus the ministration of relief acquired a new significance for Jesus' contemporaries, who were accustomed to miraculous healings. Jesus' healings liberated them from their entrapments in sickness and the resulting social and cultic segregation and included them in the movement of the rule of God. In this context, the forgiveness of sins marks the opening of a new approach to God. Thus, Jesus' healings were acts of liberation toward the kingdom of God. This aspect was thrown into relief by Jesus' quarrels with Jewish purity codes and the perception of the Sabbath in some of his healings (see Schröter, *Jesus von Nazaret*, 233–45). As such, Jesus' social and healing actions and his claiming God for the forgiveness of sins are a form of communication. Since it delivered individuals to a new form of everyday life, while being clearly eschatologically oriented, I call this form of communication helping for living.[36] Living here refers both to earthly existence as well as to God's constancy outlasting biological death. Like the other two, this third mode is also affected by disruptions: where he was not accepted, Jesus could not heal (e.g., Mark 6:5).

---

[35] See Walter Mostert, *Jesus Christus—Anfänger und Vollender der Kirche: Eine evangelische Lehre von der Kirche*, ed. Jan Bauke-Ruegg, Peter Koller, Christian Möller, and Harald Weihnacht (Zürich, ²2007), 53.

[36] By adding "for living" I incorporate the psychologically, sociologically, and intratheologically reasoned ambivalence of the concept of help (see, for an elaborate argument, Anika Albert, *Helfen als Gabe und Gegenseitigkeit: Perspektiven einer Theologie des Helfens im interdisziplinären Diskurs* [VDWI 42] [Heidelberg, 2010]).

Ecclesial continuation: The church adopted these modes of communication and elaborated them. In doing so, it faces two radical challenges.

First of all, ecclesial action, as opposed to Jesus ministry, is mediated action. It acts on the fundamental impulse given by Jesus' example. For this reason, the defining profile of the communication of the gospel—after Jesus—must be fundamentally symmetrical.[37] The gospel of the living and effective presence of God is accessible only in the symmetrical exchange between individuals. It is not an irrefutable doctrine against which the knowing can be separated from the unknowing: in teaching and learning, the position of teacher and learner can switch, which is often seen as the most rewarding feature in the teaching professions; celebrating is a fundamentally communal experience; and, finally, in the processes of helping for living, the roles are occasionally inverted: the sick help the healthy, the dementia patient may teach the caregiver a new perspective on life, and so on. This being said, the constant danger of misunderstandings inherent to human communication may imperil these processes. Due to its openness to pluriform appropriation, a long trail of devastatingly fallacious understandings of the gospel runs through Christian history, resulting in reductions to one-dimensional doctrines. The communication of the gospel must always refer to Jesus' ministry and destiny.

Second, social and cultural change requires transformation. As mentioned above, even the New Testament accounts of the Last Supper reveal a tendency to foreground the forms of symbolic communication. This development has been extensively discussed[38] under the culture theoretical concept of the "ritual." According to this discussion, imperiled or perilous communications are translated into regulated procedures. Closer analysis however reveals that this overlooks an important prerequisite: the natural recognition (in African tribes) of the life and value orientations implicit in these symbolic communications. Therefore, the inflationary reference to "ritual" in writings on Practical Theology is not particularly helpful for the closer analysis of

---

[37] This is "fundamentally" true, since communication takes place only in contexts. Consequently, the symmetry of the communication of the gospel takes on different forms between well-educated individuals in a modern democracy, between an illiterate peasant and a theological scholar in medieval estate-based societies, and between individuals in different stages of life.

[38] See Benedikt Kranemann and Paul Post, eds., *Die modernen Ritual Studies als Herausforderung für die Liturgiewissenschaft* (Liturgia condenda 20) (Leuven, 2009).

contemporary practice.[39] It is important to keep in mind that it is an empirical characteristic of contemporary life and value orientations to have a sense of optionality and consequently reservations against general validity claims; and that, furthermore, the insistence of reformatory theology on the difference between human action and the will of God has led to a fundamental sense of relativity in the domain of symbolic communication. It is therefore recommended to speak of "rituals" only in the context of premodern social interactions, in which the necessary prerequisites are fulfilled. For this reason, Thomas Klie suggests the term "rite" to designate Christian practices of symbolic communication.[40]

Conclusion: Combining the findings with regard to Jesus' three modes in which he communicates the advent of God's reign and the above reconstruction of the New Testament understanding of the "gospel" (*euangelion*), we can conclude that the gospel happens in practices of verbal and nonverbal communication. The content and meaning of these communications are revealed in reference to Jesus' ministry and destiny. This is why it is crucial to keep in mind the double meaning of the gospel as verbal communication and as a book. In terms of media theory, both forms are interactions: the former constituting a situational, open-ended mode, the latter a closed mode of interpretation. Both modes must remain in reference to each other to avoid spiritualizing one-sidedness or scholarly ossification. This relativizes the common theological ontological or subjectivity-theoretical approaches and translates their insights into a form of communication,[41] with interaction at its center.

Historical research has attempted to distinguish—with conflicting results—between the parts of the gospel relating to the earthly Jesus and the parts relating to the so-called community formations. For a communication-theoretical foundation of the gospel, these hypothetical operations are of no interest. Instead, it is striking that the three modes of communication have evidently been taken up and developed by all Christians in order to establish the truthfulness of the gospel. Its message, the advent of the kingdom of God, was given precision by referring it to the ministry and destiny of Jesus.

[39] See Thomas Klie, "Vom Ritual zum Ritus: Ritologische Schneisen im liturgischen Dickicht," *BThZ* 26/1 (2009), 96–107.

[40] Klie, "Vom Ritual zum Ritus," 104–7.

[41] See the fundamental discussion in Thomas Micklich, *Kommunikation des Glaubens: Gottesbeziehung als Kategorie praktisch-theologischer Theoriebildung* (APTLH 58) (Göttingen, 2009).

Teaching and learning, communal celebration, and helping for living have been the quintessential forms of expression of the emulation of Christ ever since. Reports of impediments to successful communications indicate that the communication of the gospel was already precarious for Jesus and failed. However, the open-endedness of the communication of the gospel offered followers fresh perspectives on life, which took form in a variety of ways. All three modes are marked by an open, inclusive momentum, bringing each participant into union with God. This momentum fundamentally requires symmetrical communication. The three modes go hand in hand: only together will they enable the experience of the loving and active presence of God.

Religion

In the following I wish to show why the concept of "religion" as a description of the subject matter of Practical Theology is today fraught with problems. Its abiding potential as a distinguishing category remains however intact. For this reason—at least within the field of Protestant Theology—it cannot be eschewed. It enables a hermeneutical distinction that allows one to understand the tensions within present-day communication of the gospel.

A look at the conceptual history (see Meyer-Blanck, "Praktische Theologie und Religion," 354–63) reveals varying meanings and functions of the term:[42] in ancient Rome, religio, together with pietas and sanctitas, described appropriate human behavior with regard to the gods, but it was no superordinated principle.[43] Only the denominational schisms of the sixteenth century forced a separation: cuius regio/cuius religio. The connection between church doctrine and personal piety grew visibly looser at the end of the eighteenth century and the beginning of the nineteenth—first among the more cultured and educated. "Religion" became a general term of German Neo-Protestant Theology, designed to distinguish between church doctrine and (dissenting) practices of faith while at the same time confirming their relationship, Christianity forming the natural matrix. In the philosophy of religion, "religion" was then divested of its connection with the church and a so-called natural religion was postulated on anthropological grounds, while still being unmistakably rooted in Christianity: only those elements of church doctrine that

---

[42] See Falk Wagner, "Religion II: Theologiegeschichtlich und systematisch-theologisch," TRE 28 (1997), 522–45.

[43] Ernst Feil, "Religion: II. Religion and History," RPP 11 (2012), 33–37, 33.

seemed to contradict reason were discarded. In the course of the nineteenth century, when other faith groups came into scholarly focus, this understanding of religion evolved to include the idea of evolution. According to this point of view, Christianity (of Protestant provenance[44]) was the highest form of religion. Other "religions" were placed in reference to Christianity, while this shows only that they were designated as such. Descriptive and normative criteria became confounded, and religion emerged as a—more or less highly developed—general human disposition or social form. Even Dietrich Rössler still uses "religion" in this anthropological and simultaneously generally Christian sense. He assumes that "religion belongs to the conditions of human reality."[45] With a view to contemporary society, he differentiates between "lived religion" (see Reglitz, *Erklären und Deuten*, 159–232) and church-theological religion.[46] This understanding of religion implicates an expansion of the subject area for Practical Theology, building on a functional understanding of religion as it has been proposed by the sociologist Thomas Luckmann.[47]

Too little attention has however been paid to the preconditions of this understanding of religion, that is, the anthropological assumption of a general religiosity, and the unquestioned Christian and ecclesial underpinning of culture. Challenges posed by other, non-Christian life or value orientations or nonreligious individuals did not come into view. Rössler's Practical Theology ignores, for instance, both Islam and Buddhism. From the perspective of conceptual history, the reason for this can be found in the transformation of a theological concept that was introduced to distinguish and integrate different forms of Protestantism into a term that was now meant to describe a general phenomenon and was reified in the process. One important implication of the original concept of religion was forgotten, however, namely the idea of progress, which Protestantism in its individualized form fulfilled as the most developed form of religion.

A much more critical stance than in Practical Theology toward the concept of religion and its performative capabilities can be encountered in the

---

[44] In the Catholic Church, a different understanding of "religion" evolved, in that it denotes the Church-approved beliefs and not individual faith (Meyer-Blanck, "Praktische Theologie und Religion," 355–56).

[45] Dietrich Rössler, *Die Vernunft der Religion* (Munich, 1976), 123.

[46] Rössler, *Die Vernunft der Religion*, 381.

[47] Thomas Luckmann, *The Invisible Religion: The Problem of Religion in Modern Society* (New York, 1967).

field of contemporary religious studies. The Neo-Protestant idea of the concept is perfectly present in this line of inquiry. With regard to non-European cultures and non-Christian "religions" it is, however, fraught with problems.[48] On the one hand, it is difficult to establish the common ground of these other "religions" which would justify the general concept of religion. Neither "God," nor "sacredness" or general transcendence are convincing candidates. A defining feature like "God," for instance, proves to be too narrow, since it excludes certain phenomena that are generally referred to as religions such as Buddhism. In the case of "transcendence," it proved impossible to establish an operative distinction between "religion" and "culture." In field research, the use of specific dimensions that together define "religion" has asserted itself.[49] This procedure manifests the construct character of "religion"—revealing considerable weaknesses in non-Western regions.[50]

On the other hand, taking account of non-European and non-Christian "religions" emphasizes how much the concept of religion has been shaped by European Christianity and Protestantism in particular. For example, after an interview about her "religion," a young Indian woman explained to a startled German sociologist,

> I have passed through a Western system of education here in Singapore, and I think I know quite well how you Western people are used to think about man and God and about "religion." So I talked to you as if "hinduism" were my "religion," so that you may be able to understand what I mean. If you were a hindu yourself, I would have talked to you in quite a different fashion, and I am sure both of us would have giggled about the idea that something like "hinduism" could be a "religion," or that something like "hinduism" does even exist.[51]

---

[48] See Gregor Ahn, "Religion I: Religionsgeschichtlich," *TRE* 28 (1997), 513–22.

[49] Particularly important: Charles Glock, "On the Study of Religious Commitment," *Religious Education* 57 (1962), 98–110.

[50] See Michael von Brück, "Meditation und Toleranz: Anmerkungen zu den ersten Ergebnissen des *Religionsmonitors* in Indien und Thailand," in *Religionsmonitor 2008*, ed. Bertelsmann Stiftung (Gütersloh, 2007), 230–36.

[51] Quoted in Joachim Matthes, "Auf der Suche nach dem 'Religiösen': Reflexionen zu Theorie und Empirie religionssoziologischer Forschung," *Sociologica Internationalis* 30 (1992), 129–42, 141.

Curiously, such fundamental objections are not heeded in the contemporary practical-theological debate, in spite of their clear warning that an unthinking use of the term "religion" may be problematic with regard to non-Christian or non-Protestant communities. Since the term "religion" reflects only specifically European and Protestant conceptions, it tends to distort the particular properties of the thus termed.

To conclude, the use of the concept of "religion" as the object of Practical Theology is fraught with difficulty. In a globalizing media landscape and a world of migration, individuals, groups, and communities meet that could colloquially be referred to as "religious," but who represent interpretative systems and concepts of life that significantly differ from those of Christian origin. Nevertheless, the concept of religion—consilient with its contemporary usage—is still important as a Protestant category of distinction. For (Western) Christianity, it extends the view beyond church doctrine and ecclesial organization to the dispositions and ideas of the individual. Its point of reference is Christian doctrine as taught by the major (Western) churches.

Indeed, the term has colloquially been vernacularized to designate different forms of life and value orientation outside of Christendom. It is however unreflectingly used to transfer Western and Neo-Protestant ideas onto conceptions of other faith groups and their values and orientations. Using the example of the transformation of Islam under colonialism, Thomas Bauer has shown that this may be perceived as a form of occupation.[52]

Spirituality

In modern sociology of religion (and Practical Theology) the concept of spirituality has partly replaced what has hitherto been called "religion." The history of this concept comprises a variety of trends that have been taken up and transformed. In the sociology of religion, "spirituality" above all describes modern, non- or hardly organized currents in which forms of transcendence are experienced, thus paying tribute to the current developments in individual attitudes and practices. From the perspective of the gospel in its Reformation sense, the unqualified adoption of this concept for the practical-theological argument presents some thorny problems.

---

[52] Thomas Bauer, *Die Kultur der Ambiguität: Eine andere Geschichte des Islams* (Berlin, 2011), esp. 198–223.

To come to grips with these, we first need to take a closer look again at the conceptual history. Like "religion," the concept of "spirituality" is of Christian origin, but became popular only during the twentieth century. It was however received in different fashions.

Originally stemming from French-speaking Catholic Orders,[53] the use of "spirituality" first found its way into Catholic Theology in the 1950s to represent the "subjective side of dogma."[54] In concrete terms, it had its field of reference in the religious retreats or other forms of praxis pietatis.[55]

In the 1970s the ecumenical movement adopted the concept to counteract the one-sidedly political orientations of the 1960s. The plenary assembly of the World Council of Churches in Nairobi "announced in a prayer: 'We are longing for a new form of spirituality to infuse our planning, thinking, and acting'" (Reglitz, *Erklären und Deuten*, 239).

The term also made its appearance in interreligious dialog, in which it designated impulses from non-Christian traditions such as Zen-Buddhism that emphasize meditation and other yogic exercises.[56]

In the English-speaking world, "spiritual" became an anthropological category, analogous to "moral," "cultural," or "mental," which will, for instance, be encountered in educational contexts.[57]

Finally, the concept of "spirituality" made its entrance into Protestant Theology and the Protestant Church, on the one hand replacing "piety," which seemed too old-fashioned, and on the other hand—relating to its colloquial use—ensuring the relationship with "lived religion."

Most of all, the concept has gained currency as a designation for modern cultural currents identified in religious-sociological analyses of contemporary lifestyles. In his analysis of "popular religion," Hubert Knoblauch uses the term in a nuanced manner, to capture contemporary developments in the

---

[53] See Ulrich Köpf, "Spirituality. I: Terminology," *RPP* 12 (2012), 224–25, 224.

[54] See Hans Urs von Balthasar, "Spiritualität," *GuL* 31 (1958), 340–52, 341.

[55] For the design of study programs in the United States building on this dogmatic and historical traditions, see the overview in Janet K. Ruffing, "Die akademische Spiritualitätsforschung in den USA: Entwicklungen einer jungen Disziplin," in *Spiritualität im Diskurs: Spiritualitätsforschung in theologischer Perspektive*, ed. Ralph Kunz and Claudia Kohli Reichenbach (Zürich, 2012), 55–70.

[56] See Hugo Enomiya-Lassalle, *Zen und christliche Spiritualität*, ed. Roland Ropers and Bogdan Snela (Munich, 1987).

[57] See Christian Grethlein, "Spirituelle Bildung–Gebet–Meditation," *NRHPG* (2002), 252–55, 252–53.

domain of transcendental experience. Following Thomas Luckmann in this, he characterizes transcendental experience as "an intrinsically social phenomenon," which is "not of a binary nature," but describing "connection and dissolution as the transgression and overcoming of that which can be perceived as a boundary or difference" (Knoblauch, *Populäre Religion*, 55). According to Knoblauch, the following indicators of modern religious practice are described by the concept of "spirituality": it is critical of institutions and organizations, it is a holistic concept, and it emphasizes the subjective experience of transcendence (see 419). In this manner, it vouches for the "authenticity" of the experience (see 271). For Knoblauch, spirituality is part of a "double subjectivization": On the one hand, people participate in the popular forms of religious culture disseminated by the media and the market. On the other hand, they have their own transcendental experiences. This explains why religious experiences, once the province of the virtuosi, all of a sudden become viral on Internet blogs and forums (see 271)—thus ending the privatization of the religious inasmuch as Internet communication dissolves or subverts the distinction between private and public. Transcendental experience is being popularized. An expression of subjectivity, it prompts people to go on pilgrimages, which have become a hallmark of such spiritual quest (see 179). A similar trend can be observed in writers and poets and their use of religious language. A review of late modern biographical writing with its acute sense of fragmentation reveals that authors astonishingly frequently resort to the religious traditions as well as motifs and words of biblical language.[58]

To conclude, Knoblauch's concept of spirituality undoubtedly captures important traits of contemporary attitudes and practices. On a number of occasions, Knoblauch also points to its close connection with Protestantism and its emphasis on personal experience replacing clerical agency. It is however not surprising that Protestant theologians display a certain reluctance in implicitly adopting the concept of "spirituality."[59] Its emphasis on human activity, for example in the form of meditation practices, threatens to eclipse the message of justification. Inversely, the attraction of such methods indicates the significance of the immediately practicable for the communication

---

[58] See Lutz Friedrichs, "Ästhetik existentieller Selbsterkundung," in *Kasualpraxis in der Spätmoderne: Studien zu einer Praktischen Theologie der Übergänge* (APrTh 37), ed. Lutz Friedrichs (Leipzig, 2008), 98–121.

[59] See also for the following Christian Grethlein, "Christliche Lebensformen— Spiritualität," *GlLern* 6 (1991), 111–20.

of the gospel. Taking this into account, the traditional forms of piety were rooted in the kind of contextual prerequisites that Manfred Seitz lists as "an unbroken tradition, the patriarchal family order, and . . . 'a general steadiness and slowness of life,'"[60] which today are seldom met. In this sense, the efforts subsumed in the concept of spirituality are invitations to Christian ways of living. Due to the specific lifeworldly circumstances, however, they are marked by a low degree of commitment and a high adaptability with regard to individual needs. It is for these reasons that I doubt whether attempts at finding "a spiritual form of Practical Theology"[61] or a form of "Christian spirituality" (Dahlgrün, *Christliche Spiritualität*, 420–22) are conceptually felicitous. A closer look reveals that they require "regularity and commitment" (421), a form of continuity that the "spiritual" quest described by Knoblauch precisely lacks.

Summary

The definition of the basic terminology of Practical Theology provides a basis for a nuanced study of the communication of the gospel in the present. The tension between redundancy and selection draws attention to the fact that communication must refer to the known while at the same time pointing beyond it. This basic insight helps understand the meaning of "gospel": Jesus' ministry in its three modes of communication, teaching and learning, communal celebrating, and helping for living, continues old traditions but places them in the new context of the beginning kingdom of God.

The open-endedness of communication means nettlesome uncertainty, but is a precondition for new insights of the communicators. In the ministry of Jesus we meet both: lack of understanding and new perspectives on life. In this respect, doctrinal fixations of the "gospel" obstruct its communication if they try to regulate it. It is rather their task to provide points of view for the communication process. A look at Christian history reveals that the pluriformity of the communication of the gospel is not a recent phenomenon, but has been with it from the start.

While "communication of the gospel" thus constitutes an empirical and theologically well-founded area of academic study, which yet remains to

---

[60] Manfred Seitz, "Frömmigkeit II: Systematisch-theologisch," *TRE* 9 (1983), 674–83, 679.

[61] See Christian Möller, *Einführung in die Praktische Theologie* (Tübingen, 2004), 20–23.

be fleshed out, the concept of "religion" appears only partly to fulfill these requirements since it is a genuinely Protestant category of distinction and integration. Applying this category to other forms of life and value orientations runs the risk of reshaping this forms with a Christian or Protestant bias. The problematization of "religion" in the field of religious studies emphasizes this danger.

"Spirituality" is employed by sociologists to describe contemporary developments in transcendental experience, which are generally anti-institutional and consciously referring to subjective experience. In this context, the concept underlines its connection to biography, which includes the transcendence of everyday experience. Furthermore, it emphasizes experience as a fundamental point of reference for many people's interest in and openness for the transcendental.

Owing to the open-endedness of communication and the importance of the specific context for the meaning of "gospel," a theory of the communication of the gospel can integrate such insights without charging them normatively. The point to note here is that the impulses the concepts of "religion" or "spirituality" in the forms outlined above carry, are in critical opposition to the fundamental Christian impulse: "religion" opens up the field beyond the church, "spirituality" claims biography and closeness to everyday life as important points of reference. Inversely, the theological vagueness of "religion" and the concentration of "spirituality" on personal conditions and activities neglect the reference to Jesus Christ in the communication of the gospel.

2. Hermeneutical Clarifications: The Pluralism of the Gospel–Differentiation of Religious Experience–Cultural-Hermeneutical Distinctions

Literature: Andreas Feldtkeller, *Theologie und Religion: Eine Wissenschaft in ihrem Sinnzusammenhang* (ThLZ.F 6) (Leipzig, 2002); Christian Grethlein, "Praktische Theologie und Mission," *EvTh* 61 (2001), 387–99; Eberhard Hauschildt, "Praktische Theologie und Mission," in *Praktische Theologie: Eine Theorie- und Problemgeschichte* (APrTh 33), ed. Christian Grethlein and Helmut Schwier (Leipzig, 2007), 457–514; "Nairobi Statement on Worship and Culture," *International Review of Mission*, 85/337 (April 1996), 184–88

In the practical-theological work of recent years, two hermeneutic models have proven particularly suitable for a nuanced description of the communication of the gospel in the present. They transform the dichotomies of the word-of-God theology into a praxis-oriented form of tension, the balance of which needs to be sought (see above, Summary of Part 1. This involves on the one hand the meaning of the gospel itself, and on the other hand the relationship of the communication of the gospel to its cultural context. More specifically, it deals with the distinction between primary and secondary religious experience and a four-part scheme of differentiation for the relationship of the gospel and culture. The material prerequisite for the deductive power of these distinctions is the pluralistic constitution of Christianity with regard to both contents and social forms.

Pluralism of the Gospel

Jesus' message was already received in different forms of emulation even by his immediate disciples. Jens Schröter distinguishes in Jesus' instructions "those that are addressed to the fellowship of his disciples, and those that address the whole of the Israel-to-be."[62] Indeed, the discipleship of Jesus formed in a variety of manners. The small circle of disciples that accompanied Jesus on his peregrination was joined by many others. They remained in their families, occupations, and homes and began to shape their lives in the light of the coming kingdom of God.[63]

The beginning of the transformation of the gospel into a written medium necessary for passing on the tradition is marked by an interesting fact with regard to pluralism: the New Testament contains four books that differ significantly due to differing interpretations of Jesus' ministry and destiny. Apparently, these four versions originated in different parochial districts, thus reflecting different situations in which the gospel was communicated. In doing so, they digest different sources producing a polyphony of voices even within each of the Gospels. In other ways as well, one encounters an astounding richness, with regard to both religious doctrine and moral rules, which was only forcibly and doctrinally reduced from the fourth century onward. It is therefore hardly surprising that right from the start Christians have

[62] Jens Schröter, *Jesus von Nazaret: Jude aus Galiläa—Retter der Welt* (Biblische Gestalten 15) (Leipzig, ²2006), 216.

[63] See Schröter, *Jesus von Nazaret*, 232–33.

pursued different ways of life. There were celibates like Jesus and Paul; the majority, however, lived, like Peter, in families.

At last, different forms of Christian community evolved, with regard to both orientation and organization. In the broadest terms possible, in Orthodox churches liturgical practice is dominant, the Catholic Church has created a complex judicial body, in Protestant Churches the role of theology as an agency for reflection is a prominent feature. Socially, continent-spanning structures like the papacy-centered worldwide Roman Catholic Church are found side by side with autonomous Free Church communities including only few members, Episcopal and presbyterial-synodal side by side with consistorial church constitutions, and so on.

These plural forms of the communication of the gospel outlined here did of course not evolve without conflict. There have been various attempts to reduce "the gospel" to a one-dimensional doctrine and form of organization. However, contrary to this, the open-endedness and constant context-relatedness of the communication of the gospel needs to be taken into account. This will be concretized by the two following hermeneutical distinctions.

Differentiation of Religious Experience

The distinction of different, but at once cross-referenced forms of religions opens the way for a deeper understanding of the communication of the gospel. The following distinctions also include discernments and suggestions from positions critical of religion.

The first hermeneutical distinction is that between primary and secondary religious experiences. Currently, the attempt to distinguish between "religion 1" and "religion 2"—with substantially different results—can be observed in German (Practical) Theology.[64] In the light of this dilemma, the distinction between primary and secondary religious experience, originally developed and religio-historically substantiated in response to the "dialog" concept of the Ecumenical Council of Churches, is more helpful. It is based on a religio-historical thesis that the missiologist and religious scholar Theo Sundermeier derived from an analysis of tribal religions.[65] Accepting the

[64] Hans-Eckehard Bahr, "Ohne Gewalt, ohne Tränen? Religion 1, Religion 2," in *Religionsgespräche: Zur gesellschaftlichen Rolle der Religion*, ed. Bahr (Darmstadt, 1975), 31–64.

[65] See Theo Sundermeier, "Interreligiöser Dialog und die 'Stammesreligionen,'" *NZSTh* 23 (1981), 225–37.

distinction between mystical and prophetic religions proposed by Nathan Söderblom and elaborated by Friedrich Heiler, he criticized the inherent evolutionary concept and redefined the two types of religion. He insisted that "primary religious experience," typical of tribal religions, is also the defining experience for today's world religions, which combines with "secondary religious experience" in various ways.

In the context of practical-theological considerations, the explanatory value of this theory for ancient form of religions, controversially discussed by Egyptologists, classical, and Old Testament scholars, is of no interest.[66] The misgivings of religious scholars can equally be ignored. The important point here is to attain a nuanced, practice-related understanding of the communication of the gospel. In other words, within the limited scope of this inquiry I pursue a heuristic objective. The usefulness of this distinction is underpinned by biblical tradition, since, as Rainer Albertz has shown in his religio-historical research into family religion,[67] here the coincidence and opposition of the two forms of experience can be observed.

Andreas Feldtkeller has adapted this distinction for media theory and redrafts it for heuristic purposes to analyze contemporary forms of religion. For practical-theological considerations it is particularly interesting that he starts from a transformation that can be described in terms of communication theory. His point of departure is the media-theoretical observation that a religion changes due to its written fixation of oral tradition. Originally based in concrete experience and encounters that were orally transmitted, a need arose to preserve these materials for posterity. This was the origin of holy scriptures, and while the oral transmission continued it now referred to the written tradition. The line of distinction between different forms of religion in this model is thus drawn between different media of religious communication, that is, oral or scriptural. Textualization is, as a rule, accompanied by theologization, which again, as Feldtkeller has shown with examples from Judaism, Christianity, Islam, and Buddhism, involves a critical review of primary religious experience (Feldtkeller, *Theologie und Religion*, 53–62). He then proceeds to elaborate this observation in the distinction between a primary, orally transmitted, and a secondary, essentially written, religious

---

[66] See Andreas Wagner, ed., *Primäre und sekundäre Religion als Kategorien der Religionsgeschichte* (BZAW 364) (Berlin, 2006).

[67] See Rainer Albertz, *Religionsgeschichte Israels in alttestamentlicher Zeit*, vol. 1 (ATD Ergänzungsreihe 8/1) (Göttingen, 1992), 45–68, 143–57, 161.

experience. It is important to keep in mind that these two forms must not be played off against each other. In fact, they overlap in concrete communication and are mutually dependent.

Primary religious experience in this model describes "the fundamental layer of human religiousness" and refers to the circumstances in which people find themselves (48). In particular, these circumstances are defined by three essential contexts: first, there is the descent community (i.e., husband and wife and intrafamilial relationships). The second one is the Earth (fertility, animals), and the third one is the organization of time (the diurnal, lunar, annual and life cycles). Secondary religious experience both critically assesses and continues primary religious experience. While primary religious experience remains in the sphere of creatureliness, the written record transcends this limitation.

The difference in mediality in which these two forms of religious experience are communicated also leads, among other things, to a difference in social reach. While primary religious experience is generally confined to the family circle and smaller communities, secondary religious experience, because of its written form, is easily communicated across wider areas. In consequence, primary religious experience is associated with greater intensity and plausibility, secondary religious experience with greater reflectivity. In Practical Theology, this hermeneutical distinction has already been applied for the rites of passage.[68] In this area, central to the religious practices of many Protestants, this distinction has proven its hermeneutical capacity, by transforming the antagonisms of earlier theory formation, which encumbered pastoral practice, into tensions.

To sum up, the communication-theoretical observations regarding the mediality of communication provide the distinction between primary and secondary religious experience as a powerful tool for a modern religious hermeneutics, facilitating the understanding of present-day Christian praxis as tension-filled but not antagonistic. Accordingly, the communication of the gospel takes place in the tension between the immediate relationships of people (descent community, Earth, time) and the discernment (in the form of scriptures) transcending these. A one-sided focus on revelatory scripture threatens to sever the connection with people's living experience. Conversely,

---

[68] Christian Grethlein, *Grundinformation Kasualien: Kommunikation des Evangeliums an Übergängen des Lebens* (Göttingen, 2007), esp. 42–52.

the reduction of Christianity to mere creatureliness runs the risk of being only affirmative and ignoring new perspectives offered by everyday experience. The awareness of the significance of redundancy and selection for communication may here prevent the emergence of false alternatives. Primary religious experience largely communicates the all-too-familiar (redundancy), while secondary religious experience provides innovative input (selection). The trick here is to keep them in balance.

Cultural-Hermeneutical Distinctions

It is of fundamental importance to be aware of the relationship of the communication of the gospel to its cultural context. Culture here generally refers to "a symbolically interpreted horizon of meaning, in which all our perceptions, interpretations, and actions are embedded."[69] In particular, the concept of culture is used "when comparing and identifying the other."[70] Practical Theology was first confronted with alterity in the context of mission studies (see Grethlein, "Praktische Theologie und Mission," 389–92) without having any conceptual consequences. Since the turn of the nineteenth and twentieth centuries, missiology had developed into an independent discipline. It has developed the concept of convivence, which equally embraces the notion of alterity and the necessity of mutual assistance which need to be brought together in constructive dialog.[71] This defines the position of mission within the framework of Intercultural Theology, and provides Practical Theology with an important incentive for its task of contextualization. On this basis, an international process of consultation in the Lutheran World Federation framed a practical-theologically progressive criteriology, in order to give a nuanced definition of the cultural relatedness of the communication of the gospel.

During the course of the third international consultation of the Lutheran World Federation's study team "Worship and Culture," which took place in January 1996 in Nairobi (Kenya), a document was issued which is of general importance for a practical-theological hermeneutics of contextualization. It

[69] Hans-Georg Soeffner, "Kulturmythos und kulturelle Realität(en)," in *Kultur und Alltag* (Soziale Welt Sonderbd. 6), ed. Hans-Georg Soeffner (Göttingen, 1988), 3–20, 12.

[70] Armin Nassehi, *Soziologie: Zehn einführende Vorlesungen* (Wiesbaden, 2008), 158.

[71] See Theo Sundermeier, "Mission und Dialog in der pluralistischen Gesellschaft," in *Mission in pluralistischer Gesellschaft*, ed. Andreas Feldtkeller and Theo Sundermeier (Frankfurt, 1999), 11–25, 22.

draws attention to a fourfold dynamic interaction between Christian worship and culture (see "Nairobi Statement on Worship and Culture"):

First, worship is "transcultural" (185). Baptism and Eucharist, Sunday service, as well as liturgical elements such as reading from Scripture, Creed, and the Lord's Prayer are shared by all Christian churches.

Second, worship is "contextual" (185–86). Each culture impacts the form of worship, and one can distinguish two modes: "dynamic equivalence" describes the fact that certain features of liturgy may be expressed in a new way by elements of the local culture. The "method of creative assimilation," on the other hand, adds individual components of the local culture to the service (186). These methods facilitate the individual's access to the understanding of the gospel by connecting it with the individual's cultural experience.

Third, worship is also "counter-cultural" (186–87). In this dimension, worship is at odds with the local culture where it contradicts the gospel.

And finally, Christian church service is "cross-cultural" (187) in that it combines the elements of different cultures. Particularly in multicultural communities this process is crucial.

These four criteria, elaborated on the basis of Sunday services, can be transferred without difficulty to all practical-theological fields of action.[72] In a nuanced manner, they draw attention to the fundamental perspectives which need to be kept in mind regarding the relationship between the communication of the gospel and the respective culture. The transcultural dimension maintains the awareness of the significance of Christian unity. The insistence on contextuality however emphasizes that the communication of the gospel always occurs and expresses itself within a specific cultural framework. Only through apposite adaptations can people partake in it. This of course must not result in the mere affirmation of the existing order, which can be prevented by taking the cultural dimension seriously. Finally, awareness of cultural reciprocity draws attention to processes that, in the face of globalizing life, are gaining increasing currency.

To conclude, at least since the study of missiological issues, the question of the relationship between the communication of the gospel and the culture in which it occurs has become ineluctable for theology. Most helpful for

---

[72] The criteria laid down here are applied two years later with regard to the rites of passage in the *Chicago Statement on Worship and Culture: Baptism and Rites of Life Passage*, reprinted in Anita Stauffer, ed., *Baptism, Rites of Passage, and Culture* (Geneva, 1998), 13–24.

practical-theological considerations and, more importantly, theory formation, a study team of the Lutheran World Federation elaborated findings from missiological studies and Intercultural Theology into a liturgical criteriology of enculturation or contextuality. Following this set of criteria, the communication of the gospel needs to be ascertained with regard to its transcultural, contextual, countercultural (critical), and cross-cultural (reciprocal) dimensions. Omitting one of these dimensions might incur a problematic one-sidedness: it might lead to a disregard of pertinent contexts or transcultural components, too much affirmation or too little allowance for multicultural factors.

Summary

In view of the communication-theoretical and theological complexity of the communication of the gospel, it is de rigueur to employ hermeneutical criteria. For one, the distinction between primary and secondary religious experience is media-theoretically evident and has been well tried in the rites of passage. To be aware of the significance of each of these forms of religious experience helps to forestall the creation of unproductive antagonisms. It is the foundation of a practice that keeps the balance between everyday experience and the written record of the fundamental Christian ideas. The second important hermeneutical device is a hermeneutics of contextuality as proposed by an international study group. It elaborates the relationship of the communication of the gospel and the culture in which it is embedded. Particularly the dimensions of contextualization and cultural criticism are important for practical-theological deliberations. The first affords serious consideration of the cultural situation, the second averts the mere affirmation of the existing cultural order.

4

THE EMPIRICAL CONDITIONS

Every form of communication, including that of the gospel, refers to a "knowledge" of reality that appears to be self-evident in each culture and social order. This "knowledge" is beyond cognition and is generally not something communicators are aware of, but is supposed to be self-evidently plausible. Only historical and/or cultural comparison draws attention to its implicit and by no means self-evident premises. The gospel, as communicative process, is a very specific form of dealing with this knowledge. It draws on it—as the similes, the meals, and Jesus' healings show—and at the same time challenges it.

Apart from this general "knowledge," there are the formations and developments of day-to-day life, which can be empirically established. Being aware of them broadens one's own horizon, which in turn has been defined by one's social background and lifestyle. In the brief review of the history of German Protestant Practical Theology, as opposed to Catholic, but also to American approaches, a problematic narrowing toward the educated middle class could be detected. Not least with respect to the diaconal dimension is it desirable to redress this narrowed view.

Finally, the development of electronic information processing has initiated a change in communication behaviors. Since this transformation is still an ongoing process, at this point only tentative observations can be made.

They are however necessary, if Practical Theology is not to remain caught in a deadlock of backward-looking affirmation, but instead become a source of guidance for future practice.

These three empirical approaches—the knowledge-sociological, the phenomenological, and the media-theoretical approach—all ultimately refer to fundamental problems of human existence. This is why the discussion of each of these will be prefaced by a brief anthropological introduction. This will be followed by a review of the historical developments without which the current situation cannot be fully understood. The chapter concludes with a critical assessment of these observations with a view to a theory of the communication of the gospel, that is, in terms of Practical Theology.

1. Communication: Under the Influence of
Reflective Modern Plausibilities

Literature: Ulrich Beck, *Risikogesellschaft: Auf dem Weg in eine andere Moderne* (Frankfurt, 1986); Peter Berger and Thomas Luckmann, *The Social Construction of Reality* (New York, 1966); Hubert Knoblauch, *Populäre Religion: Auf dem Weg in eine spirituelle Gesellschaft* (Frankfurt, 2009); Armin Nassehi, "Religiöse Kommunikation: Religionssoziologische Konsequenzen einer qualitativen Untersuchung," in *Woran glaubt die Welt? Analysen und Kommentare zum Religionsmonitor 2008*, ed. Bertelsmann Stiftung (Gütersloh, 2009), 169–203; Gerhard Schulze, *Die Erlebnisgesellschaft: Kultursoziologie der Gegenwart* (Frankfurt 1993 [1992]); Charles Taylor, *A Secular Age* (Cambridge, Mass., 2007)

At the start, I will briefly outline the human necessity of a "social construction of reality" (Berger and Luckmann, *Social Construction of Reality*). Following the broadly conceived culture-historical analysis of Charles Taylor, fundamental views of reality that, in centuries-long processes, have shaped the knowledge and therefore the communication of our contemporaries will be presented. In a complementary move, the popular religion—popular here both in the older and in the contemporary sense of the word—which accompanies these secular developments will also be considered. Next, I will take a brief glance at prominent sociological analyses of contemporary society, which is preeminently marked by the perception of the reflexivity of modern industrial society (see Beck, *Risikogesellschaft*, 14–17). It is this peculiar fracturedness that shapes modern plausibilities. At the end of this section, I will draw conclusions from these observations for the communication of the gospel.

Anthropological Foundations

The biological singularity of the so-called premature extrauterine year of the infant[1] accounts to a large extent for the extraordinary open-mindedness of human beings.[2] At the same time, humans however need certain ideas and attitudes shared by all the people they live with, in order to be able to act and build their lives. Cultural history knows a great variety of solutions for social structuring. Today, this pluriformity of lifestyles and worldviews is, in the context of intensified globalization and in particular migration, directly palpable and often leads to conflict.

In the following, the focus will be first and foremost on how human beings orient themselves in the world. Early on, human beings were evidently driven by a need to explore the relationships behind the world perceived by the senses. The world (Gr. *kosmos*) was perceived as a well-ordered structure, in which the individual has to move accordingly. This interpretation of the order is called a worldview.

Particular challenges are posed by the human awareness of personal mortality, which unsurprisingly drew great attention to the use of time. In both regards, humans have, over the course of millennia, developed beliefs that transcend the sensual world. Gods ensure the fecundity of people, cattle, and land; priests were in charge of dividing time, which they perceived in the context of the cosmos, or, more specifically, the heavenly bodies. In the course of cultural history, profound changes can be observed in these three fields of the social order, the world order, and the division of time. More specifically, the constructions of our techno-economically oriented civilization are the result of developments of the past thousand years.

---

[1] See Adolf Portmann, *Biologie und Geist* (Zürich, 1956); for the elaboration of this thesis, see Christoph Wulf, *Anthropologie: Geschichte–Kultur–Philosophie* (Cologne, 2009), 65–66.

[2] See the knowledge-sociological reception of Helmut Plessner's biological observation in Berger and Luckmann, *Social Construction of Reality*, 49–56; also compare Wulf, *Anthropologie*, 69–71.

Historical Developments

In Western societies, intrachurch discussions about the future of the church and Christianity are frequently marked by pessimistic scenarios of decadence that occasionally lead to unrealistic calls for improvement. These kinds of appraisal and postulate are usually due to one-dimensional interpretations of statistical data. At the other end of the spectrum, sociological theorizing expands the scope in the form of a general, multiply graduated concept of transcendence to such a degree that it is supposed to ring in a renaissance of religion, while, in reality, being of little benefit to the churches.

In contrast, the philosophy-, theology-, and culture-historical analysis of Canadian philosopher Charles Taylor (b. 1931) provides a historically well-grounded and internationally oriented horizon for understanding. At the center of his analysis Taylor puts a specific understanding of "secularity," into whose origin and implications he inquires.

This culture-historical approach is complemented by that of sociologist Hubert Knoblauch (b. 1959), Thomas Luckmann's former student, who takes a closer look at contemporary popular culture. He discovers in the tradition of former popular piety or popular religion a "popular," in the sense of "fashionable, widely appealing," religion, whose distinguishing mark is a new "spirituality." This "popular religion" runs alongside "secularity" without establishing a coherent link.

First let us consider Charles Taylor's take on secularity as a basic reality. The starting point for Taylor's analyses is the realization that the "world" in which the belief in God was a primary given and therefore generally shared has manifestly been lost. In that world, human beings were exposed to the influences of the cosmos and its actors like God, spirits, and so on. The belief in God and magical practices to gain protection appeared to be necessary for survival. This has changed profoundly. In his nine-hundred-page opus magnum, Taylor uses a three-partite concept of secularity:

> One understanding of secularity then is in terms of public spaces. These have been allegedly emptied of God, or of any reference to ultimate reality. (Taylor, *Secular Age*, 2)

> In this second meaning, secularity consists in the falling off of religious belief and practice, in people turning away from God, and no longer going to Church. (2)

> Now I believe that an examination of this age as secular is worth taking up in a third sense, closely related to the second, and not without connection to the first. This would focus on the conditions of belief. The shift to secularity in this sense consists, among other things, of a move from a society where belief in God is unchallenged and indeed, unproblematic, to one in which it is understood to be one option among others, and frequently not the easiest to embrace. (2–3)

In this third meaning, which I will focus on in the following, Taylor emphasizes that today the belief in God is an option to which everyone can relate on their own terms. It is this implicit freedom of choice with regard to life and value orientations that presently constitutes the framework in which the communication of the gospel takes place. It has evolved at different levels and with regard to different issues. The following two are of particular importance.

On the one hand, Taylor observes that secularity (in the third meaning) primarily occurs in Latin Christendom. He refers to the various internal church "Reform" efforts,[3] which can be observed from the eleventh century onward, and which are marked by "a profound dissatisfaction with the hierarchical equilibrium between lay life and the renunciative vocations" (61). Particularly during the Reformation this egalitarian impulse aiming at the unity of believers was emphasized (77). This was joined, around 1500, by the goal of changing the civilian habits of believers by discipline (244). A disenchantment of the "world" took place: the struggle with ghosts, demons, and so forth was replaced by educational considerations. Over the course of time, this resulted in an anthropocentric shift: efforts for faith in God were replaced by moral intent. This was connected to an "excarnation," that is, a blocking out of the corporeal dimension of communication:

> Older pre-Axial practices were swept away in a wide-ranging disenchantment. Among Protestants, the central ritual of the Mass was abolished as itself an example of illicit "magic." Carnival was suppressed. The uses of music, dancing, drama, were curtailed to various degrees of severity in the Church, and often put under heavy pressure in lay society. (614)

---

[3] Taylor, *Secular Age*, capitalizes "Reform" (first on 61) to emphasize that this marks a centuries-long overall process that extends beyond single events like the Reformation.

By this, the formerly widespread, physical experience of God was reduced. Faith in God was deferred to introspection and lost in elementary evidence.

The second important point is the triumph of science, in the wake of which the individual experiences itself no longer as "open and porous and vulnerable to a world of spirits and powers" (27) but as "buffered." Had God and his assistants or adversaries for a long time determined the courses of nature and people's lives, the discovery of natural laws now pushed this perspective back. The divine order of the "cosmos" directly impacting the individual was replaced by the immense and unfathomable space of the "universe" (325). The sacrifice as a means to welfare was systematically supplanted by purposive-rational action. This development becomes strikingly apparent with regard to health and illness: acts of penance to God have been replaced by medical technical treatment.

Both developments today make for life without reference to God. Moral discipline and the purposive-rational orientation of behavior, as expressed in the economy from the eighteenth century onward (181), have written a success story: never before has life—in spite the increase in human populations—been less imperiled by acts of violence than today. The remarkable increases in life expectancy—at least in the wealthy nations—and material welfare have occurred independent of faith in God, which has retreated into the inner sphere of the individual. The immediate and self-evident relationship to God and his divine cosmic order was transformed into a possible option for an internal relationship with God.

The predominant secular mode, however, seems to be complemented by the persistence of popular religion. In his phenomenological analysis, Hubert Knoblauch casts doubt on the disenchantment of the world attested by Taylor's culture- and idea-historical reconstruction by referring to the context of a tradition known as superstition or popular religion. He is interested in the transcendental experience that "is indeed not 'of this world' and transcends everyday experience, but which can dispense with any reference to religious legitimations and discourses" (Knoblauch, Populäre Religion, 162). It is the sphere from which UFO sightings, dowsers, aura seers, spiritual healers, guardian angels, and similar phenomena hail, and which enjoy great popularity (see 165 for exact numbers and individual experiences). They absorb former practices in a "transformation of magic" (245), providing the basis for a "popular" religion that directly opposes the hypothesis of a disenchanted world. By this and communication forms of popular culture the expression of Christian religion is changed (see 266).

It is obvious that this broad understanding of "popular religion" incurs the problems of an overstretched concept of religion. However, Knoblauch must be credited for drawing attention to the fact that developments in the history of ideas, like the techno-scientific world approach, only partly determine the life praxis of many people. Quite evidently, practices and dispositions survive in the sphere of primary religious experience which adopt former concepts of reality. They are transformed by technical views and instruments and adapted to the techno-scientific worldview. Dowsing rods are made of plastic, aroma therapies are marketed like any other commodity, and so on. The techno-scientific worldview becomes reenchanted. Secularization and sacralization run parallel in the lifeworld and complement one another in day-to-day life choices.[4]

To summarize, extremely different historical trends have produced what Taylor terms secularity in the third sense, that is, the loss of self-evident faith in God: internal church reform movements paved the way for rational, pedagogical efforts to improve life conduct; the triumph of science changed the conception of the world considerably; God's divine cosmic order directly affecting people's lives was replaced by the infinite universe. At the same time, earlier magical dispositions and practices have survived in adapted versions in modern "popular religion." Primary religious experience emerges in a new technological guise and enchants the scientific world approach.

The Current Situation

In the following, I will briefly present some important interpretive attempts of the current (communication) situation in Western societies from fields of sociology of knowledge and sociology of religion. They provide—in accord with previous methodology—a multiperspectival approach, without however claiming to be exhaustive or systematically coherent.

The first of these is the concept of pluralism, which, together with its complement individualism, constitutes the basic sign of the current situation. The pluralization of life orientations has not only accelerated, but increasingly entered public awareness. Several strands of development have interlocked and are still interlocking to reinforce one another in this trend.[5]

---

[4] See José Casanova, "Religion in Modernity as Global Challenge," in *Religion und die umstrittene Moderne*, ed. Michael Reder and Matthias Rugel (Stuttgart, 2010), 1–16, 3.

[5] See Franz-Xaver Kaufmann, *Religion und Modernität* (Tübingen, 1989), 22.

Peter Berger (b. 1929) has encapsulated this development in the striking and provocative formula of the "heretical imperative":[6] in the modern world, choice (Gr. *hairesis*) has taken the place of fate. This is equally true for the sphere of life and value orientations. An apparently orthodox modern profession of faith will thus differ from the contentually identical attitude of former times. Compared with the traditional self-evidence of former faith, the modern disposition is an expression of choice, that is, an option among many, which therefore can be reversed any time.

Ulrich Beck (1944–2014) has elaborated the classical sociological thesis of individualization further. According to him, it is educational aspirations that largely contribute to the detraditionalization of ways of life. Previously fundamental social institutions, like political parties or trade unions, become less important, while individualization increases individual pressure, since the persisting social inequalities are interpreted in terms of individual responsibility or failure.

Ulrich Beck's most momentous thesis, however, is that of the "risk society," which, published in the shadow of the nuclear disaster at Chernobyl in 1986, unsurprisingly touched a nerve. Consciously eschewing a representative assessment, he took pains to outline the social structural change that was then in the making. Beck starts from the observation that contemporary life is affected by risks that differ from the risks of past generations in two ways: they are global, thus principally concerning everyone, indeed the whole biosphere, and they are the product of successful technical developments, in brief, of modernity (Beck, *Risikogesellschaft*, 29). Formerly separated domains like technology, ethics, and politics are merging in the process, because all risk assessments now include, apart from the scientific analysis, normative assumptions about the desired way of life and considerations for the actualization of this life design. The desire of people for "security" (98) corresponds to the threat of risks. Thus, by its critical reflex to the products of modern technology, the risk society effects a new form of (secular) transcendental relevance. It puts the immediately perceptible into perspective and is to a large extent determined by possible futures (68), thus creating a space in which former, now technologically adapted, ideas about the cosmos take a hold.

---

[6]   Peter Berger, *The Heretical Imperative: Contemporary Possibilities of Religious Affirmation* (New York, 1979).

Reminiscent of Beck's coinage is Gerhard Schulze's (b. 1944) thesis of the "thrill-seeking society" (*Erlebnisgesellschaft*). Basing his examination of the individualization thesis on the analysis of empirical data, Schulze's culture sociological approach arrives at the conclusion that "individualization does not mean dissolution, but new forms of community" (Schulze, *Die Erlebnis-gesellschaft*, 24). Since the question of survival has been resolved for most people, the question of "how to design one's life ... irrespective of the objective presence of such problems" (22) now takes center stage. People are now pursuing the "project of the fine life" (35), which however entails the insecurity of how to go about this and the fear of disappointment in case of the wrong choices. Protection against this is offered by group-specific behaviors, which individuals can fall back on. Based on his observations, Schulze describes five "experiential milieus" (*Erlebnismilieus*; 259–60).

The transition from a survival-oriented society to an *erlebnisgesellschaft* has brought along an aestheticization that informs the different milieus in different ways and that Schulze interprets as "constructions that serve to provide security" (72). On closer inspection, the program of the "thrill-seeking" society contains an insoluble contradiction (see 234): human finiteness opposes the principally infinite number of life's options. This quandary is thrown into relief if one considers the problem of old age: both the review of a life full of missed opportunities and the assessment of a lifetime of limited options are bound to cause despair.[7]

The last of the more valuable perspectives on the current situation is that of individual religion. The worldwide survey of *Religionsmonitor 2008* included a study about the relationship of religion and the church on the basis of forty-nine qualitative interviews, which was carried out in Germany in 2007. In his analysis of the data, Armin Nassehi (b. 1960) relied on a communicative understanding of religion. Following Niklas Luhmann, he considers religion not as a personal trait, but as a form of sense making in which the world is observed (Nassehi, "Religiöse Kommunikation," 173) so that the perceptible and the imperceptible can be reconciled.

The interviews reveal some striking features which are typical of contemporary religious communication. First of all, the interview statements are compatible with religious communication (see 180). A second striking feature

---

[7] This problem can be increasingly encountered in literature, e.g., Philip Roth's unsparing stock-taking in *Everyman* (London, 2006).

is the systematic inconsistency of many of the utterances. "Christian and esoteric, Buddhist and animistic forms" (184–85) are combined without discred-
iting any of them. Nassehi sees in this a reflex to the generally given necessity
to cope with inconsistencies.[8] The decisive feature of these statements seems
to be the authentic communication style (see 177) and the significance of each
statement for the solution to personal problems.

To support the aptness of the communication-theoretical approach in
religious studies, Nassehi points to the great impact that socialization has on
the adult mind-set (see 193–95). As a rule, religious attitudes are shaped by
intrafamilial communication. There is one other result that merits attention:
"The more intense a person's religiosity, the more internally independent that
person seems to be of its church affiliation" (195). Nassehi assumes this to
indicate "a rather post-civic religiosity." A similar, culture-historical observation can be found in Taylor:

> The same long-term trend which produced the disciplined, conscious, com-
> mitted individual believer, Calvinist, Jansenist, devout humanist, Method-
> ist; which later gives us the "born-again" Christian, now has brought forth
> today's pilgrim seeker, attempting to discern and follow his/her own path.
> (Taylor, *Secular Age*, 532)

To summarize, contemporary society is, from a knowledge-sociological
perspective, characterized by ambivalence: gains in freedom through pluralism and individualization are challenged by the awareness of risks and uncertainty. In this situation, religious attitudes are, at least from the perspective
of church doctrine, marked by inconsistencies. The relation to one's personal
biography is an essential criterion for value orientations and life choices.

Consequences for the Communication of the Gospel

The review of knowledge- and religious sociological theories has helped one
to understand the frame of reference in which communication currently takes
place. These theories present important insights into worldviews and everyday knowledge. In communication-theoretical terms, the communication of
the gospel operates, like any other form of communication, along the lines of

---

[8] Nassehi, "Religiöse Kommunikation," here refers to television (see 187–88; compare
§12, 3.2).

redundancy and selection, that is, the taking up of the familiar, without which communication would be impossible, and the revealing of something new, which carries the communication forward. In the theological analysis of the multiperspectival framework outlined above, the Nairobi statement (see chap. 3, sec. 2) provides valuable guidance by drawing attention to the contextuality of the communication of the gospel on the one hand, and its cultural criticism or cultural distance on the other. From this, three major consequences emerge that are of particular relevance for the communication of the gospel.

The first important factor is the desire for security. First of all, before making further distinctions, the importance of the developments Taylor has outlined for current forms of communication must be emphasized. From a theological point of view, apart from material improvements, the liberation from anxiety-causing beliefs is of central importance. The disenchantment of the world from (evil) spirits, and so on, corresponds to the perspective of the incipient kingdom of God in Jesus' message.

However, a brief glance at present-day knowledge-sociological analyses (Beck, *Risikogesellschaft*, 98; Schulze, *Die Erlebnisgesellschaft*, 71–74) reveals that threat and fear return in a new guise. Both the risks of modern technology and the challenges posed by ascertaining individuality in an *erlebnisgesellschaft* fuel efforts to achieve "security." These efforts are, however, doomed to fail if total security is the goal. This is equally true of the multifarious practices that continue erstwhile popular religion in a technologically transformed fashion.

In this quandary, the Reformation distinction between *securitas*, as the human striving for safety, and *certitudo*, the God-given grace of certitude which transcends the biological life, offers a fresh, fundamentally "counter-cultural" perspective. Thus, the problem of "security" is directly related to the question of God, or more precisely, the "right" God.

For these reasons, the problem of "security" proves to be fundamental to the communication of the gospel in the present. On the one hand, it connects the communication of the gospel with a universal problem, and on the other hand, it provides the opportunity to communicate the countercultural and liberating perspective of the gospel. Modern risks stem from the future-blind fixation on present prosperity. That this is a problem of old is suggested by passages from the Bible such as the parable of the rich fool in Luke 12:16-21 and Jesus' words of wisdom on anxiousness in Matthew 6:25-34.

The second observation concerns what Taylor calls "excarnation." Taylor draws attention to the general tendency to interiorize Christian faith. The theological dissociation from magical practices suggests itself for practical as well as for theological reasons. Seeking to canalize eruptions of violence and to civilize manners in the interest of protecting the weak must also be deemed desirable. It is, after all, the instrumentally rational approach to nature and the controlled economic approach to reality that have led to general welfare and an increase in life expectancy in many countries.

Yet, Taylor emphasizes that these religious, educational, and technological reorientations entailed an "excarnation," that is, "the steady disembodying of spiritual life" (771). This is clearly at odds with fundamental Christian beliefs. Belief in the Creator as well as Jesus' ministry, in the form of healings and communal meals, sharply oppose this kind of interiorization. The question to be considered is to what extent the contemporary developments in modern electronic media continue this theologically problematic trend of disembodiment.

As concerns the communication of the gospel, this analysis suggests an opening for the dimension of the corporeal, and in a pluriform manner. We can find support for this project in "popular religion," since it incorporates the needs and objectives of primary religious experience. The long-standing connection of Protestant churches with a somatophobic bourgeois lifestyle opposes the body-related perspectives of the Gospels' incipient kingdom of God. The only vestiges of this dimension to be found in Protestant churches are singing and music.

The third important frame of reference is the biographical relevance, which Nassehi's analysis proves to be the needle's eye through which religion is approached. Traditional demands of consistency by academic theology or church doctrine are negligible compared to the perfect fit required by the individual's biographical work. People contextualize religious communication by autonomously adapting Christian, or other, traditions, and fitting them into a market-shape framework. Ecclesial forms of communication which, on the contrary, are guided by dated, corporatist standards with regard to both doctrine and praxis, lose touch with the cultural developments. This is emphasized by Nassehi's observation that particularly those interested in a religious outlook tend to expect little to nothing from the church and prefer to embark on their own spiritual quest. The communication of the gospel can therefore not simply ignore the scientific worldview. Not only does it provide the frame of reference for every communication, but also the concepts and ideas to talk about the nonobservable. However, the risks evoked by technological progress change the relationship with nature in a manner which is perfectly compatible with the biblical creationism (see 99). This is the point of contact for the adaptation of (obsolete) popular by "popular" religion as described by Knoblauch. Other than the perspective offered by the communication of the gospel, "popular religion" remains locked at the level of *securitas*, never reaching the Protestant faith in *certitudo*.

From a countercultural viewpoint, another problem of biographization is the narrowing down of perspectives to the individual's situation, and thereby largely to problems inherent in the specific social background or lifestyle. Attention to the other person, as put down in the Bible's commandment of brotherly love (Lev 19:18; Matt 5:43), is in danger of being lost. Yet, the liberation from self-centeredness can be imparted only in relation to biography. The long-prevailing model of a general church doctrine and its adoption in sermon and instruction are drawing to a close. Under the conditions of a "heretical" society and against the backdrop of global risks and the imperative of the *erlebnisgesellschaft*, the individual's biography provides the decisive point of reference for the communication of the gospel. Practical models for life will attract people, not generalized doctrine.

2. Communication: Under the Conditions of Social Change

Literature: Marianne Gronemeyer, *Das Leben als letzte Gelegenheit: Sicherheitsbedürfnisse und Zeitknappheit* (Darmstadt, 1993), 1–25; Christian Schwägerl, "Eine Schicksalsfrage, aber kein Schicksal," in *Familie, Bildung, Vielfalt: Den demographischen Wandel gestalten*, ed. Bertelsmann Stiftung and Bundespräsidialamt (Gütersloh, 2009), 17–47; Françoise Zonabend, "Über die Familie: Verwandtschaft und Familie aus anthropologischer Sicht," in *Geschichte der Familie*, vol. 1, ed. André Burguière, Christiane Klapisch-Zuber, Martine Segalen, and Françoise Zonabend (Darmstadt, 1996 [Fr.: 1986]), 17–90

The cultural philosophy and knowledge and religious sociology discussed above allow for a multiperspectival approach to the underlying conditions of contemporary communication. In this section, I will cross-check these assessments against some concrete findings concerning social change. While theoretical ambitions run the risk of neglecting the actual living conditions, the strength of these empirical data lies in capturing numerically measurable changes. By the same token, their weakness lies in answering only fairly narrow sets of questions in a slightly time-lagged manner without being able to see the bigger picture. Following a brief anthropological reminder, I will point to some historical examples for social upheavals and their impact on communication, and specifically the communication of the gospel. To conclude this section, the following changes in Western societies that can be observed across the board will be highlighted in an exemplary manner and appreciated their significance for the communication of the gospel: the increase in life expectancy, a new relationship with nature, changes in family structures, and the increase of citizens with a migratory background.

Anthropological Foundations

Human beings are creatures whose behavior is highly variable. Yet, some basic realities can be observed, which find different forms of expression depending on the cultural context. They are fundamental to communication processes. For one, humans can only live in communities. One reason for this is that they, as premature babies, are in need of assiduous attention and care. Furthermore, anthropological studies have shown that mammals like human beings need groups to survive and reproduce.[9] The apparent universality of incest taboo moreover indicates that from early on human beings experienced the fundamental need to go beyond their family of origin (Zonabend, "Über die Familie," 37–42). Only in this way could the survival of the group or tribe be ensured or the population increased. Finally, the singular feature that female reproduction is not bound to particular mating seasons, and sexual activity can take place anytime, required particular social regulations.[10] Cultural history tells us that right from the beginning diverse social forms emerged in which, for example, different conceptions of kinship were formed, which in turn led to distinct terminologies (Zonabend, "Über die Familie," 25–37). Each concrete social form primarily depended on the local economic and ecological conditions (62). All of these, of course, also shaped the forms of communication.

[9] See Claude Masset, "Die Vorgeschichte der Familie," in *Geschichte der Familie*, vol. 1, ed. André Burguière, Christiane Klapisch-Zuber, Martine Segalen, and Françoise Zonabend (Darmstadt, 1996) (Fr.: 1986), 91–115, 96–97.
[10] See Masset, "Die Vorgeschichte der Familie," 105–7.

Historical Developments

The following problem-historical examples describe four important factors that have changed the communication of the gospel through the centuries: the change in the group of addressees in tandem with a media change; a shift in the cultural frame of reference; major challenges posed for the conduct of life by an epidemic; and, finally, demographic change.

The conclusion that must be drawn from an assessment of these factors is that the fundamental Christian impetus can be preserved only by conceptual and contentual transformations. Social transformations and the resulting adaptations in communication were already present in the Christian beginnings. Jesus exerted his direct influence only in a small area, principally around the Sea of Galilee, among Jews. He evidently communicated only in oral form. Only a few years after Jesus' death, Paul expanded the reach of the communication: he communicated the contents of the gospel primarily to non-Jews, his medium of choice was the epistle. The way in which Paul met the challenge of a new audience by transforming the Jesuanic impetus already stirred up controversy in early Christian times (see Acts 15; Gal 2:1-10). Thus, both the social environment and the religious frame of reference for the communication of the gospel changed fundamentally in the transition from Jesus to Paul. This transformation is reflected in the New Testament in a conceptual shift: the central Jesuanic idea of "God's reign" becomes "God's justice" in Paul. This conceptual shift is a good example for the original imperative for contentual transformations to put forward the basic Christian ideas in changing communication situations.

While the transformation of the communication of the gospel from Jesus to Paul can be seen as a successful transition, the communication of the gospel had to meet further challenges presented by social changes as time progressed. One striking example is the transformation of the Christian initiation rite, the baptism, when entering the Germanic cultural sphere.[11] Compared to the first centuries, the social fabric of the church and the mentality began to change, and consequently the framework which gave meaning to the ceremony, while the procedure largely remained the same. The ritual of baptism had taken shape in the townships of late antiquity, in which the Christian community lived clearly separated from the surrounding pagan world. The instrumental

---

[11] For the following, also see Reinhard Meßner, *Einführung in die Liturgiewissenschaft* (Paderborn, 2001), 112–17.

word in the baptism was the systematic threefold repetition of the confirmation of faith uttered by the usually adult baptizand, "I believe." The adaptation
of the baptism in the Frankish Empire since the eighth century put it in an
entirely new context: in a culture practically devoid of urban centers, it was not
the boroughs but the monasteries that were most influential. Accordingly—
and in tune with this different mentality—it was not the Episcopal community leader who shaped ecclesial practice, but "holy men," who were looked
to for the communication of divine powers. This led, among other things, to
a different perception of the baptismal formula, "I baptize you in the name
of the Father. . . ." Whereas here formerly the calling of God's name was of
primary importance, the Franks emphasized the "I" of the priest as that of
a "holy man." In doing so—and this is the crucial change in substance—the
life-spanning process character of the baptism was forfeited; instead, it shriv-
eled into an isolated act. Time and again—motivated, for example, by Luther's
ideas about the baptism[12]—efforts were made to reclaim this process character. This, however, could not be achieved by doctrine alone. What was missing
was a principal awareness of the changed conditions of communication.

Another major change in communication conditions occurred when the
outbreak of the plague in 1348 required new ways of dealing with death. Marianne Gronemeyer (b. 1941) impressively describes the confusion that took
hold of Europe in the wake of this event. It is estimated that 30 to 50 percent
of the European population succumbed to the pandemic (Gronemeyer, *Das
Leben als letzte Gelegenheit*, 10). In one fell swoop, the communication of the
gospel, by and large functioning smoothly until then, suffered a loss of self-
evidence. The procedure of the Roman last and funeral rites of the seventh
and eighth centuries—reconstructed on the basis of records from the time—
had made dying a process that was integrated into life as the passing into the
hereafter:[13] As death was drawing near, the Viaticum, that is, Communion,
was administered; until the final death, the passion of Christ was read and
prayers for the dying were said; after death had occurred, psalms and other
prayers were said; then the body was washed and laid out; next it was taken to
church in a procession; in church, psalms and responsorial psalms were sung

[12] See Dorothea Wendebourg, "Taufe und Abendmahl," in *Luther Handbuch*, ed.
Albrecht Beutel (Tübingen, 2005), 414–23, 418–21.

[13] For more detail, see Reiner Kaczynski, "Die Sterbe- und Begräbnisliturgie," in *Sakramentliche Feiern II* (GDK 8), ed. Bruno Kleinheyer, Emmanuel von Severus, and Reiner
Kaczynski (Regensburg, 1984), 191–232, 209–13.

and mass was celebrated; the procession then proceeded to the burial site with candles and incense; the body was laid in a casket, the priest said a prayer; the grave was closed.

It is most likely that such extensive liturgy was confined to the monastic life, it however contains two normative and communicative conditions that also pertained to simpler burials: First of all, the dying person was expecting death—a sudden death was believed to be a punishment from God—and second, dying took place in the company of others. Death by the plague changed both conditions. People were in denial about the disease and frequently died solitary deaths. Likewise, the dead were buried not individually but in hidden mass graves. Judgment sermons were the theological reaction to the catastrophe—to little avail. The people responded in a variety of ways: recriminations led to atrocious pogroms of the Jews (Gronemeyer, *Das Leben als letzte Gelegenheit*, 12–13), some, mostly the rich, sought refuge in a Dionysian hedonism (11), some, in bouts of despair, buried themselves alive (10), physicians were seeking for protective measures (12), frenzied movements of penance flared up, with flagellations and similar acts of self-mortification (13). Quite obviously, the translation of the communication of the gospel as practiced in the last and funeral rites sketched above to the new challenges failed. An unbridgeable chasm between ecclesial forms and the actual needs of the people had opened up. Gronemeyer suspects this to be the cause for the intensified momentum in the already looming "decline in faith" (11).

In conclusion, the necessity for contentual, organizational, and medial transformation of the communication of the gospel informs the entire history of Christendom. Examples from Christian history show that cultural and life-world changes call for a constant reconfiguration of the communication of the gospel to preserve the fundamental Christian idea. Adhering to dated forms and formulas on the other hand jeopardizes this process of adjustment, which is rooted in the fundamental communicative nature of the gospel itself.

The Current Situation

Also in the present day, many countries are going through drastic changes. All this is taking place in circumstances that are of great concern to the communication of the gospel, which will be illustrated in the following by three examples. In these processes, the communication of the gospel has to face new challenges insomuch as basic conditions taken for granted in the Bible have changed fundamentally. The four changes addressed below concern basic conditions of human life and have started occurring in the mid-1800s. Hence the present urgency of transforming the message of the communication of the gospel.

The first of these changes is the massive increase in life expectancy, which can be observed since the end of the nineteenth century. Today, obituaries mourn the "untimely passing" of seventy-year-olds. Clearly, death is a formidable challenge that prompts individuals to reflect upon the meaning of their lives and thus provides a sounding board for the communication of the gospel. However, the predicaments arising in plague-stricken Europe are a reminder that even then there was no one-dimensional nexus of problems.

In the meantime, modern medicine and health-conscious behavior have created a sense of entitlement to living well into one's eighties. Premature deaths, even those of children, are simply experienced as a catastrophe, while the deaths of many young people in poorer countries are commonly ignored. Expressions of the communication of the gospel like the call for change, or giving thanks to God, thus find themselves in a new context and need to be redefined.

The second important shift regards our relationship with nature, or more precisely the disappearance of an agrarian lifestyle. Until the twentieth century, people were used to handling animals and had an acute awareness of the relationship between food and weather. This has dramatically changed; most people today live in cities or metropolises. Only few make their living in agriculture, forestry, or fishery. In case of droughts or floods, food is imported from other regions, at barely noticeable extra cost. The reports of the winter famines in nineteenth-century Europe make obvious what tremendous achievement this new type of economy constitutes—albeit at the price of the exploitation of poor countries and significant ecological problems. At all events, this shift places the reading of Bible texts in a new context. The formerly universally shared amazement at the miracle of creation has become as outmoded as asking God for one's daily bread.

Third, there are the changing attitudes toward the concept of family. These attitudes have changed in several aspects, the most fundamental being the optional character of family. The general fragility of partner relationships and the resulting changes in family life is another. And finally, many functions formerly an integral part of family life are now consigned to other persons or institutions. At any rate, the communication of the gospel now takes place in the context of plural lifestyles. Advocating a strong normative commitment to lifelong marriage based on Christian values is neither true to history, nor can it be made generally plausible today. Even sexual morality of the Roman Catholic Church has failed—the doctrine is simply ignored by the majority of Catholics. This being said, sexuality forms a central part of human life and can therefore not be ignored in communicating the gospel. A particular challenge is posed by the increasing number of people who remain childless and thus interrupt generational continuity. It is still an open question what this development will mean in face of the projected increase of old people in need of nursing care. They will not benefit from family help. Thus what significance does the commandment of parental love take on, which for Luther, as he interprets it in his Large Catechism, goes both ways (see BSLK 603–4)?

Consequences for the Communication of the Gospel

The most current of the changes impacting the communication of the gospel is the phenomenon of large-scale migration. The reflections on the concept of religion have already made clear that the increasing numbers of citizens with a migration background fundamentally change the context of the communication of the gospel. In conjunction with the general process of globalization driven by mass media, Western civilization's long-standing tradition of equating religion with the institutional church(es) becomes brittle. At the same time, the universality of Christian faith acquires a new form of presence. Churches only hesitantly approach the question of how to deal with people of other faiths. In the meantime, the developments hurry ahead of ecclesial debate. While ecumenical discussion groups are still debating questions of cross-denominational marriages and official church documents reject interreligious prayers, people of different religious affiliation are living in relationships, in marriages, and as families, looking for their own pragmatic solutions. Hence, the communication of the gospel must envisage the participation of individuals with other sets of values and be adapted accordingly.

3. Communication: Under the Conditions of Media-Technological Innovations

Literature: Dirk Baecker, *Studien zur nächsten Gesellschaft* (Frankfurt, 2007); Matthias Bernstorf, *Ernst und Leichtigkeit: Wege zu einer unterhaltsamen Kommunikation des Evangeliums* (Studien zur Christlichen Publizistik 13) (Erlangen, 2007); Wilhelm Gräb, *Sinn fürs Unendliche: Religion in der*

Mediengesellschaft (Gütersloh, 2002); Christian Grethlein, *Kommunika-tion des Evangeliums in der Mediengesellschaft* (ThLZ.F 10) (Leipzig, 2003); Götz Großklaus, *Medien-Zeit Medien-Raum: Zum Wandel der raumzeitlichen Wahrnehmung in der Moderne* (Frankfurt, 1995); Jochen Hörisch, *Der Sinn und die Sinne: Eine Geschichte der Medien* (Frankfurt, 2001)

Systematically, the media focus would have been well-placed in the previous section. The use of media is an important factor for a great many forms of communication, and it has a lasting effect on people's concept of reality. More-over, it changes sociality by modifying existent forms of communication and creating new ones.

There are several reasons why I dedicate a separate section to this theme. First of all, the media play an important role in communication, and this includes the communication of the gospel. That this is only a recent insight can be verified by a glance at the conceptual history. Only since the 1940s has a communication-theoretically specified concept of the media gained cur-rency (see Hörisch, *Der Sinn und die Sinne*, 68). It is not to be underestimated that weighty conceptions of Protestant Theology exerting their influence to this day were formed before this date and therefore treated their communi-cative subject-matter without communication-theoretical reflection. From a communication-theoretical viewpoint, prevailing terms like "the word of God" or "kerygma" lack in complexity and tend to obscure problematic issues rather than make them workable.

In the following, I will use a medium-range media concept. It is located between a wide concept of media as "intuitions of space and time"[14] and a nar-row concept of media, solely focusing on the technical apparatus.[15] "Media" are, in my definition, "the material conditions of human communication" (Greth-lein, *Kommunikation des Evangeliums*, 10). This allows one to think about both the technology and its use for communication in interconnectedness.

At the center of this analysis are the so-called electronic media, that is, the telephone, radio, television, and computer in their variant forms. These

[14] Mike Sandbothe, "Interaktivität–Hypertextualität–Transversalität: Eine medien-philosophische Analyse des Internet," in *Mythos Internet*, ed. Stefan Münker and Alexander Roesler (Frankfurt, 1997), 56–82, 56.

[15] See Günter Rager, Petra Werner, and Inken Oestmann, "Medien: Technische Appa-rate, Institutionen, Symbolsysteme," in *Lesesozialisation in der Mediengesellschaft: Zentrale Begriffsexplikationen*, ed. Norbert Groeben (Cologne, 1999), 57–70.

electronic media are called tertiary media. As opposed to primary (human) media, which can initiate communication without any form of technical device, and the secondary media (writing, print), for which only the sender needs an implement, tertiary media require both sender and receiver to be equipped with technical instruments. It is essential for Practical Theology to establish a relationship between these tertiary media and the primary and secondary media—as for instance the preacher or the Bible, since they have for a long time defined the communication of the gospel.

The second reason for treating the media topic separately is that it has as yet not received the (practical) theological attention befitting its lifeworldly importance. Hitherto methodological issues, such as preaching sermons without notes, or the organization of confirmation classes or pastoral care, become, when seen from a media-theoretical perspective, questions of the contextualization of the communication of the gospel (see Grethlein, *Kommunikation des Evangeliums*, 110) and thus gain greater significance. That this has received precious little attention so far may be connected not least with the traditions of the practical-theological disciplines, which developed their issues before the advent of the Internet.

In this section, I will thus proceed in the following manner. As previously, I will begin with a brief anthropological reminder, which will help understand the great attractiveness of media communication. The second passage will outline some crucial transformations of communication due to media change, specifically, the introduction of writing, letterpress printing, photography, cinematography, mass media, and, of course, the social media. These will then be examined in their impact on changing perceptions of reality. The final part will explore the consequences for the communication of the gospel. In these considerations, Nassehi's suggestion that television—and one might add: the electronic media—is connected with the tendency for inconsistency in life and value orientations must be integrated in a systematic approach.

Anthropological Foundations

The unparalleled triumph of the media, and the tertiary media in particular, can only be understood if one appreciates that they fulfill basal human dreams (see Grethlein, *Kommunikation des Evangeliums*, 43–49). First of all, they allow human beings to transcend the boundaries of time and space. This is true of the invention of the alphabet as it is of today's interactive forms of communication, from telephones to video conferences and IM (instant messaging). Today, everybody can theoretically be contacted at all hours by everybody else thanks to the new media. Furthermore, media were from the outset designed to improve awareness. Writing allows people to know about things and events which are remote in time and space. The Internet has boosted this capacity in terms of simultaneousness and graphic descriptiveness to an extent which a few decades ago seemed unimaginable. Another basic desire gratified by media is that for entertainment. From a communication-theoretical perspective, Matthias Bernstorf insists that "entertainment" is not simply a form of accessory amusement, but an essential form of communication (see Bernstorf, *Ernst und Leichtigkeit*, 48).

Above and beyond this capacity to fulfill basic needs, media have always been employed to secure the satisfaction of material needs—form a list of oil jugs to modern factory databases—and have thus become an integral part of economic management. The prosperity of the wealthy nations depends on computer technology.

Finally, media communication is fundamental to the formation of transcendental relationships: "At their origin, media exclusively and primarily served cultic functions."[16] The purpose of the cult was to express what is imperceptible to the senses, and, functionally speaking, to integrate the different aspects of life.

Historical Developments

Every new media development entails new possibilities of communication and new risks. This concerns not only technological hazards: changes in communication forms affect the very fabric of culture and society, and by association that of the church. Every (adopted) form of media innovation challenges culture and society to accommodate the welter of new kinds of communication to the existing ways of life, which, as a rule, leads to the transformation of these ways of life. The current changes instigated by computer-aided communication can presently be understood only tentatively, and, for the most part, merely in terms of predictions. Looking back at previous media innovations can increase the awareness for the present challenges, which need as yet to

---

[16] Werner Faulstich, *Das Medium als Kult: Von den Anfängen bis zur Spätantike (8. Jahrhundert)* (Die Geschichte der Medien 1) (Göttingen, 1997), 295.

be understood for the communication of the gospel. These previous changes continue to exert their hidden influence across later media changes.

The first important medial distinction is that between oral and written communication. The cultural and religious backdrop against which Jesus proclaimed the coming of God's kingdom was marked by a transition from an oral-cultic to a scriptural-hermeneutical understanding of the communication with God. The temple cult was still operational, but not least Jesus' criticism of it alerts to its fundamental shortcomings (Mark 11:15-19 par.). Economic interest had reshaped the original purpose of the temple as a place of prayer. At the same time, Judaism had already had a long scriptural tradition. The impact of such a cultural changeover induced by writing cannot be underestimated. Cultures of writing have means of remembering that are not available to oral cultures and thereby hitherto undreamt-of possibilities of differentiation and development. From a media-theoretical perspective, Judaism survived the destruction of the Second Temple thanks to the ability to refer to the Hebrew Bible.

Jesus, however, patently only communicated by speech, even though he lived in a scriptural Jewish culture based on the Torah. For him, the communication of the gospel was bound to concrete interaction, not to be evidenced in writing. On the other hand, it cannot be denied that writing enabled his continued ministry. Jesus on the other hand did not communicate through writing, thus underlining the particular significance of face-to-face communication for the discovery of God's work and love.

An even greater media shift was brought about by the introduction of the letter press. The Reformation and its connection with the emergence and spread of book printing have always compelled the attention of media theorists. Closer examination, however, presents a more complex picture. Werner Faulstich lists seven media that are responsible for the success of the Reformation: "the preacher, the letter, the handbill, the pamphlet, the book, the songster, and the theater."[17] The notable feature of the Reformation was the connection of traditional human media, like preacher, songster, and theater, with the media engendered by the letterpress. And yet, the beginning of letterpress printing was marked by a functional shift. Originally, Johannes Gutenberg (1400–1468) was seeking to emulate the ideal of calligraphy (see Hörisch, *Der*

---

[17] Werner Faulstich, *Medien zwischen Herrschaft und Revolte: Die Medienkultur der frühen Neuzeit (1400–1700)* (Die Geschichte der Medien 3) (Göttingen, 1998), 143.

Sinn und die Sinne, 134). Much more economical than the scribes, letter printing became more widely accepted, the amount of printed matter increased quickly, and the first printed books appeared. Printed pamphlets, but also song leaflets, achieved a speedy and widespread dissemination of Reformation ideas hitherto unknown. At the same time, the new technology was clearly at odds with Reformation theology's emphasis on preaching. Paintings of the period[18] show Luther preaching from the pulpit, the open Bible sitting on the parapet in front of him. The preacher, despite his reverend position, is bound to the written word, and subservient to it. In media-theoretical terms, the Reformation can thus be regarded as a revolution against a church solely oriented toward human media: the pope and his priests. By opposing it with the printed Bible, the significance of preaching was inadvertently diminished: the preacher's audience migrated from the churches to the realm of the printed word. It equally escaped general attention that book printing also changed the communicative character of the Bible. Up to that point, people knew the Bible only from lectures during service; it was a medium bound to personal communication. Mass distribution turned it into an impersonal medium, which the individual was meant to read in private. Today's museification and historicization of contemporary Bible use must be understood from this problematic development.

The next subversive media development, photography and, later, film, had a precursor in Christian history: the iconoclastic controversy. The iconoclasm, it should be remembered, was however directed at a form of image making, which, when photography appeared on the scene, was largely a thing of the past: the handcrafted, one-off picture. At the time of the iconoclastic struggle, the number of images was significantly smaller, their impact, consequently, surely much stronger.

In effect, photography and film have profoundly changed the approach to reality by producing a chemo-technologically construed reality beyond the sensually perceptible world. Periods of exposures quickly shrank from eight (!) hours in the beginning to periods escaping human perception like one-one thousandth of a second (Großklaus, *Medien-Zeit Medien-Raum*, 16). The result was a new encoding of space and time. That which was is shown as an immediate presence.[19] Past and future become one.

---

[18] An example of this is reproduced in Faulstich, *Medien zwischen Herrschaft*, 147.

[19] Roland Barthes, *Die helle Kammer: Bemerkung zur Photographie* (Frankfurt, 1985), 93.

Film has pushed these developments to new heights. Editing and rework-ing, particularly of color and sound, increase its attractiveness. With the advent of the moving image "the Gutenberg galaxy has definitely lost its monopoly: film absorbs it generously and shrewdly, leaving it behind" (Hörisch, *Der Sinn und die Sinne*, 301). A comparison with other technological innovations reveals that film represents technological progress in condensed form (see Großklaus, *Medien-Zeit Medien-Raum*, 79–80). In this manner, communication has now definitely exceeded the limitations of nature. It comes as no surprise that film is increasingly moving away from narrative concepts to image compositions in which the imagery, not the story, carries the message (25).

Against this backdrop, practical-theological studies have attempted to explain the cinema in terms of a "producer of meaning" (Sinnmaschine), that is, in a religious function. This is based on the apposite observation that movies focusing on love, nature, majesty put "the most intense primary expe-riences" center stage, experiences that "at the same time are increasingly disap-pearing from the realms of lifeworldly experience."[20] The cinema thus acquires a culture-hermeneutical function for Practical Theology.

Next, the mass media are an important social factor, even reaching into private communication. Globalization, for one, is inconceivable without the mass media—the printed media, television and radio, the Internet. Image-supported information circles the globe in a matter of seconds. Obviously, this results in the heightened asynchronous experience of synchrony, which creates considerable challenges for the selection of news items. News agencies and editorial teams follow a set of established criteria to decide which kind of information becomes news (news value theory). Some of these criteria are:

- frequency
- threshold factor (absolute intensity, increase in intensity)
- unambiguity
- meaningfulness (cultural proximity, concern, relevance)
- consonance (expectations, desirability)
- surprise (unexpectedness, uncommonness)
- continuity
- variation
- reference to elite nations

[20] Herrmann, *Sinnmaschine Kino*, 237.

- ♦ reference to elite persons
- ♦ personalization
- ♦ negativity

(see Grethlein, *Kommunikation des Evangeliums*, 61–62 for more
detail, with reference to graphics by Michael Jäckel)

Such catalogs, which may vary slightly, set the frame of reference for the communication of the gospel. At least the latter four factors are clearly at odds
with a biblical viewpoint. The belief in creation and the invitation of all people
to baptism and supper are fundamentally egalitarian, thus contradicting any
form of elite concept. Centering the communication of the gospel on Christ
opposes any form of personality cult. In contrast, television's personalization
of the political—and by association also the religious—has been empirically
proven: after watching excerpts from a political speech, respondents tend to
comment primarily on the individual politician and not on the contents of the
speech.[21] As regards the last factor, negativity—bad news is more newsworthy
than good news—the coming kingdom of God is of course an expression of
a positive affirmation of life, turning away from the fixation on the negative
aspects. Apart from these qualifications, the above factors delineate the formal conditions of effective mass media communication.

Over the course of time, the agenda-setting theory has however put the
significance of the mass media into perspective, and the models that have
emerged since 1968 have increased in complexity, distinguishing, for instance,
between media, audience, and political agendas.[22] This being said, the various
mass media not only play a pivotal role in the shaping of public opinion, but
also have a determining influence on what is communicated at all.

The Current Situation

Recently, however, the focus of attention of the public dialog has been shifting away from the mass media. As mentioned above, Internet-based forms
of communication dissolve the classic dividing line between private and public and open up spaces for new social forms. Before, however, exploring this

---

[21] Joshua Meyrowitz, *No Sense of Place: The Impact of Electronic Media on Social Behavior*
(New York, 1985), 276–83.
[22] See Beck, *Kommunikationswissenschaft*, 198.

further, the particular character of technologically mediated interpersonal communication as compared to face-to-face communication needs to be clarified.[23] The widespread tendency to view technologically mediated communication as deficient can, from a communication-theoretical point of view, not be upheld. Technologically mediated communication is certainly restricted with regard to its channels. It is generally accomplished through the medium of writing, or, in telephone conversations, phonetically, while other nonverbal signs like gestures, facial expressions, proxemics, olfactory factors, which usually accompany communication, cease to apply. In particular communication situations this can be of great advantage, as for instance in pastoral care. The absence of certain nonverbal factors may thus eliminate obstacles to communication, and for this reason Internet communication has a lower threshold than face-to-face communication. This conforms to the generally symmetrical and nonhierarchical character of the communication of the gospel. Moreover, because of, for example, the great physical distance between interlocutors, there is often no choice between face-to-face and technically mediated communication. Studies have shown that people in long-distance relationships use a variety of distance-bridging media, creating alternative forms of intimacy.[24] Currently, the so-called Internet platforms, allowing users to interact directly ("community"), are attracting much attention. The most prominent and popular of these social web networks today is Facebook, founded in 2004, and now used by several hundred million members. Users have their own profile page, on which they present themselves and can be visited by other community members. The enormous success of this platform can probably be put down to the fact that it allows users access to a great variety of interconnected applications. Close social contacts with registered "friends" and their access to specific information can be as easily maintained and interlinked as other links to the World Wide Web. As exciting as all this may sound, the limitations of Internet communication are equally manifest. It is not known how many of the users actually use their real identity and how many use aliases and/or fictitious personality traits. The use of bogus identities naturally entails many risks and opens gateways for abuse. And finally, with regard to data privacy

[23] See, for a detailed discussion, Klaus Beck, *Computervermittelte Kommunikation im Internet* (Munich, 2006).

[24] Jennifer Hirte, "In weiter Ferne—so nah: Wie Kommunikationsmedien in Fernbeziehungen genutzt werden und diese strukturieren," in *Technogene Nähe: Ethnographische Studien zur Mediennutzung im Alltag*, ed. Stefan Beck (Münster, 2000), 117–29.

and data protection, the use of these data for advertising purposes is a topic of extensive and critical discussion.

All these media shifts entail a change in the general understanding of reality. Even at the most immediate level, striking behavioral changes incurred by the electronic media can be observed. First of all, electronic communication is enormously time-consuming and affects the organization of daily life. Another aspect may be illustrated by this anecdote from school life (see Grethlein, *Kommunikation des Evangeliums*, 56–57). A class was invited to observe a solar eclipse. Eclipse glasses had been prepared, the group assembled in the schoolyard. As the time of the event approached, the students became increasingly restless: they were anxious to get back inside to watch the live coverage of the eclipse in the TV room. Quite patently, these teenagers felt that events on television were more "real" than the immediately observed phenomenon. Television also affects other forms of behavior. In his study on pastoral birthday visits, Eberhard Hauschildt observed a certain tendency for uniformity of private conversations: the "chatty conviviality" of television talk shows had obviously rubbed off on the conversation style at birthday parties.[25]

Another far-reaching change of media development is increasing speed. When trains were first introduced, whose visual extension is, in some sense, the moving picture (Großklaus, *Medien-Zeit Medien-Raum*, 122), people feared their speed might endanger the human frame. For the first time, human movement had crossed the line from using simple forces (human physical strength, horses, water) into harnessing the principally boundless powers of nature.

New dimensions of speed, however, have been reached in the timescale of the electronic media, which is measured in nanoseconds and not humanly perceptible. The manner in which this, together with accelerated forms of mobility, has impacted everyday life is for instance reflected in the rapid editing in movies or video clips. Impatience at computer uploads lasting several seconds also falls in this category. Only a few years ago, the acquisition of certain information would have lasted hours or days—on the Internet it only takes a few seconds, which now is experienced as "slow." This is connected to the observation that electronic-media communication compresses past and future into the present: "Everything tends towards being present here and

---

[25] Eberhard Hauschildt, *Alltagsseelsorge: Eine sozio-linguistische Analyse des pastoralen Geburtstagsbesuches* (Göttingen, 1996), 45.

now, happening now" (21). Since the emergence of photography, this development has gathered considerable pace. If nothing else, the constant flux of images and information hardly leaves any space for (re)collection or levelly taking the long view (see 9).

This significant loss of previously common distinctions is also true of other aspects of Internet communication. "External" versus "internal," "private" versus "public," "mine" versus "other" blur (see 8). Traditional distinctions are reaching the vanishing point where their implicit concepts of time and space fail to capture digitalized communication.

The conclusions from the above are that Jesus certainly restricted his communication of the gospel to face-to-face conversations and refrained from the then widespread use of written language, while those coming after him have always employed the latest media to communicate his message. This has entailed considerable changes, also with regard to the contents, since the media development tends to abstract communication from its natural conditions. This has effected, among other things, a new approach to the treatment of time inasmuch as past and present become simultaneous. Today, due to their time-consuming use alone, the impact of tertiary media cannot be overestimated. They shape people's view of reality, transform their attitudes toward time and space, and form the natural basis for communication. Limitations formerly imposed by nature melt away.

In many ways, mass media are in conflict with biblical views. In particular, the constant flux of images and stimuli stands in the way of tranquility and recollection, both of which are important conditions for the communication of the gospel. By virtue of their low-threshold access and new forms of participation, the social media however open up an exciting range of possibilities for the communication of the gospel.

Consequences for the Communication of the Gospel

As we have seen, the technological innovations in the media and the ways in which they have been adopted call for a theory of the communication of the gospel. In a first step, a list of media parameters imperative for the communication of the gospel today will be compiled. I will then, following the hermeneutical criterion of cultural criticism, examine tensions and contradictions arising between the present media development (and its adoptions) and the basic conditions of the communication of the gospel. To conclude, I will inquire, in the sense of a "cultural interaction," after the opportunities the new media offer for the communication of the gospel.[26]

First of all, let us take a look at the contextual framework conditions. We live in a media society. People spend great portions of the day on tertiary media, with television leading the way, followed by radio, and, of course, increasingly the Internet. The information gathered here, together with that from print media and other cultural products, makes its way into face-to-face communications in many different fashions. The communication of the gospel is inextricably involved in this process. It is, in part, explicitly practiced in tertiary media, in the form of TV worship services, radio morning prayer, prayer chats, online worship services, and so on; in part, it is referenced in mass media, as in news reports on church events, or in movies using Christian symbolism. Thus, there is no gulf between mass media communication and the communication of the gospel. The characteristic feature of the communication of the gospel by means of tertiary media is that it is principally open-access; this is easily achieved by turning on the television, the computer, or your smartphone. This is very much in tune with the basic Christian impetus, as is the fact that denominational affiliation, which is so characteristic of liturgical procedures, is of little to no importance.

Overall, it can however not be denied that the communication of the gospel is relegated to the fringes of today's mass media communication. The massive amount of images, words, and other stimuli levels the individual program, the particular contribution. Fripperies rub shoulders with the existentially meaningful, which again is drowned out by banalities. Many of the things initiated by church or theology do not find their way the public sphere of the mass media. And neither the church nor theology are quite blameless of this state of affairs, having for a long time distanced themselves, and in part still distancing themselves, from the mass media. At least in Germany, the controversies over the permissibility of television worship services are one example for this.[27]

Apart from these contextual factors, there are some fundamental contentual tensions between today's media culture and the most fundamental

---

[26] For more detail, see Christian Grethlein, "Kommunikation des Evangeliums in der digitalisierten Gesellschaft," *THLZ* 140 (2015), 598–611.

[27] See Wilm Sanders, "Gottesdienstübertragungen im Rundfunk—Hörfunk und Fernsehen," in *Handbuch der Liturgik: Liturgiewissenschaft in Theologie und Praxis der Kirche*, ed. Hans-Christoph Schmidt-Lauber, Michael Meyer-Blanck, Karl-Heinrich Bieritz (Göttingen, ³2003), 929–39, 933–34.

Christian impetus to which the communication of the gospel refers. For one, tertiary media communication presents a further step in the process of "excarnation" as described by Charles Taylor. The natural basis of our lives, to which the Christian creed refers as the creation, is falling from view. Human corporeality is reduced to the sense of sight, perhaps the sense of hearing and the sense of touch (operating keyboard or touch screen). The rapid acceleration in media development is at odds with a belief in creation that comprises rest as God's gift (Deut 5:12-15). Free time, for unrestricted awareness and contemplation, is an important prerequisite for the communication of the gospel. The constructions of reality produced by high-speed Internet communication and the rapid succession of films and programs are clearly an obstacle to these preconditions: many time-honored Christian practices of communicating with God, from prayer to chanting to reading the Bible, require quiet and time. In this context it is quite interesting to note that the cultural sciences raise a similar objection by pointing to, among other things, the problematic obsession with the present (see Großklaus, *Medien-Zeit Medien-Raum*, 101). William Powers has recommended an "Internet Sabbath."[28]

The inescapable attitudinal inconsistencies and discontinuities resulting from sensory and information overload are also in opposition to vital biblical ideas. The communication of the gospel refers to the whole human being, to every sphere of human life: God's gratuitous love transcends any particular access. Consistency here however does not mean dogmatic correctness; rather, it refers to the individual's ability to orient himself or herself and to take heart in full view of his or her gifts and imperfections, abilities, and limitations.

Finally, examination of the criteria employed in news selection reveals some theologically alarming tendencies. Focusing on elite persons clearly contradicts the equality of all people as testified by the belief in creation and expressed in the invitation of all people to baptism and supper. Mass media's desire to showcase individual bishops—let alone the pope—contradicts the theological belief in the common priesthood of each baptized individual. And focusing on elite nations subverts the positive implications of globalization. Finally, the mass news media's preference for bad news nurtures negative attitudes toward life and encourages cynical, misanthropic voyeurism.

---

[28] William Powers, *Hamlet's Black Berry: A Practical Philosophy for Building a Good Life in the Digital Age* (New York, 2010), 227.

For all the alarming developments just discussed, the opportunities offered by the social media must however not be overlooked. For a start, they contribute to the reduction of hierarchies, thus preparing the ground for symmetrical communication. While this might create some tension with respect to the ministerial and administrative structures that have formed in the churches, particularly the Roman Catholic Church, these hierarchical structures may at best be interpreted as a necessary move in the context of the estate-based societies of former times. Today, they clearly interfere with the communication of the gospel.

Moreover, social media offer the opportunity to correct, at least in part, the problematic news selection process of the mass media. In this respect, the example of some web-based communities in the ecological and political fields may show the way.

Last, but not least, the marginalization of denominational distinctions is an encouraging trend for the communication of the gospel. The biography-based communication of the social media replaces the old orientations to old-fashioned doctrinal teaching that resulted from a desire for distinction. This creates a greater pluriformity in both dispositions and behaviors, and, with this, the opportunity for open-ended and therefore innovative communication.

5

THE THEOLOGICAL
FOUNDATIONS

As shown in chapter 3, the communication of the gospel takes place in three different modes: in teaching and learning, in celebrating together, and in helping for living. All three are inextricably connected in Jesus' ministry. In the following, I will attempt to analyze the internal structure of these modes from a theological perspective.

I will start with some reflections on teaching and learning. In his book on Jesus, Jürgen Becker also begins his description of the "message of the nearness of God's reign" with a passage on Jesus' parabolic teachings.[1] Becker does this for a very good reason because it is in Jesus' parables that the new view of reality appears in its most lucid and distinct form. From the insights gained in teaching and learning processes, the significance of celebrating together and helping for living as modes of communicating the gospel becomes readily accessible. I will therefore begin with the core meaning of the communication of the gospel. This will be followed by a look at its social forms and its actualization in everyday life. Concrete analysis will show that these are only distinctions, and by no means separations. This analysis will, among other

[1] Becker, *Jesus von Nazaret*, 176–233.

things, reveal the diaconal dimension of education, the relevance of worship for daily life, and the connection of liturgy and social welfare work (diaconia).

The discussion of each mode of communication will begin with a brief anthropological contextualization. Theologically, this means firmly grounding the communication of the gospel in creation.

After a review of the biblical foundations, I will recall, by way of example, important stages of the problem-historical development up to the present: constellations in early Christianity, in the Middle Ages, during the Reformation, during the Enlightenment, and in the nineteenth and twentieth centuries, all of which provide perfect illustrations for the contextualization of the communication of the gospel, since communication is always subject to transformations according to the contextual changes. However, some transcultural approaches offer themselves which have proved successful in different contexts. Within the scope of the countercultural dimension, elenctic comparison reveals new options for new courses of action. And finally, with regard to the cross-cultural dimension, one can observe processes of cultural exchange where Christianity has entered different cultures. In accordance with the fundamentally integrative tendency of the communication of the gospel, I will then point to the—actual, but also potential—connections with the other two modes of communication. At the end, I will list some questions that have proven to be fundamental for each mode of communication in the course of Christian history.

1. The Gospel in the Mode of Teaching and Learning

Literature: Dietrich Benner, *Allgemeine Pädagogik: Eine systematisch-problemgeschichtliche Einführung in die Grundstruktur pädagogischen Denkens und Handelns* (Weinheim, [6]2010); Christoph Gramzow, *Diakonie in der Schule: Theoretische Einordnung und praktische Konsequenzen auf der Grundlage einer Evaluationsstudie* (APrTh 42) (Leipzig, 2010); Christian Grethlein, *Religionspädagogik* (Berlin, 1998), 307–541; Rainer Lachmann, "Vom Westfälischen Frieden bis zur Napoleonischen Ära," in *Geschichte des evangelischen Religionsunterrichts in Deutschland: Ein Studienbuch*, ed. Rainer Lachmann and Bernd Schröder (Neukirchen-Vluyn, 2007), 78–127; Hans Bernhard Meyer, *Eucharistie: Geschichte, Theologie, Pastoral* (GDK 4) (Regensburg, 1989); Karl Ernst Nipkow, *Grundfragen der Religionspädagogik*, vol. 1: *Gesellschaftliche Herausforderungen und theoretische Ausgangspunkte* (Gütersloh, [2]1978), 107–27;

Eugen Paul, *Geschichte der christlichen Erziehung*, vol. 1: *Antike und Mittelalter* (Freiburg, 1993); Bernd Schröder, "Von der Reformation bis zum Dreißigjährigen Krieg," in *Geschichte des evangelischen Religionsunterrichts in Deutschland: Ein Studienbuch*, ed. Rainer Lachmann and Bernd Schröder (Neukirchen-Vluyn, 2007), 35–77; Christoph Wulf, *Anthropologie: Geschichte–Kultur–Philosophie* (Cologne, 2009), 221–39

To this day, Jesus' parables and his other sayings and accounts that have come down to us initiate teaching and learning processes. In this, Jesus stands in the tradition of Jewish prophets, wisdom teachers, and rabbis. Throughout Christian history, partly practiced side by side and influencing one another, different forms and thematic accentuations of this mode of communicating the gospel between generations have evolved, often in exchange with the two other modes of communication. When reviewing the various models that have been employed to communicate the gospel in the mode of teaching and learning, one encounters two basic questions. The first is, how can the gospel be learned? And, what part does the Bible play in teaching? To start with, we will thus take a look at some basic anthropological views on learning.

Anthropological Background

As mentioned previously, human open-mindedness and sociality are the most fundamental preconditions for teaching and learning processes. They both make teaching and learning processes necessary and also shape them. At the same time, they account for the pluriformity of these processes.

The long-standing and controversial question of genetic determination proves to be too abstract and therefore of little use in our context (see Benner, *Allgemeine Pädagogik*, 70–77). Obviously, there is no human individual whose life is exclusively determined by congenital factors. On the contrary, from the moment of their birth human beings are intimately involved in the diverse types of communication and social forms of their culture. Personality-forming learning processes require the following three conditions (for more detail, see Nipkow, *Grundfragen der Religionspädagogik*). The first of these is a dependable environment, being prerequisite for the realization of an increasing, and for adult life generally necessary, autonomy (see 114). Second, there must be trust in both directions: trustfulness as well as trustworthiness. And finally, there is verbal communication, which helps the individual form an impression of himself or herself.

According to insights from cultural history now corroborated by neu-roscientific findings (see Wulf, *Anthropologie*, 222–23), human learning is a mimetic process right from the start.[2] In evolution-biological terms, human beings are marked by the ability to "identify with other persons, to see them as intentional agents, and jointly direct their attention toward an object" (222). This, however, is not mere imitation, as mimetic processes always simultane-ously produce both similarity and difference (see 236)—as is reflected in the communication-theoretical notion of the open-endedness of communication processes. Mimetic learning processes involve the whole human being, includ-ing the corporeal dimension, and are marked by intensity and permanence.

Biblical Foundations

Since teaching and learning processes are naturally embedded in everyday life, we are generally not especially aware of them. In writing-based cultures, how-ever, socializations require special training in reading and writing skills. Thus, already in the Old Testament we can encounter texts that may have their ori-gin in didactic teaching and learning processes.

Perusing the Old Testament for teaching and learning processes, the first thing that one notices is the great importance of the sense of hearing, and consequently speaking (see Isa 50:4-5). As important as the eye may be for the perception of Yahweh's deeds, the "prevalence of the ear and speech for true human understanding" is conspicuous.[3] The theological reason for this lies, apart from the context of a primary oral culture, in the salvation-historical orientation of Old Testament beliefs: the past cannot be seen any more, it can only—perhaps in writing—be verbalized. Another central term of Jewish belief, the "instruction" (*torah*), implicates teaching and learning processes. Its constitutive words proceed from God and give life (see Deut 8:3). The Psalter is therefore referred to as the "Torah of David"[4] and was, in its early stages, conceived as a wisdom "textbook."[5] This approach takes on a fully developed

---

[2] References to mimesis as a "synonym for education" (Wulf, *Anthropologie*, 213) can already be found in the third book of Plato's *Politeia*.

[3] Hans Walter Wolff, *Anthropologie des Alten Testaments* (Munich, ³1977), 118.

[4] So Reinhard Kratz, "Die Tora Davids: Psalm 1 und die doxologische Fünfteilung des Psalters," *ZThK* 93 (1996), 1–34.

[5] Erich Zenger, "JHWH als Lehrer des Volkes und der Einzelnen im Psalter," in *Religiöses Lernen in der biblischen, frühjüdischen und frühchristlichen Überlieferung* (WUNT 180), ed. Beate Ego and Helmut Merkel (Tübingen, 2005), 47–67, 47.

educational form in the sapiential literature.[6] It even contains methodological suggestions, as for instance for the chastisement of the unwilling (see, e.g., Prov 29:15).

In the Gospels, teaching and learning processes prove to be fundamental to Jesus' communication of the gospel. This is expressed by the fact that he was addressed as rabbi (e.g., Matt 26:25; John 1:38) and his followers as students (Gr. *mathetes*). In concrete terms, the proclamation of the coming kingdom of God referred to the "renewal of God's original will."[7] Jesus expresses this creation-theological perspective when he refers to the sanctity of marriage (Mark 10:2-9), or when he reverses the distinction between purity and impurity (Mark 7:15), when he redefines the Sabbath (Mark 3:4), when he heals (see part 3, chapter 7 below), and not least when he addresses God as "Father" (Matt 6:9). All these examples of course refer to primary religious experience, but by referring to God's deeds are placed within an eschatological horizon. It is striking that the addressees of Jesus teachings are people who "usually did not participate in religious teaching and learning processes."[8] The relationship between Jesus and his students was based on dialog, as shown by the queries made by his followers after Jesus' and the requests for instruction, as recorded in the introduction to the Our Father (Luke 11:1). The reason for this is given by the reference to the common Heavenly Father leading Jesus and his followers into the fellowship of the children of God (Rom 8:14-17). To be sure, there was a difference between Jesus and his students. Matthew, for instance, has Jesus ask his disciples to refuse both the title of Rabbi and teacher (Matt 23:8-12). Yet, the passion and death of Jesus manifest that his relationship with his disciples was no ordinary up-down hierarchy. On the contrary, the usual standards are turned on their head, in this regard also providing guidance for the company of those who belong to Christ: "He who is greatest among you shall be your servant" (Matt 23:11; see also Mark 10:43-45).

---

[6] Ludger Schwienhorst-Schönberger, "Den Ruf der Weisheit hören: Lernkonzepte in der alttestamentlichen Weisheitsliteratur," in Ego and Merkel, *Religiöses Lernen in der biblischen*, 69–82.

[7] Udo Schnelle, *Neutestamentliche Anthropologie: Jesus–Paulus–Johannes* (Neukirchen-Vluyn, 1991), 15; the following examples are explained on 14–22.

[8] Bernd Schröder, "Lehren und Lernen im Spiegel des Neuen Testaments: Eine Sichtung der Befunde in religionspädagogischem Interesse," in *Beiträge zur urchristlichen Theologiegeschichte* (BZNW 163), ed. Wolfgang Kraus (Berlin, 2009), 497–524, 509–10.

And finally, the most striking thing about Jesus' teachings is that they immediately refer to concrete life; they are never a scholarly exegesis of Scripture. The result is always practical activity, such as the Our Father. In keeping with the open-endedness of communication, he "placed great value on attentive listening and intuitive understanding in encounters with his followers."[9] Altogether, the contents of learning are determined by the person of Jesus: he provides the vital impulses, and—conforming to the idea of mimesis as the basic model of learning—his history is unfolded in the Gospels as the quintessential message.

Historical Forms

In the following, various forms of the communication of the gospel from Christian history will be outlined. In keeping with the multiperspectival approach of this book, the focus will be on both concrete practices as well as thoughts on teaching and learning processes. In following the historical chronology, I will present these practices and reflections according to acting persons, signs employed, specific situations, and goals pursued. In this manner, an array of markedly different models can be ascertained. The impact of the Reformation will be illustrated using the example of Martin Luther, since he not only deeply engaged in questions of education, both theologically and pragmatically, but also achieved to exert a considerable influence.[10]

To begin with, we will look at Christian teachers. As early as the second century CE, three types of teachers can be encountered: itinerant teachers, catechists, that is, appointees of parishes, and so-called free teachers.[11] The latter represented a particular form of contextualization which is traceable until the mid-third century. The works of Justin Martyr (ca. 100–165) serve as a good example to illustrate how the then customary institution of a philosophical teacher could prove seminal for the communication of the gospel. Justin presented Christianity to adult listeners in writings, verbal disputes, and oral instruction as true doctrine and practice of living, while being in contact with

---

[9] Schröder, "Lehren und Lernen im Spiegel," 510.

[10] Concerning Johannes Calvin, see Bernd Schröder, "Johannes Calvin—religionspädagogisch gelesen: Oder: Historische Religionspädagogik als Erforschung der Wirkungsgeschichte des Unterrichts in christlicher Religion," *ZThK* 107 (2010), 348–71.

[11] Ulrich Neymeyer, *Die christlichen Lehrer im zweiten Jahrhundert: Ihre Lehrtätigkeit, ihr Selbstverständnis und ihre Geschichte* (SVigChr 4) (Leiden, 1989).

but not dependent on the Christian community. Origen (184/185–253/254) provides the example of a Christian teacher turned ecclesial official (as a presbyter)—and the difficulties connected with that transition. The interesting thing about the Christian teachers of the second and third centuries is the endeavor to assert the truth claim of Christian doctrine by means of the then common philosophical methods. These, however, reveal significant divergences with regard to both content and methodology, implying a fair amount of pluriformity. All in all, the peculiar form in which the Christian "school" organized itself even in the early period displays a tendency to create loci outside parish structures for the communication of the gospel.

The catechumenate, which is evidenced in different sources since the second century, was also aimed at adult individuals (see Paul, *Geschichte der christlichen Erziehung*, 45–57). It has been described in particular detail in the *Traditio Apostolica* from the third (or fourth) century, attributed to Hippolytus of Rome. It was carried out in the following manner:[12]

(XVII) Duration of the Catechumenate: three years
Course of instruction: Christian way of life; instructions
Partaking in worship (excluding the Eucharist)

(XX) Examination of the candidates (catechumens)
Individual exorcism
Thursday: catechumens bathe and wash themselves
Friday and Sabbath: Fasting
Sabbath: catechumens assemble, pray and kneel, bishop lays on hands exorcizing them, then breathes on their faces and seals their foreheads, ears, and noses.
Night vigil with readings and instructions

(XXI) Morning of the baptism (at the cock's crow)
Praying over the (pure and flowing) water
Catechumens undress
Baptisms: first the children, then the men, then the women (who are to undo their hair and remove their jewelry)
Consecration of the oil
Positioning of the deacons
Anointing, baptism, anointing

---

[12] Roman numerals in parentheses designate the chapters in the *Apostolic Tradition*.

(XXII) In church:

    Laying on of hands, anointment, sealing, kiss

    Lord's Prayer

    Kiss of peace

    Baptismal Eucharist with three cups (wine, milk with honey, water)

    The newly baptized pledge commitment to Christ[13]

What strikes one first is the care and particularity with which this teaching and learning process was orchestrated: already the duration of three years is indicative of this. Admission to the church community was prepared in a varied manner: in different locations (the church, the place of baptism out of doors), and by different persons (bishop, deacon, parishioners). The wide array of signs employed is impressive. Ritual-theoretical analysis shows that these signs conveyed the meaning of the baptism by engaging all the senses.[14] In this way, and by way of contrast to the pagan environment,[15] the procedure left an indelible imprint on the lives of those baptized. The final phase, from Thursday to Saturday, represents a mimesis of the last days of Jesus. The close connection with celebratory elements, on the Sundays as well as the last three days, must also be emphasized.

However, already the text of the *Apostolic Tradition* contains one problem. It reports that children were also baptized, without however mentioning how they should be prepared, or, indeed, be guided afterward. It stands to reason that they were quite naturally integrated into Christian life by their baptized parents and brought up to be Christians. Yet, when infant baptism became the rule in the fifth century, the exclusively adult-oriented catechumenate, and therefore the lack of teaching and learning processes for children, caused serious problems. Infants were baptized shortly after birth, but the learning processes originally connected with the baptism were absent. This shortcoming could not be compensated by the children occasionally attending church services (see Paul, *Geschichte der christlichen Erziehung*, 68–71).

The next important step is marked by the introduction of monastic schools. In the ancient world, Christian parents interested in education had sent their children to the conventional institutions of the time. They willingly

---

[13] Summary after Christian Grethlein, "Taufe," in *Liturgisches Kompendium*, Christian Grethlein and Günter Ruddat (Göttingen, 2003), 305–28, 307–8.

[14] Rudolf Roosen, *Taufe lebendig: Taufsymbolik neu verstehen* (Hannover, 1990), 36.

[15] See Meßner, *Einführung in die Liturgiewissenschaft*, 96.

accepted that the curriculum included pagan learning contents, as for instance the classical pantheon connected with reading Homer (see Paul, *Geschichte der christlichen Erziehung*, 18–27). Only after the fall of the Western Roman Empire, and the collapse of the ancient pagan educational institutions, Christian institutions began slowly to establish themselves. In the primarily rural culture, monasteries constituted islands of scholarship amid a largely illiterate environment. This situation saw the birth of an institution specifically designed for the Christian education of children: the monastery school.

Originally, the monastic life only addressed grownup individuals with a leaning for asceticism. Spiritual advancement was paramount, (formal) education played only a mediate role. Nevertheless, we can find reports from the beginning of the sixth century of children that were brought up in monasteries. Apart from children sent there by their parents, foundlings were also taken in. In any case, it became necessary for monasteries to educate children. On the one hand, children—girls were placed in convents—were integrated into the monastic life, on the other hand, special tuition for children was conceived and delivered by a monk assigned to the task. The monastic life was at the same time a way of life and education goal; children were brought up to become a monk or nun. Monasteries operated under the name of "schola," they were "a school for life" (Paul, *Geschichte der christlichen Erziehung*, 123). The fact that some children were only temporary monastic charges, and for them becoming a monk or nun was not a matter of course, only intensified the monasteries' educational efforts. This led to the institutional distinction of a "schola interna" and a "schola externa."

The memorization of the psalms as the dominant prayers, as required in all orders, connected monastic instruction with the insights of the church fathers (130–31). Tuition and monastic life coincided to a high degree: the psalms were crucial to monastic piety not only in the liturgy of the hours, but also in all other liturgies. They were considered to be prayers by Christ, the church's prayers to Christ, and statements about Christ (132). Centuries later, we encounter this high esteem for the Psalter in the Reformation. Even today, the psalms are an important subject in Christian education.

The impact of the Reformation marks a major watershed for the history of education and schooling. The sudden absence of the apparent self-evidence of a shared religious belief required renewed educational efforts to enable the understanding of the differences and one's own affiliation (see Schröder, "Von der Reformation," 37–38). The impulse for the Reformation input to the communication of the gospel in the mode of teaching and learning processes came from a deep-set crisis in the school system, partly already existing, partly brought about by the Reformation itself (see 39–40). On the one hand, the general level of education was alarmingly low: the church visitors reported ignorance of basic Christian beliefs. On the other hand, the theological criticism of monastic life imperiled higher education, since many monasteries, and consequently their schools, were dissolved.

Theologically, the Protestant Reformers recognized the crucial importance of education. Since they believed that every person is in direct relationship with God, mediated only by Christ, and in which she or he cannot be represented by anyone else, clerics included, they also saw the need for education with regard to that relationship. This is why for Martin Luther (1483–1546) the question of the proper education had soteriological qualities—expressed in the struggle between Christ and the Devil, who wishes to suppress schools and education (see WA 15, 29–30). Distinguishing between the two regiments, Luther saw that education had a right to exist in itself, and should not be subsumed by theology.[16] In consequence, he turned to the authorities in three important writings:

> An den christlichen Adel deutscher Nation von des christlichen Standes Besserung [To the Christian Nobility of the German Nation on Improving the Christian Class] (1520; WA 6, 404–65);
> An die Ratsherrn aller Städte deutschen Lands, dass sie christliche Schulen aufrichten und halten sollen [To the Councilmen of All German Cities That They Establish and Maintain Christian Schools] (1524; WA 15, 27–53);
> Eine Predigt, dass man Kinder zur Schulen halten sole [A Sermon on the Importance of Schooling Children] (1530; WA 30,2, 517–88).

Furthermore, he addressed the homes, or more specifically, under the patriarchal structures of the time, the housefathers, with whom he believed lay the primary duty to educate their children. But he knew that many families were, for various reasons (malevolence, inaptitude, lack of time; see WA 15,

---

[16] See Markus Wriedt, "Erneuerung der Frömmigkeit durch Ausbildung: Zur theologischen Begründung der evangelischen Bildungsreform bei Luther und Melanchthon," in *Frömmigkeit und Spiritualität: Auswirkungen der Reformation im 16. und 17. Jahrhundert*, ed. Matthieu Arnold and Rolf Decot (Göttingen, 2009), 59–71.

32) not able to assume their responsibility, and urged the establishment of schools. His particular commitment was to elementary schools, his fellow campaigner Philipp Melanchthon made important contributions to the further development of Latin schools (for more detail, see Schröder, "Von der Reformation," 42–45).

Luther's *Small Catechism* is a remarkable didactic achievement. In a very elementary manner, it presents the fundamentals of Christian faith:

> The Small Catechism begins with the Decalog (Ten Commandments). Luther here provides a fundamental—theologically grounded (First Commandment!)—ethical orientation.
>
> This is followed by the Creed, the Apostolicum. Here readers obtain knowledge of their relationship to God as their Creator, their Redeemer and Renewer.
>
> The Our Father schools individuals in their personal relationship with God, while they can voice their personal wants and needs.
>
> This is followed by remarks on the baptism, the Eucharist (and, later, confession) as the most fundamental Christian practices.
>
> Morning and evening prayer (and later, saying grace) teach a Christian division of time. From an educational perspective it is interesting to note that Luther even gives instructions for the required physical executions: crossing oneself, and perhaps kneeling.
>
> The Small Catechism ends with a haustafel, a domestic code for different social situations.[17]

Conveying cognitive knowledge and the executions of Christian praxis thus blend into one another. This was of course not restricted to the home, liturgical procedures like morning prayer and other worship services formed as much part of school routine as class lessons. A particular bridging function was taken on by church songs: "Singing was part of the classes and an important link between school and worship!" (Schröder, "Von der Reformation," 56).

The impact history of the *Small Catechism* implied a relativization of the Bible's importance for school education, since the catechism was regarded as the "layman's Bible" (57). For the curriculum of his Latin school, Melanchthon also put intelligibility first and advised against the use of Isaiah, Romans,

---

[17] Christian Grethlein, *Fachdidaktik Religion* (Göttingen, 2005), 34.

and the gospel of John for school tuition.[18] Thus, central scriptures of Reformation theology were not read in school for reason of intelligibility.

Another set of important insights with regard to the communication of the gospel in the mode of teaching and learning processes can be found in the pedagogues of the Enlightenment. Since the Reformation, the cultural and political context had changed considerably: traditions and teaching contents were called into question, pedagogy established itself as a science in its own right and schooling was nationalized (Lachmann, "Vom Westfälischen Frieden," 109–10). Accordingly, Christian education in elementary schools was for the first time set apart from the rest of the lessons. Pedagogically, if not in school praxis for a long time to come, it had become crucial to think in terms of the child, not in terms of the specified learning contents. Particularly Christian Gotthilf Salzmann's (1744–1811) religious textbooks, written in the style of children's novels, presented a consistent concept of enlightened religious instruction for families employing a private tutor. The Philanthropinum in Dessau, a boarding school founded in 1774 and regarded as the model school of enlightened pedagogics, adopted a two-pronged approach. Besides Christian education, which purposely distanced itself from the church and its doctrines, there were liturgical ceremonies in "the worship of God." Evidently, for all their child orientation, the Philanthropist reformers found this form of communication indispensable.

In criticizing Christian school education, Friedrich Schleiermacher (1768–1834) contributed further important aspects for the communication of the gospel in the mode of teaching and learning processes. Even in his famous "Reden" (speeches), which he composed at the age of thirty-one, he distanced himself from Christian education in schools. This was due to his understanding of religion, which he set apart from metaphysics and ethics.[19] "Religion" is already inherent in the child's nature, as a "hidden disposition, not understood," (97) which needs to be protected against confusions like the "fury of understanding" (96). For these reasons, Schleiermacher deemed religious instruction inappropriate (see 93–94). Also in his influential lecture on pedagogy (1826) Schleiermacher criticized Christian school education for being a

[18] After Dieter Stoodt, ed., *Arbeitsbuch zur Geschichte des evangelischen Religionsunterrichts in Deutschland* (Münster, 1985), 162.
[19] Friedrich Schleiermacher, *Über die Religion, Reden an die Gebildeten unter ihren Verächtern* (Stuttgart, 1969), 38 (OP 55). Page numbers in this paragraph refer to this edition.

relic of the school's former subordination to the church.[20] For him, the legitimate place of religion and its passing on was in the family, preferably with the mother.[21] Religion, he insists, can only be transmitted in the "dynamic context of life," in other words, in open-ended communication processes.[22] His celebrated *Weihnachtsfeier*[23] (Christmas Eve: Dialogue on the Incarnation) illustrates this in a very vivid manner.

Contrary to Schleiermacher's efforts to protect "religion" from a functional appropriation, the school history in nineteenth-century Germany pointed in a different direction. The authorities took the expansion of the school system in its own hands. The distinctiveness Schleiermacher had claimed for religion was leveled under the functional imperative. This corresponded with the particular didactic endeavors with regard to religious instruction, which emerged in the nineteenth century. Their goals, character formation or conversion, were clearly beyond the possibilities of a subject restricted to a few hours per week. What is more, both state and church desired obedient subjects, which of course banished all forms of open-ended communication from school. Instead, fixed and extensive matters for memorization were established in religious instruction. The lifeworld context, hitherto naturally included in the teaching and learning processes of the communication of the gospel, receded from view.

The concentration of Christian religion as a teaching subject in state schools is a unique development in the history of the communication of the gospel in the form of teaching and learning, which can be understood only in the context of state school policy and the close connection between state and church. As a consequence, liturgical ceremonies in schools lost their importance or were discontinued altogether.

In summary, the following major relationships and issues discussed in the models outlined above should be kept in mind.

First of all, the communication of the gospel in the mode of teaching and learning is characterized by the figure of Jesus as a teacher. He provided the

[20] See Friedrich Schleiermacher, *Pädagogische Schriften I: Die Vorlesungen aus dem Jahre 1826*, ed. Erich Weniger (Frankfurt, 1983), 339.

[21] See Schleiermacher, *Pädagogische Schriften I*, 227.

[22] Martina Kumlehn, *Symbolisierendes Handeln: Schleiermachers Theorie religiöser Kommunikation und ihre Bedeutung für die gegenwärtige Religionspädagogik* (Gütersloh, 1999), 281.

[23] Friedrich Schleiermacher, *Die Weihnachtsfeier: Ein Gespräch* (KGA I,5) (Berlin, 1995), 39–100.

fundamental impetus, which has been handed down in the recording medium of the Gospels, and which is in need of constant transformation in communication media.

Second, teaching and learning take place in different locations, primarily in the home, in church, and in school, but also out of doors. For Luther and Schleiermacher—and indirectly also for the *Apostolic Tradition*—home and family were the primary locations for the communication of the gospel in the educational mode. The monastic life had family-like characteristics.

Third, the Psalms in the form of prayer and song served as an important bridge between school, church, and home.

Fourth, up to the second half of the twentieth century, there was a continuous relationship between forms of instruction and forms of liturgy in institutions introducing adults and children to the Christian faith.

Moreover, the communication of the gospel in the mode of teaching and learning involves both receptive and participatory forms of learning.

With regard to contents, the communication of the gospel—as shown in Luther's *Small Catechism*—treats of the relationship between the individual and God.

And finally, there is a basic tension—particularly conspicuous in catechism classes in school—between the impartation of certain contents and learner orientation. This already surfaces during the Reformation, but becomes more apparent in the Enlightenment.

Relationship with the Other Modes of the
Communication of the Gospel

Jesus' communication of the gospel was characterized by fact that the modes of teaching and learning, celebrating together, and helping for living were all integrated. This fact will be explored in this section with respect to teaching and learning processes. In this regard, recent developments in liturgical and diaconal education merit specific attention.

In the models outlined above, one can observe that all teaching and learning processes are closely and, for the most part, inextricably connected with communal celebration, specifically with liturgical procedures. In the first type of Christian learning, the catechumenate, the communal celebration of the baptism even formed the aim and culminating point, which was followed by the so-called mystagogic catecheses. The liturgical procedure itself became the basis of education, by virtue of the model of "mimesis." During the reformation, the fact that the *Small Catechism* results in morning, evening, and mealtime prayer also illustrates the natural relationship of learning and liturgy.

As late as the nineteenth century, we find school pedagogical reflections emphatically underlining the educational value of liturgical ceremonies. As a general state school system took hold, the relationship between school and liturgy became looser, although liturgical celebrations were common in German schools until the 1960s. In spite of this, religious instruction in schools became more and more independent. It was only in the 1990s that school teachers as well as religious educators became aware of the pedagogical importance of rites and liturgical procedures for students and Christian education again.[24] "Liturgical education" has since become a didactic and methodological issue. Fundamental acts of communication of Christian liturgy, such as prayer and receiving blessing, now attract criteriological attention in education theoretical considerations.[25]

From liturgical let us now turn to diaconal education. So far, in our inquiry into the modes of teaching and learning, we have not yet explicitly encountered the mode of helping for living. A closer look however reveals such connections.

In chapter XX of the *Apostolic Tradition*, for instance, the examination of the baptizand's moral conduct prior to final admission is depicted. Among the criteria are the honoring of widows, visiting the sick, and constantly doing good works (XX, 1). Similar injunctions hold true for the monastic life and monastic schools. The Christian labor of love is enshrined in the Rule of St. Benedict, and among the seventy-eight good works article IV (*quae sunt instrumenta bonorum operum*) lists, there are many describing helping others.

What the early Christian catechumenate and the monastic school have in common is that they regarded being a Christian as a comprehensive way of life, so that the communication of the gospel would naturally include helping others. But even in the school or class models of religious instructions these connections can be discovered, because they would traditionally deal with pertinent biblical texts such as the commandment of brotherly love or Jesuanic stories such as that of the Good Samaritan (Luke 10:25-27). In a class context, however, this would be restricted to reflection and not involve practice.

[24] See Christian Grethlein, "Liturgische Bildung: Anthropologische Voraussetzungen und Zielperspektiven," in *Mensch–Religion–Bildung: Religionspädagogik in anthropologischen Spannungsfeldern*, ed. Thomas Schlag and Henrik Simojoki (Gütersloh, 2014), 571–80.
[25] Grethlein, *Fachdidaktik Religion*, 271–80.

Almost simultaneously to the outlined endeavors to connect a religious didactics with liturgy, there were attempts to integrate social and diaconal experience into schooling. This was also due to a general dissatisfaction with a two-hour classroom subject that, for its lack of experience-orientation, did not measure up to the contents it taught. By now, so-called diaconal placements are often an integral part in church-funded German schools. In addition, there are schools in which diaconal-social learning in various organizational forms runs through all grades (see Gramzow, *Diakonie in der Schule*, 116–19). Conceptually, it is important that these learning processes are well-grounded in educational theory. Such a theoretical framework can be found in the concept of "diaconal education" (*Diakonische Bildung*):

> Diaconal education thus consists in a meaning- and value-oriented, reflective penetration of diaconal-social fields of action and challenges with respect to their communicability in social discourses.[26]

Fundamental Questions

Two religious-pedagogical questions in particular need to be fundamentally reconsidered for a theory of the communication of the gospel in the mode of teaching and learning. First, can the communication of the gospel be taught? And, what is the place of the Bible in such teaching and learning processes?

Let us first consider the gospel as a subject of teaching and learning. Religious educators have always been grappling with the question of the teachability of "religion," by which they (of course) meant the Christian faith.[27] After all, it is on this that the legitimacy of religion as a school subject depends. A close look at the concept of the communication of the gospel helps to identify the tensions and defuse them. From a communication-theoretical perspective, the gospel for one thing means a recording medium when it refers to the Gospels in the New Testament. Doubtless, they can be understood, as well as their sources in the Old Testament and antiquity, by operational learning

---

[26] Heinz Schmidt and Renate Zitt, "Fürs Leben lernen: Diakonisches Lernen—diakonische Bildung," in *Diakonische Bildung: Theorie und Empirie* (VDWI 21), ed. Helmut Hanisch and Heinz Schmidt (Heidelberg, 2004), 56–75, 68.

[27] A classic reference for this is Richard Kabisch, *Wie lehren wir Religion? Versuch einer Methodik des evangelischen Religionsunterrichts für alle Schulen auf psychologischer Grundlage* (Göttingen, 1910).

processes. With regard to the general cultural importance of Christianity, this appears to be a requirement in school education.

At the same time, the gospel is a transmission medium. To communicate the gospel means to raise awareness for the advent of God's reign, or the love of God, which will give a new outlook on life. The form of communication involved here is geared toward mutual understanding and therefore open-ended. Evaluations defeat the purpose.

If we now turn to the Bible as school subject, a brief media-theoretical discussion can here as well open up new perspectives for the controversy over the relevancy of the Bible in Christian education. Again in terms of communication theory, the Bible served for a long time as a personal medium. Until the eighteenth century few people so much as owned a Bible. Their knowledge of the Bible came from listening to Scripture during worship or looking at pictures in churches. Only the dissemination of Bibles made it possible to read them and thus turn them into an impersonal medium. This should sound a note of caution about instantly connecting the communication of the gospel with the reading of the Bible. As a matter of fact, few people today read the Bible, as only a minority of the population read books at all. The reading of books, and especially large tomes like the Bible, is milieu- and class-dependent. Yet, the communication of the gospel needs input from the Bible if it is not to lose its fundament. It needs therefore to be considered how this can be achieved without having everyone read the Bible—which would be seem illusive anyway.

This is where the concept of Bible didactics comes in.[28] For one thing, Bible didactics aim to find out which kind texts are meaningful to whom, and for another, it methodically investigates appropriate approaches. In this context, it stands to reason that presenting biblical texts as open-ended communication processes that invite participation. Methods like the "bibliodrama"[29] and the "bibliolog"[30] implement this mimetically or aurally. They facilitate a direct encounter with biblical figures above and beyond the mere reading. In this manner, the oldest forms of learning from human history and the primal

[28] See Mirjam Zimmermann and Ruben Zimmermann, eds., *Handbuch der Bibeldidaktik* (Tübingen, 2013).

[29] See Heiner Aldebert, *Spielend Gott kennenlernen: Bibliodrama in religionspädagogischer Perspektive* (Berlin, 2001).

[30] See Uta Pohl-Patalong, *Bibliolog: Impulse für Gottesdienst, Gemeinde und Schule*, 2 vols. (Stuttgart, 2009).

forms of reception from Christian history take effect. They transform the knowledge of particular texts and ideas into a form of communication capable of inspiring fresh outlooks on life. Furthermore, the varied reception of biblical texts, traditions, and motifs in literature, art, and film offers splendid opportunities for the communication of the gospel, often in the form of a "productive confusion,"[31] since the historical remoteness of biblical texts has here already been aesthetically processed.

2. The Gospel in the Mode of Celebrating Together

Literature: Peter Cornehl, "Gottesdienst VIII: Evangelischer Gottesdienst von der Reformation bis zur Gegenwart," *TRE* 14 (1985), 54–85; Gregor Etzelmüller, . . . *Zu schauen die schönen Gottesdienste des Herrn: Eine biblische Theologie der christlichen Liturgiefamilien* (Frankfurt, 2010); Christian Grethlein, "Gottesdienst und Diakonie: Evangelische Annäherung an ein schwieriges Thema," in *Die diakonale Dimension der Liturgie* (QD 218), ed. Benedikt Kranemann, Thomas Sternberg, and Walter Zahner (Freiburg, 2006), 41–57; Christian Grethlein, *Grundfragen der Liturgik: Ein Studienbuch zur zeitgemäßen Gottesdienstgestaltung* (Gütersloh, 2001); Hans Bernhard Meyer, *Eucharistie: Geschichte, Theologie, Pastoral* (GDK 4) (Regensburg, 1989); Peter Wick, *Die urchristlichen Gottesdienste: Entstehung und Entwicklung im Rahmen der frühjüdischen Tempel-, Synagogueen- und Hausfrömmigkeit* (BWANT 150) (Stuttgart, ²2003 [2002]); Christoph Wulf, *Anthropologie: Geschichte–Kultur–Philosophie* (Cologne, 2009)

As so often in Practical Theology, there are significant differences in contemporary language use and the usage in Christian history. Thus, *Gottesdienst* (divine service) is a term that Martin Luther used primarily for theological reasons,[32] but for which no clearly corresponding concept can be found in the Bible or in early Christianity (see Grethlein, *Grundfragen*, 55–65). The more general concept of "communal celebration" for this particular mode of

---

[31] See Lutz Friedrichs, "Produktive Irritationen: Eric-Emmanuel Schmitts Bestseller *Oskar und die Dame in Rosa* religionspädagogisch und homiletisch gelesen," *PTh* 100 (2011), 490–502.

[32] Programmatically elaborated in his *Vorrede zur Deutschen Messe* (Preface to *The German Mass*) (1526; WA 19,72–113).

communicating the gospel is both reminiscent of these origins and opens up a wider anthropological horizon.

As purported in the Gospels, Jesus lived with his disciples in the time of his ministry, but he also sought communion with other people. As a Jew, he naturally celebrated the feasts of his people, the Sabbath, Pesach, and so on. He visited the synagogues and the temple, prayed, and fasted at the customary times. He thus was rooted in the Old Testament tradition. After his death, the Jewish ceremonies were adopted and transformed by the early Christian community.[33] Out of this, and due to different contextual challenges, a pluriform ensemble of rites evolved, for which I will give some examples below. As regards the input from the Reformation, I will concentrate on Luther's works again, since he offers extensive and in every respect praxis-oriented responses to the question of the *Gottesdienst*. His ideas have been repeatedly referred to in subsequent periods.[34]

It should be noted that, methodologically, this line of argument runs counter to the kind of organological approach such as is currently proposed—in the tradition of Anton Baumstark—by Josef Ratzinger, for example. This theory charges the celebratory aspects of liturgy normatively. Discontinuities, like the disruptions of the Reformation, or changes due to context, are either not allowed for or regarded negatively.[35] The fiction of an organic evolution is however historically untenable[36] and stands in the way of an ecumenical science of liturgy.

From this vantage point, insights into the—possible—correspondence with the two other modes of the communication of the gospel offer themselves. The basic question that informs the history of Christian worship throughout is the issue of the distinction between true and false worship.

---

[33] Albert Gerhards emphasizes the mutuality of this exchange process in "Kraft aus der Wurzel: Zum Verhältnis christlicher Liturgie gegenüber dem Jüdischen. Fortschreibung oder struktureller Neubeginn?," *KuI* 16 (2001), 25–44.

[34] For Huldrych Zwingli's alternative, pneumatological, idea of the church service, see Ralph Kunz, *Gottesdienst evangelisch reformiert: Liturgik und Liturgie in der Kirche Zwinglis* (THEOPHIL 10) (Zürich, 2001), 33–194.

[35] See Josef Kardinal Ratzinger, "Liturgie zwischen Tradition und organischem Wachsen," *Una Voce-Korrespondenz* 35 (2005), 85–89.

[36] See Arnold Angenendt, *Liturgik und Historik: Gab es eine organische Liturgie-Entwicklung?* (QD 189) (Freiburg, 2001).

Anthropological Background

Here and in the following, I am guided by the common usage in cultural studies according to which feast and celebration form a set. Festivities transcend everyday life. The communal celebrations that go along with them are culture-historically an ancient form of communication (see Grethlein, *Grundfragen*, 130–32, 147–48). Festivities are usually connected with communal meals, expressing the life-affirming attitude and future orientation that behooves a celebration. This form of communication therefore involves all the senses (see 160–61). The semiotic distinction of codes offers a sophisticated instrument for the empirical analysis of celebrations and their complexities. Festivities provide social orientation in space and time. They implicate a certain way of managing time. Certain time rhythms are inherent to the human body, such as the wake-sleep cycles, endocrine cycles, and so on. Humans are exposed to certain environmental rhythms like the lunar cycle, the circannual cycle, and the tides. Apart from the day-night rhythm, calendar divisions may vary culturally, and those divisions regularly refer to transcendental causes.

Festivities reach their communicative point of culmination in celebrations, which usually take place in special locations, since communication is closely related to the space in which it takes place. Celebrations are structured by fixed and free communication phases. From a culture-anthropological point of view, celebrations are key to human sociality:

> They are instrumental in dealing with difference and alterity, in creating community and relationships, and they help to interpret and organize human situations. Rituals connect past, present, and future. They enable continuity and change as well as experiences of transition and transcendence. (Wulf, *Anthropologie*, 261)

In their ritualized forms, celebrations pass on crucial insights from one generation to the next. Next to language and mimesis, imaginations play an important role in this process.

Biblical Foundations

Because of Jesus' participation in Jewish life, its foundations in the Old Testament need to be outlined before reconstructing the understanding of communal celebrations in the New Testament.

Peter Wick interprets the Gospels' statements concerning "divine service" in their Jewish context. Three types of communication form the basis for the commerce between the people of Israel with God: "the sacrificial cult, prayer, and scriptural piety" (Wick, *Die urchristlichen Gottesdienste*, 50). Wick shows the fundamental importance of the sacrifice in the Old Testament as a "guarantor of the shalom" with God (37–47). During crises and in critical controversies in particular, prayer supervened (47–48).[37] Finally, "scriptural piety and the observance of the Torah" present other important forms of communicating with God, where ethical instructions play a vital role.

Due to the centralization of the cult (Deut 12), the attitude toward the sacrifice changed and it became limited to three pilgrimages per year, which resulted in the other two forms of communication taking on a special significance for everyday life. As a final mark of distinction from the cult practices of surrounding peoples, the "priority of obedience before worship" (43) must be mentioned. According to this principle, appropriate ethical behavior was prerequisite for every cult act destined to please God.

These three forms of communication from early Judaism took place, as a rule, in different locations: the sacrifice was confined to the temple, prayer to the home, and scriptural piety to the synagogue. For everyday practical life, the home was naturally most important: daily routine was organized by three prayers (morning, noon, evening) and the prayer before the shared meal.[38]

By looking at the Christian reception history of church liturgies, Gregor Etzelmüller takes a different approach. Reconstructing various Christian liturgical families he finds two distinct cultic concepts expressing themselves in Christian liturgies: the deuteronomical and the priestly scriptural concepts, whose differences become particularly apparent in the respective festival calendars (see Etzelmüller, . . . *Zu schauen*, 497). There is thus no uniform conception of the communal communication with God even in the Old Testament. Instead, we encounter theologically and communicatively diverse types of communal celebration explicitly performed in the face of God.

In contrast, the striking thing about the New Testament is the general lack of cultic terminology. This is, for instance, rather apparent in the descriptions

---

[37] The difficulty here again is that the Old Testament does not provide any concept corresponding to our idea of "prayer" (see Rainer Albertz, "Gebet II: Altes Testament," *TRE* 12 [1984], 34–42, 34).

[38] Albert Gerhards and Benedikt Kranemann, *Einführung in die Liturgiewissenschaft* (Darmstadt, 2006), 62.

of or the references to the Lord's Supper.[39] Also, the figure of the priest, so important in ancient cult, is absent from the Gospels. The designations for functionaries in the New Testament—*apostolos, episkopos, diakonos*—were "not taken from the contemporary language of administration or cult, but were developed from terminologically largely undetermined word radicals."[40] The reason for this is certainly the principal reference to Christ, who considered his ministry to be *diakonia* (Gr. "service"; Luke 22:27). While naturally taking part in temple and synagogue services, he however upset the cultic mind-set in three important instances: by rejecting the distinction between clean and unclean (Mark 7:1-23); by criticizing the economic basis of the temple cult (Mark 11:15-17); and in claiming the power and authority to forgive sins (Mark 2:5-7). These acts challenged the fundamental functions of the temple. Their aim of course was to emphasize the presence of God's caring attention in all of life's situations. Thus, Jesus approvingly quotes Hosea 6:6 (Matt 9:13; 12:7).

One can here detect—as well as in the Old Testament—a close proximity between communal celebrating and the communication mode of helping for living, since assisting the oppressed and the poor is fundamental to communal celebration. The meaning of "divine service" implicated herein was succinctly captured by Paul in the term of *logike latreia* (Gr.; Luther: *vernünfftiger Gottesdienst*)[41] clearly indicating that intelligibility was an important criterion for that which was said in congregation (1 Cor 14:23-33).

Finally, two practices emerged after Jesus' death in which the presence of the risen Christ was celebrated, namely the Eucharist and the baptism. By celebrating the communion of the assembled with the risen Lord or the initiation of a new member, they open up an eschatological horizon. Both rites have precursors in religious history while simultaneously relating to Jesus' ministry. And again, from a communication-theoretical perspective, the integration of all senses in these rites must be highlighted.

---

[39] Roloff, "Heil als Gemeinschaft," 176.

[40] Jürgen Roloff, "Amt/Ämter/Amtsverständnis IV: Im Neuen Testament," *TRE* 2 (1978), 509–33, 510.

[41] In his German translation of the Bible of 1545.

Historical Forms

In the course of Christian history, the biblical pluriformity of forms of celebration was not only continued, but became further differentiated regionally and, later, denominationally.[42] In the following, I will present from this wide multiplicity only a few examples in which the biblical impulse was transformed to serve in new contexts. The fundamental forms of communal celebration will at least briefly be touched upon: the baptism and the Eucharist, benedictions, preaching service and festive services, and the liturgical treatment of time (liturgy of the hours).

First, let us turn to the significance of the Lord's Supper. We know very little about the Christian celebration practices of the first two centuries. In a pagan context, the baptism arguably played a central role, since it rather powerfully expresses Christian identity in combining all three modes of the communication of the gospel. The same is true of all other forms congregation in which the Eucharist, Scriptural reading and interpretation and offertory collection took place (see Just. *1 Apol.* 65–67). The temporal structure of the Jewish communities was kept, but redefined. In terms of the history of religion, communal celebration, with the Eucharist at its center, was transformed into a complex cultic pattern. This is exemplified in the changing of the Lord's Supper (see Meyer, *Eucharistie*, 73–115).

Already in the New Testament a discord as to the proper form of the celebration led to conflict among the Corinthians. As a result, a separation of the Eucharist from the meal (see 1 Cor 11:34) took place. This initiated a fundamental transformation which completely changed the nature of the communication and became prevalent over time: the Lord's Supper, at which Christians ate and drank together, became the cultic rite of the Eucharist, which was separated from the communal meal (see 87). This entailed a ritualization, that is, the carrying out of repetitive acts of symbolic communication. Giving thanks to God as the provider of food and drink became less important (see 93). Probably due to the growing distance to Jesus' earthly ministry, one can observe an increasing accentuation of the anamnesis of Christ from the second century onward.

---

[42] I am focusing on the development in Western Christendom; for an introduction to the development in Orthodoxy, see Hans-Dieter Döpmann, "Gottesdienst im orthodoxen Kontext," in Schmidt-Lauber, Meyer-Blanck, and Bieritz, *Handbuch der Liturgik*, 129–39; Bieritz, *Liturgik*, 336–70.

Another important step in the transformation of the biblical foundations was the emergence of offices. The cultic character of communal celebrations brought with it the establishment of offices, most prominently that of the bishop. While in early Christian house communities the pater (or mater) familias, and later also to some extent charismatics, presided over the congregation, now the task of community leader exclusively fell to the bishop. The—probably[43]—first record of the three-partite structure of bishop-presbyter (priest)-deacon can be found at the beginning of the second century in the letters of Ignatius of Antioch. They fulfilled different functions, while the bishopric was the central one.[44] Without the bishop, neither baptisms nor the love feast, or agape, which probably meant the Eucharist (Ign. *Smyrn.* 8:1-2), could be performed. The prominent position of the bishop must above all be understood from the desire for unity which characterized Ignatian theology.[45] This regionally varying but overall intensifying institutionalization of offices and their liturgical functions impacted the forms of communal celebrations.

This development can, for example, be studied in one of its Western end products, the basic structure of the Roman-Latin mass.[46] This liturgy is the expression of a contextualization within a hierarchically organized society, and the challenge to preserve the unity of the church. The countercultural aspects inherent in early communal celebrations disappeared under the weight of clerical ceremony, as did the teaching and learning processes that formed part of those early congregations.

While the discussion of the Eucharist focused on inner-church matters, the following look at the role of benedictions will take us to forms of communication in which people, full of hope, brought their everyday needs before God. Benedictions thus primarily concerned the home. In the Middle Ages, however, one can observe the church's tendency to adapt intrafamily blessings for its purposes. There was moreover a continuous increase in the number of benedictions that were practiced on the peripheries of church liturgies. Particularly two important life transitions that were celebrated within the family saw benedictory adaptations by the church: marriage and burial. The churching of marriage began only in late antiquity to the early Middle Ages.

---

[43] See Hermut Löhr, "Die Briefe des Ignatius von Antiochien," in *Die Apostolischen Väter: Eine Einleitung*, ed. Wilhelm Pratscher (Göttingen, 2009), 104–29, 105–9.

[44] See Löhr, "Die Briefe," 119–21.

[45] Löhr, "Die Briefe," 117.

[46] Gerhards and Kranemann, *Einführung in die Liturgiewissenschaft*, 75.

Before taking a closer look at this development that already took monogamy for granted, it is important that the Old Testament also reports other forms of marriage: the patriarchs and kings of Israel were polygamous, and there was the levirate marriage for widows. And in the New Testament we even find voices critical of marriage altogether (see, e.g., 1 Cor 7:1-9).

Joining couples in wedlock had been the privilege of the paterfamilias or his deputy (see Tob 7:13-14), and this remained the status quo during the first centuries of Christian communities. The first instance in which the Eucharist is mentioned in connection with Christian marriages is probably in Tertullian, at the turn from the second to the third centuries. In the fourth century we find the blessing of the bride (*benedictio nuptialis*), together with her veiling (*velatio nuptialis*). These rites were—and this was a new thing—performed by the priest.[47] The slow transition from the bond of marriage which was entered *in facie ecclesiae* to marriage as ecclesial act took, depending on the region, well into the second millennium, and only came to a conclusion at the Council of Trent where the canonical form of marriage was confirmed (DH No. 1814).

A similar development can be observed for burials. Until the fifth or sixth centuries, Christian burials seem to have been, as was the Roman custom, the charge of the families. Only slowly did these customs, which were at odds with belief in the resurrection, vanish; church officials were now in charge of the ceremony. And in monasteries particularly extensive procedures were put in place. In terms of religious hermeneutics, these new ecclesial acts referred to primary religious experience. This is equally true of the rapid spread of benedictions.

In this context, however, two important circumstances need to be kept in mind: for one, life in those days was a highly precarious thing. Magical practices, in tandem with benedictions, promised protection. Furthermore, the spread of Christianity into the Franco-German realm promoted a reification of transcendental ideas, since the majority of the population was illiterate and keen on seeing life improvements take place instantly. Corresponding with the Jewish Berakot, thanksgiving had dominated the blessings in early Christian times. Now it was petitions, exorcisms, and an attitude toward magic

---

[47] See Bruno Kleinheyer, "Riten um Ehe und Familie," in Kleinheyer, Severus, and Kaczynski, *Sakramentliche Feiern II*, 67–156, 90.

that was pretheologically interested in the correct execution of formulas and procedures.[48]

The Reformation marks another significant incision: it was not least the excessive system of benedictions that provoked Martin Luther's protest. In his *Von ordenung gottis diensts ynn der gemeine* (1523) he sharply criticized this and other issues (see WA 12,35). His first criticism was directed against daily office. These prayers included reading from the Bible but no interpretations, which, Luther insisted, were necessary for the word to work (see WA 12,37). His second criticism shows that this was also a matter of content. Sermons on Acts of the Saints—which is probably what Luther had in mind—did not comply with christological standards. Finally, he vilified the concentration on righteousness through works since this obscured the message of the grace of God. In concrete terms, Luther condemned, among other things, the practice of having mass read for money in the absence of the congregation.

In contrast, he programmatically placed the relation to Christ at the center of the "divine service." All the rest seemed disposable—as his fundamentally conservative attitude toward existing morals shows. Whatever seemed to obscure the gospel—like the sacrificial tenor of the Canon prayer—needed to be thoroughly eradicated. Therefore all of Luther's liturgical suggestions are informed by the catechetical perspective which is most evident in his *Deutsche Messe* (1526). The relation to Christ did not only concern sermons and church service. As opposed to the great number of saint's days in the Roman church, it also led to a concentration of worship to Sundays and Christ's feast days.[49] This reform also brought about a strong verbalization of the communication of the gospel. In one respect, however, Luther provided an important incentive for the emotional arrangement of the communal celebration, namely by foregrounding congregational singing.[50]

In the wake of the Reformation a further issue surfaced: the question of instructing people in religious matters. Udo Sträter puts the case quite convincingly by detecting in the Lutheran churches of the seventeenth century "a crisis of churchliness, which manifested itself in a crisis of ecclesial

---

[48] Christian Grethlein, "Benediktionen und Krankensalbung," in Schmidt-Lauber, Meyer-Blanck, and Bieritz, *Handbuch der Liturgik*, 551–74, 557.

[49] See Frieder Schulz, "Die Ordnung der liturgischen Zeit in den Kirchen der Reformation (1981)," in *Synaxis, Beiträge zur Liturgik*, ed. Gerhard Schwinge (Göttingen, 1997), 359–83.

[50] See Johannes Schilling, "Musik," in Beutel, *Luther Handbuch*, 236–44.

proclamation."[51] Particularly the sermons did not fulfill the Reformation desire to awaken and strengthen the congregation's faith. And neither did the various proposals for meditations,[52] which were even meant to replace sermons to some extent. To make matters worse, criticisms of the church began to emerge in the eighteenth century, and the church service had to compete with the emerging periodicals like the "Moralische Wochenschriften"[53] (moral weeklies) whose intent was to both entertain and instruct, women in particular. It is hardly surprising that in this situation, in the last third of the eighteenth century, a number of theoretical and practical suggestions for the reform of church service are put forward.[54] Apart from proposals concerning liturgical procedure and songbooks, the attention focused on the sermon, with regard to both its purpose and structure. Addressing this issue, Johann Spalding's (1714–1804) publication *Ueber die Nutzbarkeit des Predigtamtes und deren Beförderung* (On the Utility of the Preacher's Office and Its Improvement) made a significant impact and saw three reprints between 1772 and 1791.

In the first part, Spalding ventilates the idea of the utility of the preacher's office from the title in two ways. One essential question is that of "religious instruction," which immediately draws the attention to the important role of the parents in a family.[55] Leaning on moral doctrine, Spalding on the other hand seeks to establish the value of the sermon for society in general. The layout of the sermon hinged on the distinction between theology and religion, which had become commonly accepted during the Enlightenment.[56] The sermon was meant to address only that which "actually impacts the soul and the life."[57] Dogmatic tenets like those of justification or original sin were excluded.

[51] Udo Sträter, *Meditation und Kirchenreform in der lutherischen Kirche des 17. Jahrhunderts* (BHTh 91) (Tübingen, 1995), 30.

[52] Sträter, *Meditation und Kirchenreform*, 100–118.

[53] See Werner Faulstich, *Die bürgerliche Mediengesellschaft (1700–1830), Die Geschichte der Medien*, vol. 4 (Göttingen, 2002), 236–42.

[54] See Alfred Ehrensperger, *Die Theorie des Gottesdienstes in der späten deutschen Aufklärung (1770–815)* (SDGSTh 30) (Zürich, 1971).

[55] Johann Spalding, *Ueber die Nutzbarkeit des Predigtamtes und deren Beförderung* (¹1772; ²1773; ³1791), ed. Tobias Jersak (SpKA I/3) (Tübingen, 2002), 52–53.

[56] See Albrecht Beutel, "'Gebessert und zum Himmel tüchtig gemacht': Die Theologie der Predigt nach Johann Joachim Spalding," in *Reflektierte Religion: Beiträge zur Geschichte des Protestantismus* (Tübingen, 2007), 210–36, 222–25.

[57] Spalding, *Ueber die Nutzbarkeit*, 134–35.

Denominational differences were also minimized. The emphasis was put on a life-embracing, intelligible, and therefore productive exposition of the reasonable Christian moral doctrine. The preacher, who should not be a priest, but a "trusted friend" (Ger. *vertrauter Freund*)[58] of the congregation, was supposed to preach with a determined hold on the daily life of his listeners. It is quite apparent that "instruction" is at the center of this understanding of worship. Accordingly, Enlightenment theologians emphatically promoted the introduction and spread of the confirmation.

The final aspect I would like to address in this section is that of religion as a festival religion. Every culture has its festivals. Official cult and actual life praxis are often intricately interwoven. A prominent example for this is Christmas. Its Christian roots reach back into the fourth century in Rome, where December 25 was celebrated as Natalis Solis Invicti.[59] In addition, there were several pagan traditions feeding into the celebration; consequently, several motifs combined to shape the festival liturgy (see Grethlein, *Grundfragen*, 251). Over time, the range of festivals around Christmas expanded and a rich liturgical life and a variety of customs emerged.

The way the Christmas festival established itself in nineteenth-century Germany[60] merits particular attention because it has since radiated into many different countries. The reason is that, at the time, a specifically bourgeois festival culture developed that is still in place today. Ecclesial traditions, public festival culture, and family traditions blended into one another, which becomes particularly evident in the mutual adoption of festival insignia. The Christmas tree, for instance—first iconographically present in a copper engraving from 1505 by Lucas Cranach—moved in the course of the nineteenth century from public spaces like guildhalls to the living rooms of families. The winter of the 1870–1871 war moreover gave the Christmas trees, which adorned the shelters of the German soldiers fighting the French, an additional nationalistic glow. Before long, the nativity scene, for a long time displayed only in churches and other public buildings, also entered the family homes. As Kristian Fechtner summarizes, "Christmas sees a life-worldly

---

[58] Spalding, *Ueber die Nutzbarkeit*, 64.

[59] Hansjörg Auf der Maur, *Feiern im Rhythmus der Zeit*, vol. 1: *Herrenfeste in Woche und Jahr* (GDK 5) (Regensburg, 1983), 166.

[60] See Ingeborg Weber-Kellermann's seminal *Das Weihnachtsfest: Eine Kultur- und Sozialgeschichte der Weihnachtszeit* (Luzern, 1978).

privatization, minimization; it is, as it were, intimized."[61] What emerged was indeed a festival in which primary and secondary religious experience were united. In the form of the Christmas festival thus, the communication of the gospel in the mode of communal celebration established itself in the bourgeois families of the nineteenth century as a religious festival. The Christmas celebrations in the home related to the church festival and therefore to the biblical festival legend; the celebrants however quite often distanced themselves from specific church teachings like the immaculate conception or the dogma of reincarnation. They were therefore religious in the sense of religion as an intra-Protestant term of distinction.

On the margin, it is interesting to note that this festival culture also influenced the form of the Hanukkah festival in Jewish families. This is not surprising in view of the all-embracing framework of bourgeois culture; and the shared symbolism of light certainly helped. Thus, the Christmas tree also found its way into Jewish homes.[62]

Finally, another link between the private celebrations and the festive church service was provided by the songs.

In summary, the following important contexts and problems should be kept in mind. The first important development occurred in the second century CE, when the primary task of communal celebrations became to keep the anamnesis of Christ alive. As a consequence, congregational proceedings became increasingly disengaged from daily life. Furthermore, functional needs, the problem of the unity of Christian communities, and political as well as cultural contexts led to the implementation of offices, which in turn introduced hierarchical structures into communal celebrations. Parallel to these organized ecclesial procedures, practices of popular piety evolved, which were more or less loosely connected with church practice (e.g., medieval benedictions, religious festivals in the nineteenth century). They strongly related to everyday life, but were in danger of weakening or losing the relation to Christ. In this manner, the whole of Christian history is marked by a peculiar tension between forms of communal celebration oriented, in a secondary religious fashion, by the Bible or church traditions, and other forms of primary religious experience that sought to express vital human needs. This hiatus is

---

[61] Kristian Fechtner, *Im Rhythmus des Kirchenjahres: Vom Sinn der Feste und Zeiten* (Gütersloh, 2007), 68.

[62] Thomas Nipperdey, *Deutsche Geschichte 1866–1918*, vol. 1: *Arbeitswelt und Bürgergeist* (Munich, [2]1991), 405.

often bridged by aesthetic forms of expression like song and music, or dramatic forms such as mystery, passion, or nativity plays.

Relationship with Other Modes of the Communication of the Gospel

The forms of communal celebration have changed fundamentally and in various ways on all levels. The Lord's Supper, which satisfied hunger and thirst, was replaced by the ritually elaborate Eucharist offering a thin wafer and—in Reformation churches—a sip of wine. Evening congregation turned into a highly sophisticated liturgical year defining the rhythm of our society to this day. The home parlor turned into a church building. The fellowship of coequal disciples split up into a priestly hierarchy on the one and the congregation on the other side. All this of course had significant consequences for the two other modes of communicating the gospel.

First, let us take a look at the mode of teaching and learning, in what I would describe as a movement from mimesis to the education of the people. As shown for the baptism on the basis of the account in the *Apostolic Tradition*, early Christian practice was dominated by mimesis, a mode which involved the whole human being. The same can be said for the weekly communal meal: the participants joined the table fellowship beginning in the ministry of the earthly Jesus. From the beginning, the congregation also practiced verbal forms of teaching: reading and interpreting Scripture. The early Christians also adopted all forms of communication available at the time, which led to teaching and learning processes outside the weekly congregations.

The medieval development of liturgy cuts off the connection between the communication of the gospel in the mode of communal celebration and the mode of teaching and learning. Mass celebrated by ordained priests in a language unintelligible to most of the attendees afforded the uneducated churchgoers at best the opportunity to marvel at the splendor of the proceedings. It is worthwhile to note that during this period not only the connection with teaching and learning was lost, but the communal character of celebrating too was compromised. The widespread practice of what was called "eye communion," that is, a practice arising since the twelfth century of merely looking on during elevation without actually receiving the bread (see Meyer, *Eucharistie*, 233), carried the severance of the filling meal and the liturgical procedure of the Eucharist to extremes. Reserving the chalice for the priest alone, another practice from around the same period (see 498), further compromised the communication of the gospel.

Logically, this is what brought on the protest of the Reformation. However, the former mimetic procedure of communal celebration was replaced by the cognitive from of listening to the sermon. Enlightenment theologians adapted this approach to the changed cultural context and sought to relate their sermons closely to life in the interests of public instruction. This spelled the end of the countercultural perspective of the communication of the gospel.

This kind of adaptation of the communication of the gospel reached its peak in the normative bourgeois framework of the Christmas festival in the nineteenth century. The childlike form of the festival and the sentimentality that went with it overcame the cognitive reductionism of the merely verbal sermon. Simultaneously, however, the new customs of the Christmas tree and crèche threatened to eclipse the relation to Christ.

If we now turn to the connection between the mode of helping for living and the mode of celebrating, Ulrike Suhr's statement might, after what we have just said, come as a surprise: "In the Lord's Supper we can detect the closest proximity of divine service and clerical welfare work."[63] This make's sense, if we think of the Eucharist in terms of the original Lord's Supper as a communal meal. In a society in which a great many suffered from hunger, a communal meal is the expression of mutual care (see Just. *1 Apol.* 67,6–7), intimately connecting the acts of celebrating and helping. This can also be observed in the act of intercessory prayers. In addition, sermons included ethical admonishments, lessons emphasized the significance of love of neighbor for the imitation of Christ.

In the course of the cultic ritualization and clericalization of communal celebrations, this dimension of performativity however waned.[64] Bringing in the eucharistic offerings and sharing them out among the poor was ritualized and thus removed from the context of daily life, profoundly changing the attitude toward the needy, the principal improvement of whose conditions was of no more interest.

[63] Ulrike Suhr, "Gottesdienst und Diakonie," in Schmidt-Lauber, Meyer-Blanck, and Bieritz, *Handbuch der Liturgik*, 673–84, 682.

[64] See Helmut Schwier, "Liturgie und Diakonie—einige Überlegungen im Licht des 'performative turn,'" in *Diakonie und Bildung*, ed. Johannes Eurich and Christian Oelschlägel (Stuttgart, 2008), 265–77.

Even the Reformation did not manage to restore the connection between the modes of communal celebration and helping for living. Not least did the justification-theological criticism of the entwinement between clerical financial interests and liturgy pose a serious obstacle. The reticence toward the performative dimension of celebrating inherent in a predominantly verbal and doctrinal practice also proved unfavorable.

Thus, to this day, the restoration of this relationship remains eminently desirable. Ecumenical experience in the context of "healing rites"[65] is however drawing attention again to the sensually perceptible representation of the liberating character of the communication of the gospel.

Fundamental Questions

False or true worship—the Old Testament already poses this question. Finding answers to this question has been at the heart at every biblically oriented theory of communal celebration as a mode of communicating the gospel; it is the fundamental question of the meaningfulness or absurdity of liturgical action.

It is striking that the Bible does not terminologically distinguish between true and false worship. In the LXX as well as the New Testament *latreuein* and *latreia* (Gr.) can designate both false worship (e.g., Exod 20:5; Rom 1:25) and appropriate communication with God (e.g., Exod 3:12; Rom 12:1). Indeed, both forms use the same methods, such as sacrifice and prayer. The distinction is only contentual. By quoting Hosea 6:6, Jesus takes his definition directly from the prophets (Matt 9:13, 12:7). Ethical behavior in daily life becomes constitutive for the communal celebration. A pointedly worded statement of this tradition can be found in James 1:26-27.

The separation of everyday life and cult must be emphatically rejected. This is what the communication-theoretical reconstruction of Jesus' ministry clearly suggests. Communication of the gospel happens in three modes: if the connection between them is disrupted, the communion with Christ, as expressed in the early Christian, performative mode of the baptism and the Lord's Supper, is lost.

In this light, the historical development of liturgy should give theological cause for concern. As a consequence, cultural processes of differentiation need to be reexamined. There is quite obviously a tension between the basic

---

[65] See Grethlein, *Grundinformation Kasualien*, 358–89.

Christian impulse that involves the whole person and the role differentiations necessitated by modern life. In this situation, separating cult from daily life can be seen as a form of contextualization; it however eclipses the countercultural perspective of the communication of the gospel. Striving after the connection of the three modes of communicating the gospel taps into this impulse and urges a fundamental reform of worship and church.

3. The Gospel in the Mode of Helping for Living

Literature: Anika Albert, *Helfen als Gabe und Gegenseitigkeit: Perspektiven einer Theologie des Helfens im interdisziplinären Diskurs* (VDWI 42) (Heidelberg, 2010); Erich Beyreuther, *Geschichte der Diakonie und Inneren Mission in der Neuzeit* (Lehrbücher für die diakonische Arbeit 1) (Berlin, 1962); Christian Grethlein, "Benediktionen und Krankensalbung," in *Handbuch der Liturgik: Liturgiewissenschaft in Theologie und Praxis der Kirche*, ed. Hans-Christoph Schmidt-Lauber, Michael Meyer-Blanck, and Karl-Heinrich Bieritz (Göttingen, ³2003), 551–74, 565–74; Gottfried Hammann, *Die Geschichte der christlichen Diakonie: Praktizierte Nächstenliebe von der Antike bis zur Reformation* (Göttingen, 2003); Ulrich Luz, "Biblische Grundlagen der Diakonie," in *Diakonisches Kompendium*, ed. Günter Ruddat and Gerhard Schäfer (Göttingen, 2005), 17–35; Gerhard Schäfer and Volker Herrmann, "Geschichtliche Entwicklungen der Diakonie," in *Diakonisches Kompendium*, ed. Günter Ruddat and Gerhard Schäfer (Göttingen, 2005), 36–67; Peter Zimmerling, *Studienbuch Beichte* (Göttingen, 2009), 13–41

In communicating the gospel in the mode of helping for living, Jesus combined his social, or healing, activity with the promise of the forgiveness of sins. In the course of Christian history, these two things fell apart. This section will thus take a look at the developments connected with the concepts of the diaconate and diaconia on the one hand, and confession and penance (and later pastoral care) on the other. In this manner, the concept of helping for living, which integrates both these forms of care, draws attention to an open problem. Today the concept of help or helping, despite the high esteem in which clerical welfare work is held, carries ambivalent connotations. From a psychological perspective we receive warnings of a possible "psychological self-exploitation, which notoriously overcharges the help-er,"[66] from a sociological point of view, power relations must be taken into account.[67] Theologically, Gerhard Uhlhorn already listed the ways in which Christian charity may be compromised (summarized in Albert, *Helfen als Gabe und Gegenseitigkeit*, 51–53): some help to gain honor and reputation, to gain some advantage, to earn religious merit, or to distract themselves from their own problems.

As against these fallacies and misunderstandings, one should remember the theoretical framework in which the concept of "helping" is used in this context: as a mode of communicating the gospel to be found and substantiated in Jesus' ministry.

Again, in the first step, I will outline the anthropological backdrop against which this mode of communication deals with alterity.

Anthropological Background

Helping another person is a special form of dealing with alterity, insofar as every person is different.

Under the influence of Darwin's theory of biological evolution, in which the "war of nature" and the "struggle for life" designate the essential forces of natural selection,[68] social action appeared to hamper this selection process. More recent insights from the neurosciences however emphasize the funda-mental importance of social behavior for human evolution.[69] In view of the human dependence on community, it is hardly surprising that, in terms of evolutionary biology, a strong, and, as a rule, positive emotional bond ties the members of a family group or clan together. The character of this affiliation of shared identity can culturally differ, as is illustrated by the many different forms of kinship in human history.[70] A comparison with other large mam-

---

[66] See Gerd Theissen, "Die Bibel diakonisch lesen: Die Legitimationskrise des Helfens und der Barmherzige Samariter," in *Diakonie—biblische Grundlagen und Orientierungen: Ein Arbeitsbuch* (VDWI 2), ed. Gerhard Schäfer and Theodor Strohm (Heidelberg, ³1998), 376–401, 377.

[67] Theissen, "Die Bibel," 378.

[68] See also, for the following, Albert, *Helfen als Gabe und Gegenseitigkeit*, 189–91.

[69] Joachim Bauer, *Prinzip Menschlichkeit: Warum wir von Natur aus kooperieren* (Hamburg, ³2007), 37.

[70] See François Zonabend, "Über die Familie: Verwandtschaft und Familie aus anthro-pologischer Sicht," in *Geschichte der Familie*, vol. 1: *Altertum*, ed. André Burguière, Christiane

mals suggests that prehistoric human groups "comprised at most a few dozen individuals."[71] To the present day, there is strong empirical evidence for the particular importance of family ties.[72]

In comparison, the relationship with people outside one's own social group is marked by ambivalence. On the one hand, the universal occurrence of the incest prohibition makes it necessary to open the clan or family for members of other groups. It is "humanity's first step toward social organization."[73] And there is, on the other hand, the stranger anxiety phase in the human baby, which usually occurs in the sixth or seventh month, when the infant distinguishes between those it is familiar and feels safe with, and strangers it rejects as dangerous. A similar tendency to discriminate between one's own and the strange other as a form of definition can be observed when different families or tribes are living together. As groups started to settle down, this increasingly caused violent conflicts between families, tribes, and clans. The institution of the right to hospitality is an attempt to bridge the difference between one's own and the other. It is not possible to say exactly which behavior, in our dealing with strangers, is congenital and what is culturally transmitted. However, "sign stimuli like the submissive gesture or display behavior (hierarchy-regulating stimuli),"[74] which can be observed to this day, seem to be congenital. These stimuli-reaction patterns domesticate the potential for violence inherent in the confrontation of strangers.

It is this background that lends particular evolutionary biological and cultural anthropological plausibility to the invocation of family relationships when speaking of "the children of God" (e.g., John 1:12). The universal human experience of bonding in the family of origin, an essential source of primary religious experience, is, at the level of secondary religious experience, expanded by the Hellenistic notion of being conceived by God. As a consequence, helping for living extends beyond immediate kinship. This observation finds

---

Klapisch-Zuber, Martine Sengalen, and François Zonabend (Darmstadt, 1996 [Fr.: 1994]), 17–90, 25–37.

[71] Masset, "Die Vorgeschichte der Familie," 96.

[72] See Frank Schirrmacher, *Minimum: Vom Vergehen und Neuentstehen unserer Gemeinschaft* (Munich, ²2006), 43–44.

[73] Zonabend, "Über die Familie," 37.

[74] Karl Ernst Nipkow, *Bildung in einer pluralen Welt*, vol. 1: *Moralpädagogik im Pluralismus* (Gütersloh, 1998), 223.

further support in the, equally evolutionary biologically evidenced, human capacity for empathy.[75]

Biblical Foundations

Helping for living is a mode of communication which runs throughout the Bible like a golden thread. The central texts, such as the example of the Good Samaritan (Luke 10:30-35) or the description of the Last Judgment (Matt 25:31-46), are engraved deeply into our cultural memory. In some places in the Old Testament the family or tribal restrictions described above filter through. But with the kingship of David, the people of Israel become the all-determining factor. The transition is marked by the—historically inaccurate—acknowledgment by the tribes of Hebron before David: "'Indeed we are your bone and your flesh'" (2 Sam 5:1). The New Testament, prepared in pre- and post-exilic texts of the Hebrew Bible, extends this to potentially include all of humanity.

The Old Testament provides the fundamental notion for the understanding of the communication mode of helping for living in the commandment of love of neighbor (Lev 19:18). They are preceded by the protective provisions for the poor, for strangers and the handicapped (the deaf and the blind) (Lev. 19:9-10, 13:14), which are essential for the sanctification of daily life. Increasingly, this kind of ethical instruction was believed to correspond with God's actions (Luz, "Biblische Grundlagen der Diakonie," 20), a tradition reflected in Luke 6:36: "Therefore be merciful, just as your Father also is merciful." The priority of right ethical behavior over ritual acts finds its theological justification in the prophetic message: it is because God himself takes a stand for the poor and the disenfranchised that the faithful must follow him—mimetically—and must not plunge others into poverty or act unjustly. These insights led to the early Jewish "works of love," as inspired by passages such as Micah 6:8, a tradition that was immediately taken up by the first Christians (see Matt 25:31-46). Confession of sins and God's forgiveness are also reported in the Old Testament. Their festive expression is Yom Kippur, the great Day of Atonement (see Lev 16). Testimonies of confessions occur in narrative (see 2 Sam 12:13) or poetic (see Ps 32) form (see Zimmerling, *Studienbuch Beichte*, 17).

---

[75] Alfred Gierer, *Im Spiegel der Natur erkennen wir uns selbst: Wissenschaft und Menschenbild* (Reinbek, 1998), 199.

As for the Old Testament, there is the same methodological difficulty in the New Testament that different concepts describe what I, with regard to Jesus' ministry, refer to as "helping for living." In the New Testament, the beginning of God's reign and the concepts derived from the stem *diakon-* (Gr. "to serve") add new emphasis to this mode of communication. It is however worthwhile to begin with the act of "helping" (Gr. *boethein*) itself, to understand this mode of communicating the gospel better. In the Gospels, the term occurs in two miracle stories: in the healing of the (apparently) epileptic son in Mark 9:14-29, and the recovery of the sick daughter in Matthew 15:21-29. In both cases, the drama of the situation is thrown into relief: helping for living is not a simple sleight of hand, but an open-ended communication in which the communicating parties are caught up in a struggle with one another. In the course of the communication, Jesus readjusted his views, particularly noticeable in the healing of the sick daughter: he did not maintain the ethnic exclusion he first put forward—"I was not sent except to the lost sheep of the house of Israel" (Matt 15:24). The mother's pain changed his mind, and the daughter was healed.

The interesting thing about these stories is that they both describe emergencies in which the family cannot help any more. But it is the family's will to help which leads to the encounter with Jesus and the consequently the healing. The family members' faith, or the solicitation of faith, precedes Jesus' healing acts. Faith is also at the center of the healings in which Jesus "saves" (Gr. *sozein*; e.g., Matt 9:22).

The mode of helping for living appears in a new light in those texts in which "serving" (Gr. *diakonein*) is the principal aim of Jesus' ministry (e.g., Mark 10:45a, and 10:43-44, in which "servant" [*diakonos*] and "slave" [*doulos*] are paralleled; see Luz, "Biblische Grundlagen der Diakonie," 20). The principal goal of these actions is the mission, or transmission of what he has been charged with. This attitude is graphically illustrated in the account of the foot washing (John 13:4-5), even though here *diakonein* is not explicitly mentioned.

A similar criticism of generally accepted plausibility is contained in Jesus' story of the widow who contributes her mite to the temple treasury (Mark 12:41-43). In spite of her threefold marginalized position—as a woman, a widow, and a pauper—she nevertheless serves as a model. One of the practical results from this message is the community of goods which is reported in the Acts of the Apostles (Acts 2:42-47; 4:32-35). Dispelling the doubts of earlier research, Luz emphasizes the realism of this account (see Luz, "Biblische Grundlagen der Diakonie," 25–26). In these reports we find the financial side of helping as well as their intimate relationship with the shared meals. They moreover underline that being ready to help is a fundamental concern for all Christians (28).

Difficulties in organizing help however soon led to the institution of a separate function, that of the (male and female) deacon (parallel for both sexes, see 1 Tim 3:8-12; see also Luz, "Biblische Grundlagen der Diakonie," 32). Finally, Jesus' healing actions were continued in the first Christian communities (Mark 6:7-13). James 5:14-15 offers some insight into the early Christian practice of treating the sick (Grethlein, "Benediktionen und Krankensalbung," 566): attending to the physical needs—anointment as a potent ancient medical intervention—and spiritual attendance in the form of prayer and forgiveness of sins—are equal parts in caring for the afflicted. This rite combines all three modes of communicating the gospel: the helping integrating communal celebration as well as prayer as a form of Christian speech.

Historical Forms

Considering the broad base of biblical texts, it is not surprising that the mode of helping for living informs all of Christian history, albeit in varying forms. Early in that history, with the diaconate and the ritual of repentance two institutions would emerge that continued the basic notion of the communication of the gospel in a transformed manner. At the same time, the differentiation between—in today's terminology—diaconal and pastoral care threatened to compromise the unity of the communication of the gospel which was characteristic of Jesus' ministry. In his miracles, which comprised physical help as well as forgiveness of sins, the full compass of God's love became manifest.

Conceptually, this tension can already be observed if one looks at the origin of the two in this context most commonly used Protestant concepts, "diaconia" and "pastoral care" ("Seelsorge" [care of souls], the equivalent in German Protestant Theology today, is still closer to the Latin *cura animarum* [cure/care of soul]). The notion of "caring for souls" (Gr. *epimeleia tes psyches*) was introduced by Plato (*Apol.* 29e2) and in a Christian context first used by Basil of Caesarea in the fourth century.[76] This use could however not prevail against the pastoral (shepherding) analogy. It was only Martin Luther

---

[76] For the following, see Jürgen Ziemer, "Pastoral Care: I. The Term," *RPP* 9 (2011), 583.

who resolutely established *Seelsorge* in German theological usage,[77] while *dia-konia* (Ger. *Diakonie*) essentially hearkens back to Jesus own conception of his ministry.

Let us first take a look at the different stages of the diaconate. In the first Christian document outside the New Testament, probably written late first century CE, the diaconate appears in tandem with the episcopate (1 Clem 42:1-5). Before the establishment of the monarchal episcopate, both offices were held in high esteem. Similarly, Ignatius of Antioch mentions in his letters, written only little after Clemens,' bishops and presbyters as well as deacons (Ign. *Trall.* 2:1-3). On the one hand, the deacons' crucial role in providing for the material needs of the parishioners as laid down in Acts 6:1-3 is clearly underlined. Another important function was to collect the alms during the communal festivity on Sunday and to share out the leftovers of the meal to the needy. As the Jewish fellowship meal became separated from the Eucharist, the importance of this liturgical function dwindled. The connection between communal celebration and helping for living, which is so crucial to the communication of the gospel, became tenuous and was reduced to symbolic formulae. The Lord's Supper was transformed from a communal meal to a cultic act. The relationship between the communal feast and the daily life with its trials and tribulations was only maintained in dogmatic assertions.

Moreover, a distinct hierarchization of the offices can be observed, which was only to increase as time went on. In the course of this development, deacons were reduced to being mere clerical assistants to the bishop, losing their initial autonomy in the relatively short span of little more than fifty years (Hammann, *Die Geschichte der christlichen Diakonie*, 44). While the subsumption of the diaconate into the ministerial hierarchy led by bishop and presbyter (priest) admittedly consolidated its authority, the deacon's actions now subject to the bishop's directives. Gottfried Hammann critically concludes that "the sacred tended to replace the social, the cult tended to replace charitable activity" (66). This development reached its high-water mark with the Roman Pontifical in the ninth and tenth centuries whose certificate of ordination placed deacons under three obligations: "1. liturgical altar service, 2. perform baptism, 3. preach sermon" (109). Practical helping for living was only implied in the consequences from the sermon.

---

[77] See Gerhard Ebeling, "Luthers Gebrauch der Wortfamilie 'Seelsorge,'" *LJ* 61 (1994), 7–44.

After the diaconate, let us now turn to the function of repentance. From the beginning, the fundamental event in Christian existence was the baptism. It was the door to a new life in Christ and was therefore connected to the forgiveness of sins which the baptizand had committed in his non-Christian life. This soon begged the question of how to deal with transgressions perpetrated after baptism. This concerned primarily the renunciation of false teachings (Ign. Smyrn. 5:3), the forgiveness of sexual transgressions (Eus. *Hist. eccl.* IV 23:6), and the readmission of those who had become apostates under persecution (Eus. *Hist. eccl.* V 1:45-46).[78]

Individual groups like the Montanists and the Novatians claimed the strict prohibition of a second repentance (Heb 6:4-6) and justified this by elitist notions of purity. Their view did however not prevail since it opposed the Jesuanic approach according to which forgiveness of sins like healing is a help for living.

The Christian church however allowed a second repentance (*Herm.Vis.* II, 2:1-8). The procedure included public confession, penance, and the subsequent readmission into the Christian community. But even this procedure could not be kept up in the face of growing parishes and due to the fact that being Christian increasingly became the norm. The pragmatic compromise resulting from this was that the second repentance was deferred to the end of life: "Repentance increasingly becomes a preparation for dying and a therapeutic during illness."[79] In this process, penance became privatized and was in the long run transformed into private confession. The result was a new form of communication, increasingly ritualized and regimented by canon law: (auricular) confession.

This development was encouraged by the Scotch-Irish Church that had never known public, once-only repentance (see Zimmerling, *Studienbuch Beichte*, 21–23). The monastic Irish Church granted repentance as often as a Christian had sinned. Penance was to be done according to tariffs (*libri poenitentiales*) that assigned precise acts of contrition to each transgression. This form of individual confession, which now left the monastery and was soon to be adopted by the Frankish bishops, can be thought of as the beginning of Christian pastoral care (*Seelsorge*). The confessor truly became a spiritual

[78] Martin Ohst, "Repentenance: IV. Christianity 2. Church History," *RPP* 11 (2012), 113–19, 114.

[79] Hermann Lins, "Buße und Beichte," in Schmidt-Lauber, Meyer-Blanck, and Bieritz, *Handbuch der Liturgik*, 319–34, 322.

director (*Seelsorger*), however without being interested in the individual person, but only in the enforcement of universal norms.[80]

Overall, a transformation took place which stayed abreast of the contextualization of Christianity and its new implicitness. Jesus' call to repentance, originally meant to encourage his followers to change their lives, his helping for living, in which attending to physical needs and forgiveness of sins were integrated, became the church's instrument for moral education. As a matter of consequence, from the ninth century onward, the duty of confession was linked to specific seasons and acquired a life-structuring regularity.

The next important shift took place in the context of monastic charity work. After the collapse of the (Western) Roman Empire and in the course of the Christianization of the Germanic tribes, the church faced a structural problem with regard to their helping for living. Hitherto, the church had been an urban phenomenon, now it had to face the challenges of rural structures. This called for reorganization.

In the first instance, this caused a void, which the bishops were unable to fill. As a legal requirement, the tithe was introduced, which the bishop was to split up into four parts, "one part each for himself, for the clergy, for the upkeep of the churches, and for the poor" (Hammann, *Die Geschichte der christlichen Diakonie*, 105). The actual allocation, however, depended very much on the individual bishop. The dispute over whether this levy was due to the church or the state authorities lasted for centuries (105). In this situation, a different institution provided Christian charity with a fresh impetus: the monastery.

The Benedictine order had already explicitly enshrined helping action in their powerful monastic rule (see 107), recognizably referring to Matt 25:31-46: the monks understood their commitment to helping the needy as following Christ's example. Both physical care and spiritual accompaniment were to be provided for those admitted to the monastery. On admission of a patient to the monastic hospital, confession was taken, as a form of medical history, so to speak.

The monastic reform which started from Cluny at the beginning of the tenth century continued this impetus. A new form of community emerged, striving after the communication of the gospel in the mode of helping for living, with regard to both physical afflictions and the relationship to God. Charity, which had originally been the deacon's charge, had now become

---

[80] See Rössler, *Grundriß der Praktischen Theologie*, 157.

incorporated into monastic life. The Benedictine *ora et labora* found an ideal sphere of activity in helping for living, as contemplation and action here interlock (see 125). This impetus was furthermore taken up outside the monastery by brotherhoods and female communities; hospitals arose in many places to care for the poor, the elderly, and the sick. In all of these nonclerical or church-independent initiatives we find a strong connection between a collective lifestyle and helping for living.

Further impetus came from the Reformation. The diaconal commitment of the Reformers can be understood only against the background of the following developments, issues, and insights.

First of all, on the basis of Germanic notions of rulership as well as Christian principles, Charlemagne (742–814) had already prioritized caring for the poor (Beyreuther, *Geschichte der Diakonie*, 20). There was, therefore, a principal awareness of the government's duty to help, without, however, it being consistently put into practice.

Second, settlement patterns were changing and urbanization had significantly increased since the fourteenth century. In the cities, magistrates were in charge of the care for the poor. They drew on the diaconal infrastructures created by the brotherhoods and béguinages mentioned above. Pious citizens established further charities for poor relief.

Third, the cities grappled with the "uncontrolled growth of mendicancy" (Hammann, *Die Geschichte der christlichen Diakonie*, 158). In the course of the return to the poverty of Jesus (Poverty Movement), the thirteenth century saw a rise of mendicant orders (first the Dominican and Franciscan orders, then the Carmelites and the Augustinian Eremites), whose members made a living by doing simple chores, accepting donations, and begging. Since economic fluctuations caused by the spread of the money economy deprived many people of their livelihoods, "real" beggars began to join their ranks, thus posing formidable challenges to the magistrates. This problem was "solved" by strictly concentrating on the resident beggars, and systematically keeping out the external poor by brute force.

Fourth, the justification theologians' rejection of righteousness through works guided the way in which Reformers thought about helping action: the focus was not on the alms givers and their good works anymore, but on the neighbor in need (see Schäfer and Herrmann, "Geschichtliche Entwicklungen der Diakonie," 47). For Martin Luther, clearly right preaching and the understanding of the gospel were at the center of his reform efforts. Furthermore, there was education, and of course the Christian commandment of charity.

With regard to the latter, Luther, like the magistrates, however observed many forms of malpractice by idleness and insisted on the value of labor as a cure (WA 6,450–51). Helping thus provides an important impetus for future living, particularly since Luther believed that a profession was a calling from God (see Hammann, *Die Geschichte der christlichen Diakonie*, 201). In both educational matters as well as his demands on helping action he appealed to state authority and thus played a decisive role in the establishment of systematic urban poor relief. Due to the desolate situation of the church, Luther conscripted the councilmen as Christians (see Hammann, *Die Geschichte der christlichen Diakonie*, 204) and thus, in spite of the strict separation of the two spheres, effectively treated church and state as one body when it came to caring for the needy. This approach was put into practice even more radically, namely without any reservations whatsoever, by Huldrych Zwingli in Zurich (see 221).

With regard to the communication of the gospel, two problems present themselves at this point: One, since Luther's interventions, a strong connection between church and state institutions in the mode of helping for living has firmly established itself in Germany. As institutions are subject to administrative logic, the gospel's inclusive dimension of helping for living, which includes our relationship with God, has lost most of its impact. And two, the Reformers' theological criticism of righteousness through works is fundamental. Historically (not systematically!) this has put the mode of helping for living on the backburner, as documented for instance in the *Confessio Augustana* (art. 7). This is evidently a problem, since it reduces the communication of the gospel by one constituent dimension.

Another form of care, helping by educating, came into being in the wake of the Thirty Years' War, which had destroyed the hitherto existing structures of poor relief. A fresh impetus with regard to both contents and organization came from the German Pietist movement. In his influential *Pia desideria* (1675), Philipp Jakob Spener (1635–1705) had already drawn attention to the hardships of the poor. The practical suggestions of his theology formed the basis for diaconal action. His point of reference was the Jerusalemite community of goods (Acts 6) and the Old Testament obligation of the tithe.[81] He castigated the social hardships as "a dark stain upon our Christianity."[82]

---

[81] Philipp Spener, *Pia Desideria (1675): Deutsch-lateinische Studienausgabe*, ed. Beate Köster (Gießen, 2005), 60.

[82] Spener, *Pia Desideria*, 62.

One in particular who took up Spener's challenge was his friend August Hermann Francke (1663–1727). Supported by the Prussian king, Francke built the Glauchaschen Anstalten (later: Franckesche Stiftungen [Francke Foundations]) on the outskirts of the eastern German town of Halle. From the very outset, this institution emphasized a strong connection of Christian impetus, care for the poor, and a strong educational as well as economic orientation. Francke and his collaborators succeeded in building up a unique, diaconally oriented school city. One of the main purposes of this project was to relieve the distress of deprived children by integrating them into a Christian community. In this endeavor, charity and enterprise—the foundations ran their own pharmacy with sales and distribution and a printing shop and publishing house—went hand in hand. Diaconal action was integrated into the institution's educational community. Educators were also *Seelsorger*. Francke's particular commitment to the education of girls, outstanding for the time, should not go unmentioned.

Another feature that was remarkable by the standards of the time was the strong ecumenical rationale of his work. As early as 1695 he established first connections with Russia; relationships with North America and South Africa resulted from his connections with Holland and England, and further connections with East India through his Scandinavian relationships; in the East, his contacts reached as far as Constantinople (see Beyreuther, *Geschichte der Diakonie*, 38).

Francke's educational methods were already put under critical scrutiny by some of his contemporaries.[83] The constant observation the children were under served the purpose—in the context of a theology of original sin and conversion—of breaking the children's will. This notwithstanding, Francke's combination of poor relief and education introduced an important form of helping for living which was to provide an attractive peg for the contextualization of the communication of the gospel in the "Century of Education" (Ger. *das pädagogische Jahrhundert*), the period of the European Enlightenment.

The history of female deacons and their role in diaconal activity also constitutes an important development. The New Testament tells us that women played an essential part in the communication of the gospel at the time. The first witnesses to Jesus' resurrection were women (Mark 16:1-8). According

---

[83] See Peter Menck, *Die Erziehung der Jugend zur Ehre Gottes und zum Nutzen des Nächsten: Die Pädagogik August Hermanns Franckes* (Hallesche Forschungen 75) (Tübingen, 2001).

to current text-critical conclusions, Paul knew a female apostle, Junia (Rom 16:7), and a deaconess, Phoebe (Rom 16:1).[84] However, even in the New Testament we encounter voices wishing to exclude women (1 Cor 14:34-35; 1 Tim 2:11-12). The only undisputed domain for women in early Christianity was that of practical help, as evidenced by the offices of widows (viduage) and deaconesses[85] and their liturgical duties primarily during the christening of women (who had to be naked). In the context of Old Testament and ancient—but emphatically not Jesuanic—ideas of purity,[86] the female ideal was modeled on (Mary's) virginity because it was thus that Eve's original sin could be prevented (e.g., Tertullian, *De cultu feminarum* I,1). Clearly, there were always women who became prominent, like Hildegard of Bingen or Catherine of Siena, but all in all, women were excluded from church offices outside the convent.

Neither did the Reformers see a necessity to take remedial action. Luther saw no formal objections to female ministers, but the pushback of traditional hierarchy prohibited the implementation of a new order.[87] Invoking the charity work of widows in the New Testament, Calvin even went so far as to demand the establishment of a female diaconate, but he failed to gain the acceptance of the Council of Geneva (see Hammann, *Die Geschichte der christlichen Diakonie*, 276–77, 289).

The first substantial advance in this direction was only made during the diaconal awakening at the beginning of the nineteenth century. As a young minister, Theodor Fliedner (1800–1864) attempted to improve the funds of his impoverished parish in Kaiserswerth (a small town close to Düsseldorf in

---

[84] See Anni Hentschel, *Diakonia im Neuen Testament: Studien zur Semantik unter besonderer Berücksichtigung der Rolle von Frauen* (WUNT II 226) (Tübingen, 2007), 181, 184.

[85] We first encounter the female form *diakonissa* in the texts of the Nicean Council (see Anni Hentschel, "Frauendienst—Frauenamt: Zur Frage nach einem Diakonissenamt im Neuen Testament," in *Dienerinnen des Herrn: Beiträge zur weiblichen Diakonie im 19. und 20. Jahrhundert* [Historisch-theologische Genderforschung 5], ed. Jochen-Christoph Kaiser and Rajah Scheepers [Leipzig, 2010], 38–56, 41).

[86] See Franz Kohlschein, "Die Vorstellung von der kultischen Unreinheit der Frau: Das weiterwirkende Motiv für eine zwiespältige Situation?," in *Liturgie und Frauenfrage: Ein Beitrag zur Frauenforschung aus liturgiewissenschaftlicher Sicht* (PiLi 7), ed. Teresa Berger and Albert Gerhards (St. Ottilien, 1990), 269–88.

[87] See Karl-Heinrich Bieritz, "Die weyber nach den mennern: Der reformatorische Gottesdienst und die Rolle der Frau," in Berger and Gerhards, *Liturgie und Frauenfrage*, 229–52.

western Germany) by traveling to collect money. On his travels, he became acquainted with Elisabeth Fry's work with female prisoners in England, and the deaconess office of Dutch Mennonites.[88] Back in Germany, he began—with instrumental support by his wife Frederike, and when she died in 1842, his second wife Karoline—to establish various diaconal activities: care for women and girls released from prison, foundation of a knitting and elementary school, foundation of a seminary for female educators and, later, female elementary school teachers, foundation of a hospital, and so on (see Beyreuther, *Geschichte der Diakonie*, 62–71). In all these diaconal activities, women were deployed. The *Bildungsanstalt für evangelische Pflegerinnen* (Seminary for Protestant Nurses), founded in 1836, became particularly important: Fliedner referred to the graduates as "deaconesses" and managed to secure their special social status (see 66).

The backdrop to this was provided by the process of industrialization, which, while not having gathered as much momentum in Germany as in England, nevertheless brought with it incisive social changes, particularly for women. In these circumstances, Fliedner on the one hand managed to professionalize nursing care in the deaconesses' mother house, and on the other hand he provided unmarried women the opportunity of professional employment and integration into a Protestant community (see Schäfer and Herrmann, "Geschichtliche Entwicklungen der Diakonie," 57–58). As in the case of Francke, Fliedner's project spread across national borders. Educational and diaconal activities went hand in hand. The result was a large institution, branching out in many directions.

The final form considered to be historically instrumental is that of the Inner Mission movement. During the first half of the nineteenth century and under the influence of the Pietist and Revivalist movements, further initiatives were formed which combined the diaconal with the educational-missionary impetus. These efforts were conceptually and organizationally consolidated by Johann Hinrich Wichern (1808–1881).[89]

Wichern gained his first hands-on experience of the deep distress of many children and families as a senior teacher of the Altona Sunday school, whose function included home visits. From these experiences issued his desire

[88] For the following, also see Jutta Schmidt, *Beruf: Schwester: Mutterhausdiakonie im 19. Jahrhundert* (Geschichte und Geschlechter 24) (Frankfurt, 1998), 84–216.

[89] See Traugott Jähnichen, "Johann Hinrich Wichern: Eine Erinnerung anlässlich seines 200. Geburtstages," *ThLZ* 133 (2008), 355–70.

to establish a rescue home, which he was able to put into effect in 1833, when he founded the Rauhe Haus in Hamburg. In his practice, Pietist devoutness and recent pedagogical insights like those of Johann Heinrich Pestalozzi went hand in hand. Every child admitted to the Rauhe Haus was welcomed by Wichern with the words: "My child, I know everything, but you are forgiven" (quoted in Beyreuther, *Geschichte der Diakonie*, 93). Another thing that was important for Wichern, was the child's freedom. In 1839, a *Bruderhaus* (fraternity home) was added, in which the educators of the rapidly expanding children's charity, later referred to as "deacons," were trained. Wichern sent them out to be town missionaries, carers, hostel and hospice wardens, thus making sure his ideas were disseminated. Wichern's concept of the Inner Mission aimed at the "organizing of all manifestations of life—of the people, the state, the family, the society, of science and art, and also of the social and economic life toward the Kingdom of God."[90] And indeed, the Inner Mission became a major organization in its own right.

In summary, the following important relationships and problems outlined in the models above, should be kept in mind.

First of all, there is an unmissable tendency in the history of the Christian church to prioritize the two other modes of the communication of the gospel over the mode of helping for living. This is clearly indicated by the development of the diaconate into a subordinate office in the early church as well as the emphasis on preaching and the Reformers' criticism of works righteousness.

In contrast, helping for living always organized itself outside the church hierarchy. Monasteries, pious brotherhoods, female communities, and finally independent associations assumed the responsibility disdained by the church. All of these organizations reacted in very specific terms to the states of emergency and social injustices of their times.

In this context, the strong connection between Christian community and helping for living should be noted. This comes as no surprise when one considers the basic challenge of any helping action: to deal with alterity. It is being firmly anchored in a community and its shared lifestyle which enables involvement with the other. Lifestyle and religious style characterize the forms of

---

[90] Kurt Nowak, *Geschichte des Christentums in Deutschland: Religion, Politik und Gesellschaft vom Ende der Aufklärung bis zur Mitte des 20. Jahrhunderts* (Munich, 1995), 127–28.

social interventions and charity work accordingly. This means that in each case, the integration of physical care and spiritual accompaniment, which is constitutive for this fundamental form of Christian communication, finds itself reshaped.

Finally, the relationship between diaconal activity and the state has remained an issue ever since the Christian church(es) had been accepted and privileged by the state. Charlemagne had already claimed poor relief to be an imperial charge, and Luther and most of all Zwingli appealed to state authority to meet its social responsibilities. Last, the diaconal movements of the eighteenth and nineteenth centuries would have never achieved such a wide impact without state support.

Relationships with Other Modes of the Communication of the Gospel

The impetus of Jesus' healings for the communication of the gospel has undergone various significant transformations. The different needs of different times required different forms of helping for living. Reconstructing these forms, one generally encounters connections with the other two modes of the communication of the gospel, as for instance the mode of communal celebration in the Lord's Supper, or the involvement of teaching and learning processes in early Christian rites of baptism, processes that today are didacticized under the heading of "diaconal education." In the following, I will enlarge upon these insights with the help of two examples that illustrate the potential of the communication of the gospel in the mode of helping for living beyond concrete help.

The first of these is the tendency for professionalization. The early emergence of the diaconate as a distinct function of Christian community already points to the implicit tendency of the helping mode to form professions. It is true that a similar tendency can also be observed in the two other communication modes with regard to the teachers and the directors of festivities, the officiants. But at least since the diaconal awakening in the mid-1800s the mode of helping witnessed a much stronger and more differentiated professionalization. It is striking how the many initiatives which created rescue homes, elementary and industrial schools, hospitals, and care homes frequently led to the foundation of seminaries, schools, and so on, in which the necessary staff was trained. The diaconal initiatives thus moved significantly beyond their initial aims. New professions were created, such as nurses, educators, geriatric nurses, and social pedagogues. Today's diaconal training facilities are reminders of these origins. Appropriate help for living requires specialized knowledge in modern society, eclipsing to a large extent the original revivalist impetus. However, diaconal or other church institutions seek to complement all functional training with religious education.

The second important connection is that with the mode of communal celebration: for people in precarious circumstances, festivities and celebrations constitute an important recess from their everyday activities, and often offer an opportunity for integration that in daily life is difficult to attain. In any case, communal celebrations facilitate interesting exchange processes, in which asymmetrical communication can be overcome and mutually enriching experiences can be made. In view of these observations, it seems hardly surprising that the diaconal history of the nineteenth century is in many ways closely connected with the emergence of the Sunday school and, later, the German *Kindergottesdienst* (children's service). Wichern was not the only one to gather formative experience for his later diaconal work in the context of the Sunday school. Sunday school developed into a liturgical celebration, while never giving up important pedagogical methods like group work. The transfer of the experiences made here to other forms of liturgy (for adults) however failed.

Today, one of the most useful concepts to inspire the practice of communal celebration is the concept of inclusion stemming from the fields of therapeutic or inclusive pedagogy. A good example for this can be found among the responses to a call for written submissions issued by Katharina Stork-Denker in the context of liturgy-theoretical research into the concept of participation. An approximately fifty-year-old woman writes of her experience as a sporadic participant in worship:

> One service that has recently impressed me profoundly was a Pentecostal service, which was organized in the context of a meeting lasting several days of disabled and non-disabled people. . . .
>
> In the preliminary meetings, in which both disabled and non-disabled persons participated, we first tried to come to grips with the text, the Pentecostal story, and then went on to think about how we could interpret the story in a manner so that it would be accessible to all, regardless of their intellectual capacity. This meant appealing to as many senses as possible and activating the community with movements. For instance, we introduced the "sound from heaven as of a rushing mighty wind, which swept

through the whole house" with breathing exercises. Or everybody was given a toy pin wheel at the end of the service, to illustrate the power of the wind and the Holy Ghost. . . .

What impressed me most in this service was the cheerfulness and the directness, but at the same time the seriousness, with which everybody took part.

Everybody was included through music, movement, conversations, everyone according to their abilities. I was also impressed by the unorthodox way in which ecumene was practiced.[91]

This Pentecostal service draws attention to the potential that helping for living holds in store for communal celebration. It is of course no accident that the service took place outside the customary Sunday morning procedures, since the limited scope for communication in the traditional service excludes certain groups of people from the outset. In the service from the report, however, the celebration as a collective activity was not simply a dogmatic postulate, but actually put into practice. A form of communication that involves all the senses is essential for the mentally handicapped, but it is equally beneficial for the cognitively more gifted. Such an inclusive form of liturgical celebration is naturally ecumenically oriented, since all—purportedly—schismatic distinctions are of an exclusively cognitive nature.

Fundamental Questions

Helping for living constitutes undoubtedly an integral part of the communication of the gospel since Jesus' ministry and is therefore an integral part of Christian life. In spite of this, it never managed to become a permanent fixture in the organized church. The question therefore is: how is helping organized? In a second step, one needs to look at the relationship between professional forms of help and those of daily life.

Let us first take a look at forms of organization. In the first instance, the commandment of charity means each and every Christian. The emergence of certain problems during the Christian community's first century however led to establishing of a separate diaconal function. Ever since, Christian history has been marked by the coexistence of individual and organized help.

---

[91] Quoted in Katharina Stork-Denker, *Beteiligung der Gemeinde am Gottesdienst* (APrTh 35) (Leipzig, 2008), 225–26.

Organized help became particularly important in cases where individual help did not suffice any more, as in cases of immiserization as a result of wars or drastic economic change.

Taking a survey of the reactions to such challenges, it becomes apparent that the typical form of organization, which had since Charlemagne been primarily parochial, proved too inflexible. On the other side, social forms which were on the fringes of or partly even outside the ecclesial hierarchy proved more successful, like monasteries, brotherhoods, female communities, orders of deacons or deaconesses. Extending their reach beyond the confined spaces of the territorial church or the diocese, they were able to provide help in the face of wholesale disasters.

Conversely, a diaconal weakness surfaced in the communication of the gospel when such alternative structures did not develop. The Reformation is a striking example of this: only the Pietist reform managed to initiate a fresh departure, which was eyed suspiciously and in part hampered by the church hierarchy. From a point of view which includes helping for living in the communication of the gospel, the local forms of church organization are thus in dire need of complementation. Granting this, another area reveals itself, in which diaconal activity of (individuals and) organizations is in better accord with the fundamental Christian impetus than the institutional churches. Even in the early church, helping reached beyond the members of the Christian community. In the final analysis, helping for living is possible only in a literally ecumenical sense, that is, within a scope that encompasses the whole world and everyone living in it. The diaconal awakenings since the eighteenth century, for instance, very quickly crossed denominational borders to encounter people with different life and value orientations. The perceived superiority of the Christian culture however precluded the possibility for dialog and gave the idea of mission an imperial slant.

The second important question is that of the forms in which helping has professionalized itself and in which it appears in daily life. The double structure just outlined—as individual practice or in organizations—poses a particular challenge for individual helpers, since professional help not only requires expertise but also is subject to certain economic and technical conditions. This poses an obstacle to the spontaneous help that is part of being Christian.[92]

---

[92] See Corinna Dahlgrün, *Christliche Spiritualität: Formen und Traditionen der Suche nach Gott* (Berlin, 2009), 310–26.

The founding fathers (and mothers) of the German diakonia in the nineteenth century tried to solve this problem by referring back to the diakonia of early Christianity, while, historically speaking, effecting wide-ranging transformations. This attempt however enjoyed merely a limited success. Today, only a small number of nurses, educators, and social workers are members of diaconal (or other) orders.

At the same time, my problem-historical survey has revealed that there is a significant relationship between membership in a Christian-oriented community and successful helping for living. It is thus in this field of tension that one has to reflect upon the organized forms of diakonia. The historical knowledge of the various forms in which these communities organized themselves frees up copious space for creative solutions. They range from the final vows of the monastery through the more open sociality of the Beguines to smaller communities simply united by a concrete diaconal project.

Summary of Part II

Against the backdrop of the problem-historical reconstruction of Practical Theology I define as its object the communication of the gospel in the present. From its beginnings, Practical Theology has insisted on its orientation toward contemporary life. The following concepts are in need of clarification.

First, the concept of communication allows for a connection with nontheological disciplines. The multiperspectival approach to the phenomenon provides wide and flexible access to the lifeworld. The fundamental openendedness of communicative processes with regard to life and value orientations is doubly determined by redundancy and selection. Open-endedness therefore does not mean arbitrariness, but affords the prerequisite for innovation.

Second, the concept of "the gospel" connects practical-theological study with theological theorizing in its various disciplines. The communication-theoretical reconstruction of Jesus' ministry and destiny yields three basal modes of action in which the gospel is communicated: teaching and learning, celebrating together, and helping for living. These modes take up universally human forms of communication and place them within the horizon of God's all-embracing love. The communication of the gospel thus needs to be investigated from the angles of both the empirical sciences and theology.

Third, the concept of "religion" owes its emergence to the separation of church doctrine and Christian practice; as a Protestant concept of distinction it is however informed by their connection. The presently common widening of the concept to include decidedly non-Christian forms of life and value orientation runs the risk of implicitly imprinting its Christian nexus onto them.

Fourth, in the sociology of religion and in Practical Theology, the concept of "spirituality" has of late been placed alongside of "religion" or has replaced it altogether. This is due to the realization that institutions and organizations today play a lesser part in the individual quest for life and value orientations. Both concepts mark important lifeworld changes and allow relevant distinctions.

After the clarification of concepts, the theory of communication of the gospel in the present requires potent hermeneutical criteria for its analyses. Two hermeneutical models offer themselves to capture the pluriformity that has marked the communication of the gospel since the beginnings of Christianity.

The first one, the media-theoretical transformation of the distinction between primary and secondary religious experience, while at the same time preserving their connection, prevents academic contrapositioning. This distinction heightens the awareness for tensions in the communication of the gospel and for the challenge of dealing with them in a constructive manner. In communication-theoretical terms, the redundancy afforded by primary religious experience is the indispensable basis and springboard for secondary religious processes of selection. These, in turn, necessarily remediate the primary experience's attachment to creatureliness.

Second, the liturgy hermeneutical distinction between transcultural, contextual, countercultural, and cross-cultural dimensions of the communication of the gospel allows for a differentiated look at its transformation and can be transferred to other forms of the communication of the gospel. It is grounded in the fundamental Christian impetus.

The empirical framework within which the gospel is presently communicated can be determined in three steps:

First, Taylor's concept of secularity and Knoblauch's conception of popular religion in a complementary manner trace out the fundamental culture-historical and knowledge-sociological conditions of present-day communication (of the gospel). Protracted processes of reform in Western Christendom, growing scientific knowledge and resulting technological achievements have made the belief in God optional. This optionality is accompanied by a longing for meaning and wholeness, which adopts transformed versions of earlier forms of magical approaches to the world. Two fundamental factors of communication in the domain of life and value orientations are striving for security and biographical relevance.

Furthermore, a profound change in living conditions can also be observed in every other domain. Particularly significant for the communication of the gospel are increasing life expectancy, transformations in the social forms of the family and work, as well as worldwide migration. All these affect the organization of everyday life that up to the middle of the nineteenth century had been taken for granted and appeared to be cast in iron.

Finally, new social forms are clearly in the making owing to the adoption of media-technological innovations. Their effects on communication are already clearly visible in the younger generations and are likely to take on greater significance in the long term. This concerns the problematic tendency for "excarnation" (Taylor) as much as great opportunities for symmetrical communication.

It is in the context of these processes that the communication of the gospel takes place. It is therefore necessary to distinguish carefully between the opportunities for new approaches and the developments that disagree with the fundamental Christian impetus.

Last, and from a theological perspective, the—exemplary—historical reconstruction of the three modes of communicating the gospel yields forms of contextualization—but also lapses in the countercultural dimension of the communication of the gospel.

In the various models of teaching and learning we encounter a great variety of places for learning and didactical approaches. The current German focus on schooling is an exception in Christian history, creating serious communication-theoretical problems.

The striking feature of the mode of celebrating together is the fairly common coexistence of official ecclesial forms of celebration and the private practice of most people. The tension between primary and secondary religious experience is here particularly palpable, and is for example expressed in the pluriformity of liturgical practices.

In the course of church history the mode of helping for living, in spite of being so fundamental to everyday life, has been overshadowed by the other two modes of communicating the gospel. This mode is marked by a particularly close relationship between action and community. In concrete practice, communities often contextualize this dimension of the communication of the gospel in opposition to the organized churches. In the contemporary context, therapeutic or inclusive pedagogical approaches merit specific attention.

PART 3

Methods for Communication of the Gospel

The history of the discipline (see part 1) has shown that for German Practical Theology contemporary relevance is key. It evolved as a theological discipline to confront the growing chasm between church doctrine and the reality of life and value orientations of ordinary people, as well as the awareness thereof.[1] The tension resulting from this difference posed new challenges to pastoral practice. By now, this problem has caught up with theology as a whole, if it accepts the Reformers' insight that communication is constitutive of theology.[2]

Since the transition from the nineteenth century to the twentieth, German practical theologians have turned to empirical research in order to gain insights into the cultural and social contexts of theology and church. In the course of this process, changes with regard to the purpose of Practical Theology have therefore imposed themselves. The first practical theologists like Carl Immanuel Nitzsch opened up the pastoral-theological orientation by resolutely turning toward the church. At least since the 1960s, even this

---

[1] The open communication of this difference is supposedly the really new thing in cultural and Christian history. Church doctrine and popular piety probably always varied significantly.

[2] Grethlein, "Theologie und Didaktik."

seemed to be too "parochial": the marginalization of the church and the generalized pluralization called for a further reaching out. Fashionably focusing on
"religion" however only partly solved the problem: based in Christian theory,
(Protestant) Christianity was still taken to be the standard form of "religion."
Criticism from scholars of religion has drawn attention to the problematic
nature of this concept.

It is because of these circumstances that "the communication of the gospel" suggests itself as the definition of the subject matter of theology (see
part 2). In relation to the present, this term both opens up and specifies the
field of study of Practical Theology. Moreover, profiling the "communication
of the gospel" by referring to the biblical accounts of Jesus' ministry and destiny shows that the gospel as the message of the beginning of God's reign,
that is, God's effective love, is fulfilled in communicative processes, in concrete
terms: in the modes of teaching and learning, celebrating together, and helping for living. These modes need to be organized in their particular contexts
in such a manner that everybody can participate in them.

In this respect, a great variety of social forms and activities have evolved
across the globe, differing according to political conditions, and social and cultural contexts. A detailed presentation of these forms at this point is however
beyond the scope of this book.[3]

The case is different for the forms of communication in which people try
to reach mutual understanding. It is of course in principle true that the gospel
can be fulfilled in any form of communication, as long as it aims at understanding and is not deformed by agendas of oppression or exploitation. Nevertheless, in the course of Christian history some forms of communication have
crystallized that seem to be particularly suited to discovering and ascertaining
God's unconditional love.

Reviewing Christian history in this perspective, one cannot fail to notice
that the treatment of time and space is hugely important in opening up the
space necessary for these forms of communication. The liturgical year and
church buildings are impressive evidence of this fact. Since they form a fundamental framework for the communication of the gospel today, we will take a
look at them first, before addressing the practical methods of communication.

When one tries to establish concrete methods of communication against
this background within the framework of the three modes of communicating

---

[3] The original German version provides such a detailed presentation for Germany.

the gospel as developed in part 2, three modes of contact with God suggest themselves: the mode of teaching and learning communicates about God, celebrating together communicates with God, and helping for living taps into God's strength. God here is neither "concept" nor "experience," but concretely subject, goal, and origin of communication.

6

UNDERSTANDING TIME
AND PLACE

Communication always takes place in a specific context, which can be ana-lyzed in terms of perspective. Generally, space and time, gender, age, and social background or lifestyle of the communication partners play significant roles in communication processes. In addition, there is the specific situation, which may for instance be marked by sickness or health, climate, and other concomitant circumstances.

In the following, I will concentrate on time and space, or, more specifi-cally, times and places of the communication of the gospel. Here is why. First of all, epistemologically they are, as Kant has shown,[1] fundamental. Second, throughout Christian history these connected forms of intuition have received continuous and assiduous attention. In accordance with the contextuality of communication, their organization has yielded great pluriformity. At the same time, the concept of space and time was also changed by the Christian impetus. Moreover, knowledge-sociological analysis of contemporary society has established that security is a basic need for many people. Reliable times and places are important preconditions for certainty.

---

[1] Immanuel Kant, *Kritik der reinen Vernunft*, ed. Ingeborg Heidemann (Stuttgart, 1973 [²1787]), 80–118 (Die Transzendentale Ästhetik).

The ecclesiastical year and church buildings have developed in processes lasting centuries, involving cultural adaptations and dissociations. Both dominated Western culture for a very long time, but for some time now they have been in competition with different rhythms of time and different places. In view of these developments, a new balance between cultural context and the fundamental Christian impetus needs to be found. In doing so, however, one needs to be aware of the fact that Western culture is impregnated with Christianity and that our Christianity has been shaped by non-Christian culture, so that mere juxtapositions are too simplistic.

1. Times

Literature: Kristian Fechtner, *Im Rhythmus des Kirchenjahres: Vom Sinn der Feste und Zeiten* (Gütersloh, 2007); Christian Grethlein, "Potenziale liturgischer Zeiten heute," in *Normalfall Sonntagsgottesdienst? Gottesdienst und Sonntagskultur im Umbruch* (PTHe 87), ed. Kristian Fechtner and Lutz Friedrichs (Stuttgart, 2008), 180–89; Hansjörg Auf der Maur, *Feiern im Rhythmus der Zeit I. Herrenfeste in Woche und Jahr* (GDK 5) (Regensburg, 1983); Ursula Roth, Heinz-Günther Schöttler, and Gerhard Ulrich, eds., *Sonntäglich: Zugänge zum Verständnis von Sonntag, Sonntagskultur und Sonntagspredigt* (Ökumenische Studien zur Predigt 4) (Munich, 2003)

In the first part of this section, I will bring to mind the fundamental conditions facing every culture and their concept of time. Next follows an investigation of the biblical angles on time, which reflect general temporal structures but put them into theological perspective. After this, I endeavor to interpret the ecclesiastical year as an attempt to correlate primary religious experience and the fundamental Christian impetus and transform them into workable daily praxis. The remainder of this section will focus on contemporary challenges.

Cosmological-Anthropological Foundations

Time is a cultural concept that refers to cosmological or biological givens (see, for the following, Grethlein, "Potenziale liturgischer Zeiten heute," 180–81). The most basic phenomenon prompting human time divisions is the alternation of day and night, that is, of lightness and darkness. This change marks the transition from activity to rest and is quite often experienced as precarious and therefore accompanied by ritual.

Another fundamental cosmological phenomenon is the changing of the moon, which throughout cultural history has frequently prompted festivities and of course the monthly cycle of our calendar.

A further important cycle in most regions of the world is the changing of the seasons, with its immediate effect on vegetation and the animal world and consequently the human food supply. Since this is most quite simply bound up with the sheer physical survival of the people, it quite naturally gave rise to seasonal festivities.

Finally, there are the different stages of an individual's life: the human body is inscribed with a temporal structure. The most elementary stages are birth, sexual maturity, mating, and death, and they are often celebrated in rituals.

All these temporal rhythms are socially important. Accepted time arrangements are important for the integration of a sociality. Their social significance requires supreme authority, often wielded by priests.[2]

The issues of time and fundamental life and value orientations are connected by their relationship to mortality. The specific organization of time, as a look at cultural history reveals, is each culture's expression of its fundamental attitude toward life and death.

Biblical Perspectives

On the one hand, many biblical texts refer to specific times of the day when speaking of contacts with God. Morning and evening in particular were regarded as good times for the sacrifice (see, e.g., Exod 29:38-43; Num 28:1-8). In the New Testament, the communication with God was guided by the daily rhythm: morning (Mark 1:35), noon (Acts 10:9), and evening (Acts 3:1) were the times for prayer. Equally, the seasons played an important role in the Jewish festival calendar. At this point, however, we encounter a semantic transformation: it was not the seasons that were celebrated, but events in the history of the people were remembered in the rhythm of the annual cycle.

Furthermore, there was a specific way, today however only accessible in historical reconstructions, of dealing with the lunar phases.[3] It seems that

---

[2] Norbert Elias, *Über die Zeit: Arbeiten zur Wissenssoziologie* II, ed. Michael Schröter (Frankfurt, ⁴1992 [1984]), 20.

[3] See, for the following, Klaus Bieberstein, "Vom Sabbat und Siebten Tag zum Sabbat

the Jewish Sabbath began with a Babylonian Festival of the Full Moon (*šab/pattu*). At the same time, the Babylonian lunar phases were, after the calendar reform in the seventh century BCE, divided into seven-day periods. Both of these Babylonian time rhythms were adopted in Israel and transformed into a context—which has been ascertained elsewhere in the ancient Near East—of rest from work. Thus emerged in the priestly tradition the weekly Sabbath as the expression of "the rhythm of the creation, which needed to be discovered and which—in order to partake of a Divine privilege—one needed to join in."[4] Its introduction—as can be seen in Nehemiah 13—was fraught with considerable difficulty: what was, in creation-theological reasoning, a gift from God, was transformed into a commandment enforced by penalty.

The early Christians took the Sabbath as a given. Jesus taught in the synagogue on that day (e.g., Mark 1:21), and so did Paul (e.g., Acts 13:14-47). Jesus however emphasized the—original—social and humane character of the Sabbath (see, e.g., Mark 3:1-6). After his death, the "first day of the week" (1 Cor 16:2), the Sunday, began to take the place of the Sabbath. Erich Spier reconstructs this process of transformation in four stages:

I. The Sabbath is the only holiday also for Christians.
II. Sabbath and Sunday become holidays on an equal footing.
III. The Sunday replaces the Sabbath . . .
IV. The Sunday is celebrated by adopting contentual and formal aspects of the Sabbath.[5]

Apart from the adoption of given time rhythms outlined above and the emergence of the special position of first the Sabbath and then the Sunday, the Bible gives evidence of a fundamental relativization of all temporal structures. The Old Testament already speaks of the "day of the Lord," which will end time (see, e.g., Ezek 30:3); this is taken up by the authors of the New Testament, who knew that the time is "fulfilled" (Mark 1:15; Gal 4:4). Right at the beginning, the Revelation warns that "the time is near" (Rev 1:3). This

---

am Siebten Tag: Zur Vorgeschichte des christlichen Sonntags," in Roth, Schöttler, and Ulrich, *Sonntäglich*, 15–29.

[4] Bieberstein, "Vom Sabbat," 27.

[5] Erich Spier, *Der Sabbat* (Das Judentum. Abhandlungen und Entwürfe für Studium und Unterricht 1) (Berlin, ²1992), 109; see 109–18 and 129–35 for more detail on the development of the Sabbath practice in Christian churches.

relativization of cosmological and biological time marks all Christian thinking about time—sometimes almost forgotten, then again startlingly present.
In any case, it resists a static fixation of temporal order and opens up perception for a sphere that is not subject to a linear time structure.

The Liturgical Year

That which has been known as the ecclesiastical, or liturgical, year since the
sixteenth century in fact evolved in a complicated and regionally differing process over the course of centuries. Since the fourth century, extensive festivities
emerged, first around the annual celebration of Easter, and later also around
Christmas. In these contexts, the baptism played an important role, although
this celebration had before not been connected to a specific season. It now was
primarily celebrated at Easter or at Epiphanias (Christmas). Attached to this
were preparatory periods of penitence (and fasting), the Passiontide and the
Advent season.

The smallest structural units of the liturgical year were the Sundays. In the
beginning, they were celebrated as the "weekly Easter." By embedding them
into larger time units, they were however interpreted in various other ways.
Since the early Middle Ages further semantic attributions can be detected.[6]

To this day, there is ambiguity as to the significance of the Sunday. Liturgical interpretations as "weekly Easter" stand side by side with the ethical
claim of rest from work and the focus on the sermon. What they however
share in common is the problem of communicating with contemporary culture. In the Middle Ages, the Sundays were furthermore joined by numerous
saint's days, which the Reformers regarded critically since they saw no biblical
foundation for them. Luther was also aware of the relativity of feast days (see
WA 50: 559). Nevertheless, he particularly valued the Sunday as a day of congregation and emphasized its social significance—a functional view.

New Time Rhythms

Since the nineteenth century, several changes in the social time rhythms can
be observed that are relevant to the temporal structure of the communication
of the gospel (see Grethlein, "Potenziale liturgischer Zeiten heute," 185–86).

---

[6] Arnold Angenendt, *Geschichte der Religiosität im Mittelalter* (Darmstadt, 1997),
427–28.

The most fundamental determinator is the economic understanding of time (catchphrase: "time is money"), which prevails in many spheres of human life. This is connected to the acceleration, which can be observed in the systems of transport and general communication. This is of major consequence for the communication of the gospel, which requires, at least potentially, greater temporal coherence.

The electrification of the cities since the second half of the nineteenth century has to some extent dissolved the separation of day from night. New forms of nightly conviviality emerged. Moving the New Year's Day service in the morning to New Year's Eve is one example of the liturgical consequences of these developments.[7]

The introduction of the working vacation at the end of the nineteenth century also changed the landscape by adding to the general feasts times of rest, which can be individually arranged. Working hours also shifted. The weekend, occasionally beginning early on Friday afternoon and lasting until Monday morning, began to be established in the 1960s and put the Sunday morning service in a new position in the temporal structure.

Finally, the transitions of the phases in life changed. In the course of the centuries, they were embedded in church ritual: at birth the baptism, on reaching sexual maturity (and until fifty years ago connected with this also the entry into working life) the confirmation, the wedding on entering into matrimony, and at death the Christian burial. For some time now, these transitions are being stretched in an unprecedented manner. Ample medical advance and after-care programs accompany birth, the transition into adult life today is stretched out by an adolescence not uncommonly lasting up to twenty years. The forming of love relationships now takes years, generally starting out with the formerly critical sexual relationship. Intensive medical care prolongs the process of dying.

Suggestions for Reform

The singular nature of the Christian view on time as opposed to other conceptions is expressed in the fundamental relativization of time. In a society that subjects time to the economic calculus, it manifests itself in functionless

---

[7] See Kristian Fechtner, *Schwellenzeit: Erkundungen zur kulturellen und gottesdienstlichen Praxis des Jahreswechsels* (PThK 5) (Gütersloh, 2001), 137–38.

presence. As such, the following suggestions for reform for the temporal con-textualization of time take on explosive countercultural force.

As regards the difference of day and night, it is apparent that evening or late night services have been enjoying great popularity for quite some time. The festivities of Christmas Eve, just as those of the Easter vigil, refer to the particular situation of the evening or night (or daybreak): in a culture in which electric light reduces the difference between day and night and with this between activity and rest, the conscious enactment of the dark becomes particularly attractive for many people. This is a perfect opportunity for the communication of the gospel if one remembers that in biblical times the day began in the evening: with the period of rest. It is at that time, when one's activities no longer get (so much) in the way, that the individual is particularly responsive. In theological terms, beginning the day in the evening conforms with the insight of the gift-character of life from the doctrine of justification.

Concerning the annual cycle, Kristian Fechtner's suggestion to dis-tinguish the official liturgical year from the one that is actually practiced, provides a culture-hermeneutically interesting starting point (Fechtner, *Im Rhythmus des Kirchenjahres*, 57). According to this, he proposes to structure the year in the form of a "four-field model" (59). He defines the well-known festival groups anthropologically and adds two further points of focus: the first group, Christmastide, focuses on "beginning to live" (61); the second one, Eastertide, is guided by the idea of "out of death" (91); one of the new groups is the "Pentecostal time," which, under the motto of "emerging into life," should also integrate vacation experiences; and the equally new "Late Period of the Liturgical Year" (125) under the heading of "to mature in faith" comprises Thanksgiving, Reformation Day, Halloween, the Day of Prayer and Repen-tance, and *Totensonntag* (the commemoration of the dead on the fourth Sun-day before Advent).

2. Places

Literature: Thomas Erne and Peter Schüz, eds., *Die Religion des Raumes und die Räumlichkeit der Religion* (APTLH 63) (Göttingen, 2010); Gotthart Fermor et al., eds., *Gottesdienst-Orte: Handbuch Liturgische Topologie* (Beit-räge zu Liturgie und Spiritualität 17) (Leipzig, 2009); Rainer Volp, *Liturgik: Die Kunst, Gott zu feiern*, vol. 1 (Gütersloh, 1992), 181–225, 279–300, 347–406, 501–26

This section starts with places that have a particular significance for human communication. In the next step, these basic anthropological and culture-historical conditions will be put into the perspective of biblical tradition. Both, fundamental human experience throughout history and cultural achievements as well as their critique, have played formative roles in the history of Christianity.

Recent changes in social communication have led to a reshaping of space, transgressing the narrower sphere of the church. Compelled by cost-cutting measures and inspired by the "spatial turn"[8] of the cultural sciences, church buildings experience a renaissance of fresh attention.

Anthropological-Culture-Historical Foundations

Conspicuously,

> human beings seek out specific locations, natural or man-made, for certain purposes: the silence of the forest, mountain heights, cascading waterfalls, the wide expanse of the sea. This means that the individual is hoping for a certain kind of stimulus from a special place, if he is enveloped in an atmosphere of a particular kind. This place may "speak" to them better than any other.[9]

Already in antiquity, we can observe the interplay between cultic ideas and geographical space. A very good example of this is the importance of space marked by mountains or water. Many creation myths begin with the emergence of a great world mountain. Striking mountains are frequently holy places (e.g., Mount Kailash, Mount Fuji) and/or believed to be the residence of the gods (Mount Olympus, Jotunheim).[10] Moreover, there were places in which people felt particularly close to the Godhead, or were even sensually aware of its presence. Frequently, edifices of all kinds were erected as a reminder of this. In other regions, the world began with the separation of sweet water and

---

[8]   See Jörg Döring and Tristan Thielmann, eds., *Spatial Turn: Das Raumparadigma in den Kultur- und Sozialwissenschaften* (Bielefeld, ²2009 [2008]).

[9]   Hermann Reifenberg, *Fundamentalliturgie*, vol. 2 (Klosterneuburg, 1978), 315.

[10]   See Irene Mildenberger, "Berge," in Fermor et al., *Gottesdienst-Orte*, 45–48, 45.

sea water (as in the Sumerian and Babylonian epics).[11] In many places, foun-
tainheads and rivers were thought to be dwelling places of gods and demons.

Thus, the specificity of geographical space appears to be particularly conducive to human ideas of transcendence. In view of this impact of space on
human affectivity, it is therefore hardly surprising that specific places were
revered as "holy." The politically significant manifestation of this is the idea of
granting sanctuary.[12]

Biblical Perspectives

On the one hand, the biblical records draw directly on the primary religious
experiences mentioned above, which can be briefly exemplified for the significant places of mountains and water: Yahweh is referred to as the Lord who
"came from Sinai" (Deut 33:2).[13] He was supposed to dwell in Mount Zion
(Isa 8:18), on which the temple therefore was built. In the New Testament,
mountains also play prominent roles: Jesus withdrew into the mountains
for prayer (Matt 14:23); he gave an important speech on a mountain (Matt
5:1 and 8:1); on the so-called Mount of Transfiguration a theophany occurs
(Matt 17:1-9).

Similar incidences can be observed for water: in the beginning the Spirit
of God is hovering over a primeval ocean (Gen 1:2); the waters of the Sea of
Reeds parted to enable the Israelite exodus (Exod 14:21); and God appeared
to Ezekiel by the river (Ezek 1:1). In the New Testament, the preacher of
repentance preaches on the river Jordan; and the baptism was undertaken by
and with the water from the river (Acts 8:36); the thirsty are promised the
water of life from a fountain (Rev 21:6).

On the other hand, the significance of places for the communication with
God are fundamentally relativized. Jesus critically put the temple—just as the
Sabbath—into ethical perspective (Matt 21:12-17). And the gospel was also
communicated on pagan grounds like the Areopagus (Acts 17:16-34). This
explains the cultic reticence of the early Christians: congregating in the name
of Jesus Christ was important, not the place. Both forms of treating space,
relating to traditional ideas of space and their relativization, inform further
Christian history.

---

[11] See Jürgen Ebach, "Anthropogonie/Kosmogonie," *HrwG* 1 (1988), 476–91, 484.

[12] Martin Affolderbach, "Asylorte," in Fermor et al., *Gottesdienst-Orte*, 23–27, 23.

[13] Also see, for the following, Mildenberger, "Berge," 46–47.

Church Buildings

After Christians had at first quite naturally congregated in the temple (Acts 2:46; 5:12; see John 10:23) and the synagogues, they increasingly began to gather in homes (Acts 1:13-14; 12:12) and outdoors. House churches were formed.[14] It seems likely that the focus on the congregation and the excentric orientation toward God and Christ equally marked these gatherings right from the beginning.

The first Christian buildings—Hadrian gave permission for the erection of small churches in 138 CE—were the graves of martyrs. They were centers of attraction for church services, especially for the martyrs' memorial services. Sepulchral churches boomed in the fourth century leading directly to the relic cult, insofar as, being customary approximately from the sixth century onward, body parts were deposited in altars or other places in the church.

In Dura Europos, a city on the Middle Euphrates, a so-called house church has been excavated and dated ca. 230 CE, which clearly displays a functional orientation toward the basic practices of the congregation. Removal of an interior wall had made room for a bigger assembly hall (see also, for the ground plan, Volp, *Liturgik*, 185, 188). Among other things, there also was a separate baptismal room with a basin. The illustrations of biblical texts in this room are iconographically particularly interesting.[15] Otherwise, the decoration of church interiors with images—which would be fiercely disputed in centuries to come—goes mainly back to the adornment of catacombs.

From the fourth century onward, the new—recognized—status of Christianity expressed itself in intense building activity. The preferred form for large public buildings, the basilica, was also the form of choice for church buildings (for an example, see Volp, *Liturgik*, 192–97), less so central-plan buildings: "Rome's monumental imperial architecture"[16] became the model for church architecture. Gatherings in private homes were transformed into a public display of the hierarchical state cult. Churches were partitioned

---

[14] See Markus Öhler, "Das ganze Haus: Antike Alltagsreligiosität und die Apostelgeschichte," *ZNW* 102 (2011), 201–34.

[15] For a more detailed exploration, see Ulrich Mell, *Christliche Hauskirche und Neues Testament: Die Ikonologie von Dura Europos und das Diatesseron Tatians* (NTOA 77) (Göttingen, 2010).

[16] In particular, the mutual citation of architectural designs is elaborated by Christian Freigang, "Church Architecture: II. The West 2. Middle Ages," *RPP* 3 (2007), 38–52, 39.

accordingly: parts which were reserved for the clergy, and a separate part into which the so-called layperson (Gr. *laos*) was allowed. Recourse to these architectural informs all further history of church architecture. In the course of time, the towers, steeples, or spires were added, first probably simply staircases to access the galleries, then came the bells and the organ, both originally rejected as pagan.

New constructional technologies provided fresh input, while changes in both construction techniques and forms of piety and belief were interacting. Developments in technology and craftsmanship changed the face of architecture: the Gothic skeleton structure was not only statically more efficient than the old Romanesque style, but it also provided better illumination of the church interior thus creating new possibilities for the art of glass painting.

The Reformation proffered a new intellectual approach, which only in part exerted its influence in praxis. In his famous sermon on the occasion of consecration the *Schlosskirche* in Torgau in 1545, Luther emphasized the functional character of the church (see WA 49,588): the church is therefore not a house of God in the sense of a temple, but a space of communication.

In concrete terms, it was the function of the church house to facilitate the hearing of the word of God. This is also why the pulpit moves to the center of the congregational space. The introduction of the pews was to support attentive listening. In addition, it underlined the dignity of the common priesthood, since previously only the clergy had been seated during service (see Volp, *Liturgik*, 368). The hitherto open spatial situation was thus changed fundamentally. Most notably, the forms of participation were drastically reduced: whereas before people could move freely to kneel, pray, and so on, now everybody had to sit and listen. Pews offered the additional benefit of solving the community's financial problems, because a fee was exacted for each seat. In consequence, the seating order in church reflected the social hierarchies of the local congregation—a problematic by-product of an initially otherwise motivated building measure.

Furthermore, Luther suggested that the altar again be used as the table for the Lord's Supper. In the reformed churches this was strictly implemented, on the one hand because of their understanding of the Eucharist as memorial meal, and on the other because their wish to clearly dissociate themselves from any paganizing tendencies.

Only a few decades further on, changing attitudes toward life found eloquent expression in new types of church buildings in the Baroque period (see

Volp, *Liturgik*, 375). In the nineteenth century, however, the massive techno-logical and economic changes, in tandem with the emergence of new forms of constructional engineering (steel framing and concrete structures), led to confusion and insecurity in the German Protestant churches. First, there was an attempt, with the so-called Eisenacher Regulativ[17] of 1861, to find orienta-tion by relying to the time-honored Gothic and Romanesque styles of the past. Thirty years on, in 1891, the so-called Wiesbadener Programm distanced itself from such "Catholicizing" tendencies and designated the church as "an assembly hall of the celebrating community."[18]

After the collapse of 1918, German church architects began to strike new paths. The most influential figure at the time was architect Otto Bartning (1883–1959), whose concept of *Raumspannung*[19] (spatial tension) aimed to reflect the tensions of the liturgical celebration. His ideas were best expressed in his—unrealized—blueprint for a *Sternkirche* (1922), whose interior pro-vided separate spaces for liturgical and preaching services.

The cataclysm of World War II however curbed all further development. After 1945 the main objective in a devastated Europe was to rebuild or replace destroyed churches. New ideas again came from new building materials and techniques (see, also for numerous illustrations, Volp, *Liturgik*, 384–400). At the same time, talk of "the end of church architecture" (402) became com-mon, leading to a debate on the integration of liturgical church space into bigger buildings (403). However, the dissolution of a separate liturgical space into a multipurpose room could not be sustained in the long run, as it could not provide the necessary balance between primary and secondary religious experience.

The Catholic Church also made efforts to attain a spatial concept that was able to integrate the insights of the liturgical reform movement. These attempts effected, among other things, the following changes, which were implemented to benefit communal celebration: the focus on a free-standing altar—without side altars; celebration "versus populum"; and the introduction

---

[17] Reprinted in Wolfgang Herbst, ed., *Quellen zur Geschichte des evangelischen Gottes-dienstes von der Reformation bis zur Gegenwart* (Göttingen, 1968), 203–6.

[18] Also reprinted in Herbst, *Quellen zur Geschichte*, 207.

[19] See Julius Posener, *Otto Bartning: Sein Begriff 'Raumspannung,' vornehmlich im Bereich der Kirche*, Arbeitsstelle Gottesdienst 23 (2009/1), 37–40.

of the communion procession, causing the elimination of the communion rail, which had separated clergy and laity.[20]

New Formations of Space

The basis of all contemporary thinking about church architecture is the awareness of its relationship to the urban (or small-town) environment. Historically, churches were the "nucleus of the district" (Wolfgang Grünberg).[21] With the separation of residential and working environments they have lost important functions.

It is against this background that I view the rise of so-called specialized churches as an attempt to respond to the diversification in both social organization and urban planning. Typical German examples for this are the so-called city churches and youth churches. Particularly interesting with regard to the contextualization of the communication of the gospel are superhighway chapels (*Autobahnkirchen* and *Autobahnkapellen*).[22] While in this case the location of churches along thoroughfares (lines of communication) opens up new horizons beyond the organized church, the following example widens the concept of space. On closer analysis, televised church services reveal themselves as multioptical events:[23] First of all, they take place in the local community. Second, they are on television. Third, they are celebrated by viewers in their homes. The television mediates between the location of the community in which the service is being filmed and celebrated, and the location in which people follow the service on their receiving set and participate in it. At the same time, the number of viewers constitutes a new form of public within the terms of a mass society. In communication-theoretical terms this means that here the space of home and family regains liturgical quality, after liturgy had for a long period been confined to the church. These may be the first signs for a

[20] See Albert Gerhards, "'. . . Zu immer vollerer Einheit mit Gott und untereinander gelangen' (SC 48): Die Neuordnung der Kirchenräume durch die Liturgiereform," in *Liturgiereform: Eine bleibende Aufgabe: 40 Jahre Konzilskonstitution über die heilige Liturgie*, ed. Klemens Richter and Thomas Sternberg (Münster, 2004), 126–43, 135.

[21] Quoted in Heinrich Fucks, "Stadtteilkirche," in Fermor et al., *Gottesdienst-Orte*, 334–37, 335.

[22] Thomas Erne, "Autobahnkirche," in Fermor et al., *Gottesdienst-Orte*, 41–44.

[23] See Günter Thomas, "Fernsehen: Der Fernsehgottesdienst als multitopisches Ereignis," in Fermor et al., *Gottesdienst-Orte*, 98–102.

new contextualization of the communication of the gospel which stays abreast of such social changes as increased mobility and demographic ageing.

Suggestions for Reform

Rainer Volp summarizes his detailed analysis of church architecture thus:

> Western church architecture documents a complex and constantly chang-ing semiotic system. Here, the mutual challenges of tradition and innova-tion within a framework of cultural givens become particularly evident. (Volp, *Liturgik*, 406)

The following perspectives reflect the problems of this contextuality as well as the chances: first, there is the tendency to use or even appropriate church buildings for new purposes, and, second, a strand of education that emerged on both sides of the Inner German Border in the 1980s, and which in part took its cue from approaches in museum education, the so-called *Kirchraumpädagogik* (church space education).

Church buildings have found new uses after being sold to other Christian communities or given to secular associations and societies for cultural use; they are converted into lodgings, restaurants, offices, exhibition spaces, urn burial plots. The functional view of church buildings, clearly present in the Bible and Christian history and adopted by the Reformers, allows for scope. Approaching this scope from the angle of the communication of the gospel in the three modes discussed can help define it more precisely. Communal cele-brating is, after all, only one mode in which the gospel can be communicated. A public housing project within the confines of a church building may on the other hand create a space that helps for living.[24] And even if they are now used differently, one should not underestimate the impact that the function of a church building has on the topography of a place. And finally, for a church that is highly integrated into society these sales are a powerful reminder of the countercultural dimension of the communication of the gospel, which calls for change. The biblical image of the pilgrim people of God opposes local immobility.

---

[24] See Petra Bosse-Huber, "Verkaufte Kirchen," in Fermor et al., *Gottesdienst-Orte*, 204–7, 206.

Equally, church buildings hold great potential for the communication of the gospel in the mode of teaching and learning. This is where *Kirchraumpäd-agogik* or *Kirchenpädagogik* (church education) picks up and offers prolific didactic approaches. Church spaces are decoded as texts of bygone genera-tions and their topicality is discovered. In a situation in which explicit forms of the communication of the gospel have become inapproachable to many young people, conventional teaching practices, as for instance on the basis of written texts, lose their relevance. "Religion" as a school subject quickly degenerates into a historical, hard-to-decipher relic. Church buildings on the other hand offer learning processes which appeal to all the senses and motor skills, which can be adapted depending on the location. A category taken from religious science, the so-called walkthrough (*Begehung*), provides the methodological basis for individual learner approaches. Corporeality as the precondition for apperception stimulates symmetrical communication.

3. Summary

On principle, the gospel can be communicated any time and any place. This notwithstanding, Christians have created particular times and specific places. Interestingly, these places and times are even quoted in digital communica-tion. One look at the pertinent websites reveals "churches," "altars" on which virtual candles can be lit, and references to the Christian year, thus taking into account the fundamental anthropological conditions of communication.

In Christian history, the church year and church buildings occasionally acquired a problematic center position. The so-called Sunday Command-ment, decreed by Leo X in 1517 and made legally binding in the Codex Juris Canonici four hundred years later, has in the meantime also failed in the real-ity of the Roman Catholic Church. As much as the Christian year and church buildings have for a long time defined Western culture, their influence is now dwindling. Different temporal rhythms now mark people's lives, like week-ends and vacations; skyscrapers, the beacons of economic power, now tower high above churches in many cities. In this situation it is vital to follow the tradition of the Reformers and recall the functionality of Christian concepts of space and time. Suggestions for a new profiling of the Christian year as well as a rescheduling of certain services are steps in this direction, just as the attempts to find new uses for church buildings or their didactic disclo-sure. Theologically, the aim is not cultural dominance, but an advancement of the communication of the gospel. Communicating the gospel, it needs to be emphasized again, comprises not only the act of celebrating together, but also helping for living and teaching and learning. Functional changes of churches can thus be interpreted as accentual shifts in the communication of the gospel, instead of regarding them as desecrations or profanations.

7

COMMUNICATING ABOUT,
WITH, AND FROM GOD

The modes of communication presented in chapter 5 can be allocated to concrete forms of communication. The necessarily exemplary selection from the abundance of instances in Christian history is informed by the following two criteria: first, the elementariness of the form, which also shows itself in further ensuing forms of communication; and second, its significance in Christian history, and chiefly in the Protestant churches.

Despite the medial shift, this kind of review reveals a striking continuity, albeit in connection with transformation within the individual communication form. This, however, comes as no surprise if one takes account of their anthropological and culture-historical foundations. These forms are also present in other life and value orientations and open up a wide field for comparative Practical Theology, which we can go into here only by the way and for illustration. Both the religion hermeneutical distinction between primary and secondary religious experience, and the culture hermeneutical distinction between the transcultural, contextual, countercultural, and cross-cultural dimensions, reveal tensions within the individual methods. This can also be demonstrated only by way of a few examples, but can in principle be shown for all forms of communication.

The order in which these methods will be discussed does not—just as in chapter 5—imply a reasoned sequence. This being said, telling, praying, and blessing however provide access to the communication of the gospel in an exceptionally elementary fashion. It is upon these forms that the forms of talking (with each other), singing, and healing repose. In turn, their theological extensions are preaching, celebrating the Lord's Supper, and the baptism as the characteristic communication forms of the Protestant Church. These allocations do not constitute a compelling systematization, but the attempt to describe communication as it occurs in dynamic day-to-day living, that is, as individual practice, in an organized fashion. The fact alone that the different forms of communication blend into each other, defies rigid systematization.

A crucial element of the communication of the gospel is its inherent inclusiveness: the communication of the gospel is principally and permanently open to everybody. Baptizing infants and mentally impaired persons is positive evidence for this fundamental inclusiveness. This imposes very concrete demands on the methodological design, demands that can here be described only in general terms and not be elaborated in full detail.

1. Teaching and Learning: Communicating about God

Literature: Wilfried Engemann, *Einführung in die Homiletik* (Tübingen, [2]2011), 174–203; Rainer Lachmann, "Vom Westfälischen Frieden bis zur Napoleonischen Ära," in *Geschichte des evangelischen Religionsunterrichts in Deutschland: Ein Studienbuch*, ed. Rainer Lachmann and Bernd Schröder (Neukirchen-Vluyn, 2007), 78–127; Christoph Morgenthaler, *Seelsorge* (Lehrbuch Praktische Theologie 3) (Gütersloh, 2009), 239–54; Helmut Schwier and Sieghard Gall, *Predigt hören: Befunde und Ergebnisse der Heidelberger Umfrage zur Predigtrezeption* (Heidelberger Studien zur Predigtforschung 1) (Berlin, 2008); Harald Weinrich, "Narrative Theologie" (1973), in *Grundfragen der Predigt: Ein Studienbuch*, ed. Wilfried Engemann and Frank Lütze (Leipzig, 2006), 243–51

The basis for the communication of the gospel in the mode of teaching and learning is (narrative) telling. It is through narrative that people learn about the work of God and learn to understand their lives in a new way. Since narratives always imply views of the world and conceptions of humanity, talking about this is key for mutual understanding.

Against this background, preaching can be understood as an elaborate form of communication that correlates telling and talking (about what one has been told). It is in this way that people are alerted to the advent of God's reign or God's unconditional love.

While these three forms of communication foreground communication about God, this should not be confused with a problematic distance toward their point of reference. In fact, analysis of concrete communication acts reveals that the authenticity of the communicators is crucial. Communicating about God involves much more than simply addressing facts and circumstances: it leads to communications geared toward understanding directly involving the communicators and their life orientations. They correspond in large measure to the importance of biographical relatedness in contemporary life and value orientations.

The medium of choice for this form of communication is the Bible: it presents the previous history and the shaping of the fundamental Christian impetus. In order to meet its requirements, this storage medium needs to be interpreted in a manner that preserves the gospel as a transmission medium. This purpose is also increasingly fulfilled by electronic media.

Telling

Narrative telling is a time-proven cultural form for the communication of past events and future projections. It is the central form of communication in the Bible. And it is equally essential for the communication of the gospel in the present. Methodologically, it is especially taken into consideration in Christian pedagogy and homiletics.

In a first step, let us briefly consider the anthropological and culture-historical basics: Narrative telling is a fundamental form of communication which was already used in preliterate cultures to communicate about past and future, thus giving orientation in space and time and providing a framework for social integration.[1] This is why views on life and value orientations, as for instance those on the beginning and end of world and life, as well as

---

[1] Michael Scheffel, "Erzählen als anthropologische Universalie: Funktionen des Erzählens im Alltag und in der Literatur," in *Anthropologie der Literatur: Poetogene Strukturen und ästhetisch-soziale Handlungsfelder*, ed. Rüdiger Zymer and Manfred Engel (Paderborn, 2004), 121–38, 131.

identity-forming past events, were narrated.[2] As long as this was an oral process, it at once involved interpretation and updating. Narrators and listeners formed a mutually inspiring communication community.

Narrations soon found expression in images that depicted important events from the narrative and contributed to the interpretive process. Narratives were equally performed in ancient theater, highlighting their mimetic character that enhanced the lasting effect of the narrative.

This now leads us directly to the importance of narration in the Bible: not only the major parts, but in particular the most central texts in the Bible have been handed down in narrative form. And what is more, the Gospels as the basis for the congregation of Christians are narratives, which is of course in line with the ministry of Jesus, who communicated the advent of God's reign chiefly in narrative forms like the parables. From a communication-theoretical perspective, narratives are designed to be retold according to circumstance—which matches the open-ended character of the communication of the gospel.

The mimetic character of biblical narration finds its most powerful expression in the Last Supper. Right from the beginning, the narrative of this meal was passed on in different versions. In fact, this meal has been consistently mimetically repeated through the ages until today. With regard to Paul, Peter Wick suspects, "Most likely, each time the Lord's Supper is celebrated, it is not understood as a new meal, but as the continuation and extension of the meal Jesus celebrated with his disciples."[3]

In the same manner, the baptism is an expression of such mimetic recollection. Like Jesus, the individual undergoes an act of water-washing which expresses the communion with God. It is therefore not surprising that in the early church—as reported in the *Apostolic Tradition*—the last days preceding the baptism were observed in analogy to the last days of Jesus Christ: the baptizands participated mimetically in Jesus' destiny.[4]

Before we take a look at the emergence of methodological approaches resulting from these observations, let us first become clear about some systematic determinants. While in the United States narrative mode ("story")

[2] See, for classical antiquity, Jonas Grethlein and Antonios Rengakos, eds., *Narratology and Interpretation* (Trends in Classics Suppl. 4) (Berlin, 2009).

[3] Peter Wick, *Die urchristlichen Gottesdienste: Entstehung und Entwicklung im Rahmen der frühjüdischen Tempel-, Synagogen- und Hausfrömmigkeit* (BWANT 150) (Stuttgart, [2]2003), 208.

[4] See Roosen, *Taufe lebendig*, 21.

had already been an important theoretical presence in theology,[5] it was a literary scholar, Harald Weinrich, who, in 1973, first provided a major impetus for German theologians. Catholic fundamental theologian Johann Baptist Metz took up the cue providing a theologically differentiated reading, which revealed that particularly the problem and significance of suffering cannot be expressed appropriately without narration.[6] Metz draws attention to the—potentially—subversive character of narratives: by telling of a different reality, they criticize the reality at hand and unlock the necessary strengths for change. In the Easter narratives, this becomes manifest at its most radical: they open up a new horizon beyond the accepted natural boundaries of biological finality and thus categorically question the claim to absoluteness of any form of limitation. In other words, by being intrinsically critical of political rule, narratives take on a political dimension.

Moving on to methodology, storytelling has traditionally always played an important role in religious pedagogy and its predecessors. Christian Gotthilf Salzmann (1744–1811) already recognized its value. For the Christian instruction in schools, the first didactic advances came from teachers and pedagogues. In tension with the catechetical instruction given by priests or parsons, school teachers began to provide instruction in biblical history in Germany during the second half of the nineteenth century. Influenced by the religious psychology of Wilhelm Wundt, religious pedagogues like Richard Kabisch[7] recommended stories to excite the children's imagination. In the context of the word-of-God theology there was a catechetical concentration on biblical stories.

Methodological elaboration of biblical storytelling led to two approaches: Walter Neidhart[8] emphasized the importance of the imagination in preparing a story. He incorporated the historical-critical insights into a specially constructed frame narrative, thus creating an avenue to the students' receptive abilities. This of course entails the danger that occasionally the products

[5]   See Dietrich Ritschl, *Zur Logik der Theologie: Kurze Darstellung der Zusammenhänge theologischer Grundgedanken* (Munich, ²1998 [1984]), 47.

[6]   Johann Baptist Metz, "Kleine Apologie des Erzählens" (1973), in *Grundfragen der Predigt: Ein Studienbuch*, ed. Wilfried Engemann and Frank Lütze (Leipzig, 2006), 217–29, 225.

[7]   Kabisch, *Wie lehren wir Religion?*

[8]   See, e.g., Walter Neidhart and Hans Eggenberger, eds., *Erzählbuch zur Bibel* (Zürich, 1975).

of the imagination eclipse the purport of the biblical story. Dietrich Stein-wede,[9] in contrast, insisted on the central importance of the biblical text. The function of the story was merely to unfold it. This approach however begs the question whether the hermeneutical difference between the audiences—an adult audience in antiquity and contemporary children—is always sufficiently considered.

In practice, the following scenario for narrative structures has established itself, which can be easily identified in a great many biblical stories, and which makes good sense from a learning-psychological perspective:

> Phase One: introducing the situation (time and space), in which the story plays
> Phase Two: introducing the protagonist and his problem
> Phase Three: intensifying the conflict
> Phase Four: retarding the action by introducing a failed solution, by diverting the attention to a side scene or the like to increase suspense
> Phase Five: resolving the problem[10]

One method playing on the mimetic character of narratives is the "bibliodrama."[11] Stimulated by insights form theme-centered interaction and gestalt therapy, a method has been developed which allows the enactment and experience of stories with the whole body and all the senses. This method is particularly used in adult education.

The communicative potential of storytelling has also been discovered for the preaching of sermons. There is, for one, the narrative element at the beginning, which, in concentrated form, establishes a strong link with day-to-day life. On the other hand, the whole of the sermon can be a recounted story (see Engemann, *Einführung in die Homiletik*, 185–86); in this case, the structures and verbal style suggested by religious pedagogy have proven successful.

On the whole, the telling of biblical stories becomes more and more attractive in today's media society as a form of face-to-face communication.

---

[9] Dietrich Steinwede, *Zu erzählen deine Herrlichkeit* (Göttingen, 1965).

[10] Christian Grethlein, *Methodischer Grundkurs für den Religionsunterricht: Kurze Darstellung der 20 wichtigsten Methoden im Religionsunterricht der Sekundarstufe 1 und 2* (Leipzig, ²2007 [2000]), 38–50, 39.

[11] For a seminal text, see Samuel Laeuchli, *Das Spiel vor dem dunklen Gott: "Mimesis"—ein Beitrag zur Entwicklung des Bibliodramas* (Neukirchen-Vluyn, 1987); see also Gerhard Marcel Martin, *Sachbuch Bibliodrama* (Berlin, ³2011).

Furthermore, narrative structures can also be encountered in other forms of communicating the gospel: the great confessions of Christian faith, as for instance the Apostles' Creed, contain narrative passages. Evidently, one cannot speak of God in a Christian sense without telling of his work. The Christian year, church buildings, and church music as well as ethical precepts can be understood as indirect forms of such confession.

The significance of images for the communication of the gospel can hardly be overestimated. The first Bible illustrations already appeared in late antiquity, marking the beginning of a genre still flourishing today.[12] In the Middle Ages, many people learned about biblical stories only through the images in churches. To this day, images carry great weight in education, be it in children's Bibles, in the form of comic book Bibles, or single illustrations. They facilitate a first encounter with biblical messages, make them memorable and vivid, and transform them into present-day situations. They may, on the one hand, limit the imaginative scope for what has been merely heard; on the other hand, they widen the scope for interpretation.

Books and movies also offer a wide range of adaptations, distortions and modifications of biblical stories, which keeps biblical themes and insights ever-present beyond the domain of the (organized) church. The basis of this presence in culture is the communicative form of the narrative.

Talking

The basis of communication is talk or conversation and the desire for mutual understanding. A great many talks, conversations, or dialogs can also be found in the Bible. In a pluralistic situation, speaking with one another plays a crucial role for life and value orientations; and this corresponds with the practical-theological struggle for appropriate dialogical methods.

If we first look at the anthropological and culture-historical basis, we will find that the ability to speak is a skill connate in (almost) every human being. It has emerged from an evolutionary process until it was fully formed approximately thirty-five thousand years ago. The primary purpose of speaking is to achieve social agreements and communicate for mutual understanding. In Western culture, the conversational form of the dialog has acquired a particularly preeminent position. In a dialog, the dialog partners in their argument

---

[12] See Reiner Haussherr, "Bible Illustrations: I. Manuscripts and Miniatures," *RPP* 2 (2007), 26–30.

(Gr. *dialegesthai*) approach the truth. In the Socratic dialogs delivered to us by Plato we find the kind of argumentative dialog culture, which has served as a model for rhetoric and didactics ever since.

A brief glance at the type of dialog or conversation we find in the Bible reveals that it is full of highly diverse types of dialogs, often controversies about life or death, as for example, when Nathan confronts the adulterer David (2 Sam 12:1-14), or Job's heated debate with his "friends." Equally, we find conversations between God and man, as, for instance, when Moses persuades God to change his mind in Exodus 32:7-14, or, the other way round, when God teaches the discontented Jonah (3:9-11).

Jesus himself, in the prophetic tradition, put across major part of his message in the form of a verbal dispute. In doing so, he communicated the gospel in the face of objections. One is struck by his capacity to put complex problems without ceremony into the fresh perspective of the coming of God's kingdom. But for all that, he too was able to listen to argument and revise his position (as reported in Matt 15:24); and it is interesting to note that the question in this confrontation was one of inclusion, namely whether Jesus' ministry should be confined to the Israelites. The mother's distress and faith swayed Jesus and his initially dogmatic insistence on exclusion.

Trying to establish the systematic determinants of the role of dialog, by and large, Christian history reveals little capacity for dialog in the sense of an open-ended effort at achieving mutual understanding: christological and Trinitarian quarrels degenerated into bitter, power-political struggles, dissenters in faith were executed, and so on. There were, however, also attempts to communicate the gospel dialogically.

As part of the ecumenical movement, many and varied dialogs developed between different confessions aiming for unity. The Leuenberg Agreement of 1973 resulting in a "Church Fellowship" between Lutheran, Reformed, United, and pre-Reformation Churches of the Waldensians and Czech Brethren is evidence for the successful outcome of one such struggle for unity (see, e.g., Gal 3:26-27).

Dialogues are also held with representatives of non-Christian faith groups. These efforts are not least due to a striving for world peace and social integration. The basis of dialog here is the respect for different life and value orientations in the dialog partner.

There is currently a worldwide discussion as to whether and to what extent the traditions of different life and value orientations correspond with each other or are compatible.[13] Especially with regard to the Christian relationship to Buddhism there are studies alerting to the potential of Buddhism to transform Christian faith.[14] It remains however to be established whether this is only indicative of a small interreligiously interested elite trying to legitimize their lifestyle, or whether this actually provides a systematic framework to capture lifeworld changes in life and value orientations.

As regards methodology, in Christian instruction and pastoring, open dialog is now seen to be fundamental to the communication of the gospel. This was first conceptualized in catechetics in the form of the so-called Socratic method. As early as 1735, Johann Lorenz von Mosheim (1694–1755) recommended this approach (Lachmann, "Vom Westfälischen," 98–99). In a Socratic dialog the customary roles of teacher and student dissolve. In practice, however, this posed formidable difficulties (see Lachmann, "Vom Westfälischen," 119–20), since the premised ideal communication situation rarely matched the instructional reality. Class conversation was regimented and thus divested of all opportunity for person-related communication. Only with the differentiation of instructional conversation forms, the potential of the form "discussion" came into view.

While religious pedagogy favors talking in groups, pastoral care concentrates on the conversation between two persons—which does not rule out the general possibility of group pastoring. Here, too, the possibilities of conversation were only (re)discovered in the context of civic conversation culture. In the course of engaging with and largely adopting the methodical setting from psychoanalysis, and due to a fresh impetus from the pastoral care movement in the United States, a differentiated apparatus of counseling techniques in pastoring was developed (see Morgenthaler, *Seelsorge*). Particularly those parts of the communication relating to the attitudes and emotions of the conversation partners are analyzed and reflected upon. The person-centered psychological approach of Carl Rogers (1902–1987)[15] provides important pointers. It is based on the following principles:

---

[13] See Perry Schmidt-Leukel, *Transformation by Integration: How Inter-faith Encounter Changes Christianity* (Norwich, 2009).

[14] See, e.g., Paul Knitter, *Without Buddha I Could Not Be a Christian* (Oxford, 2009).

[15] Carl Rogers, *Client-Centered Therapy: Its Current Practice, Implications and Theory* (Boston, 1951).

Appreciation: the partner is treated with fundamental and unconditional affirmation and appreciation, i.e., with consideration and respect for the total person. . . .

Empathy and the verbalization of emotional conversation contents: this means to empathize with the world of the other person, to understand problems from the point of view of their frame of reference, and also to intuit the affective parts of this point of view. . . .

Genuineness and congruence: To be empathic towards another person does not mean to abandon oneself to their inner emotional world. . . . Genuineness here means congruence of thinking, feeling, and acting in a pastoral encounter. (Morgenthaler, *Seelsorge*, 246–48)

The reflection of the content-related parts of the pastoral communication of the gospel become less important in this approach. This, however, was the main emphasis of earlier concepts of pastoral care. But concepts like "proclamation" or "break (*Bruch*)"[16] fail to comply with the dialogical, and therefore symmetrical, structure of person-related communication in keeping with the fundamental Christian impetus.

Finally, there are further forms of communication changing the face of conversation. New forms of electronic communication lower the thresholds otherwise encountered in face-to-face communication. They are therefore particularly well-suited to present in manifold ways the "rumor"[17] that underlies the communication of the gospel. Regional churches and parishes have already begun to grasp these newly available opportunities.

A very special form of joining in conversation is to share in silence, sometimes referred to as meditation. An image, a cantata, or a biblical passage sometimes find appropriate expression in shared silence. The reason for the conversation is served, insofar as it comes from and ends in the silence.[18] As experience shows, exceptional places like churches, and certain times like the evening are particularly conducive to shared silence as a concentrated form of

---

[16] See Eduard Thurneysen, *Die Lehre von der Seelsorge* (Zürich, ⁴1976 [1946]), 114–28; compare Wolfram Kurz, "Der Bruch im seelsorgerlichen Gespräch," *PTh* 74 (1985), 436–51.

[17] See Josuttis, *Praxis*, 57–69.

[18] See Wulf, *Anthropologie*, 166–69.

communicating the gospel. Here, the communication about God passes over into the communication with God.

Preaching

Preaching is a, for many people probably *the* characteristic form of communication in the Protestant Church. Preaching stands in the tradition of general culture of oratory. Throughout Christian history the writings collected in the Bible have been an important point of reference for sermons. Its basic problems pervade Christian history and give cause for homiletic reflection.

Methodologically, dialogicity is key to gaining an appropriate understanding of the sermon. In this context, the reception-aesthetic perspective provides an approach that also extends to practical consequences for the composition of a sermon. Accordingly, increasing homiletic attention is devoted to sermons for the rites of passage, in which the concrete situation is of particular significance. Overall, the following comments on preaching integrate the points made above with regard to narration and conversation and condense it for the liturgical context. In doing this, the communication about God, which is generally accomplished by interpreting the Bible, opens up into a communication with God.

First, the anthropological and culture-historical foundations: for any society, public speaking is an important instrument (in striving) for social integration. In the Roman Empire, and therefore the context of early Christianity, specific forms of oratory had evolved in three fundamental places of social life: in the court of law, in the popular assembly, and in public festivities.[19] Its three functions—to instruct, to move, and to delight—remain an important legacy of ancient rhetoric to this day.

The most immediately important influence for the development of the Christian sermon was the lecture in the synagogue. It referred to a passage from the Hebrew Bible and practically-ethically oriented.[20] Another important form worth mentioning is the then common popular-philosophical discourse (Gr. *diatribe*), which treated questions of practical life in a down-to-earth manner. Christianity thus emerged in a context of a highly developed culture of oratory.

[19] See Hans-Martin Müller, *Homiletik: Eine evangelische Predigtlehre* (Berlin, 1996), 11.
[20] See Müller, *Homiletik*, 12.

From the perspective of Christian history, preaching owes its existence to the significance of the Bible. In the same manner, a sermonic culture developed in other communities that base their faith on holy scriptures. The texts require public exposition and updating.

The Bible contains a great variety of speeches. The most prominent of those are Jesus' Sermon on the Mount (Matt 5–7) and the missionary addresses of Paul in Acts of the Apostles, most notably his Areopagus speech (Acts 17:16-34), which contains rhetorical devices of the diatribe. It however remains a matter of contention whether and to what extent these speeches are a product of editorial interventions or whether they also contain points of tradition-historical interest. Be that as it may, the spatial conditions were different from those of today: there were no church buildings, nor pulpit or ambo. Neither were there any specially assigned preachers.

Turning to the systematic determinants for the sermon, a survey of the early Christian history of preaching[21] reveals a pluriformity of design, and problems that engage homiletic thinking to this day—sermons were preached at various times: on Sundays and holidays, but also on work days, in the morning and in the evening. Their length could vary between a few minutes and above an hour. They closely followed the biblical passage (homily) or treated a subject of general interest (*Themapredigt*). Every now and then, the absence of parishioners was criticized, at other times the large attendance praised. Unrest and distractions—as for instance by beautiful women—were also sometimes reprimanded.

The Reformers emphasized the importance of the listening congregation. The sermon was meant to consolidate their faith. Originally, the metaphor of "the word of God" represented the living communication necessary for this consolidation. This understanding, however, and the practice of preaching soon ossified in the constant efforts for theological correctness. The ensuing crisis led to a fundamental discussion in the seventeenth century as to the sermon's appropriateness.[22] The appearance of devotional literature also reduced the importance of the sermon. Unfortunately, certain theological standpoints talking up the office of the preacher, or taking the sermon to be "the word of

---

[21] See, for the following, with reference to many sources, Laurence Brottier, "Predigt V: Alte Kirche" *TRE* 27 (1997), 244–48, 245–46.

[22] See Sträter, *Meditation und Kirchenreform*, 97–98.

God" reinforced these tendencies and, contrary to their intentions, further depreciated the sermon.

It was Ernst Lange who developed a fresh approach with his concept of the communication of the gospel. His ideas are illustrated by the schema of his journal for sermon preparation, *Predigtstudien* (sermon studies), which is published to this day. Preparatory work is carried out in three steps for each of the two revisers:

> A outlines the "resonances" of the text in a "starter," then develops the perti-
> nent passage from the Bible "in its historical situation and mindscape," and
> finally frames the goal of the sermon.

> B in a first step reviews the work of reviser A, reconstructs the "homiletic sit-
> uation" through "the awareness and theological interpretation of currently
> existentially important life experience and politically-socially relevant ques-
> tions," then formulates the goal of the sermon to which "communicative
> connections" are added.[23]

To divide the sermon preparation up between two revisers makes the tension between biblical text and current lifeworld productive for homiletic work. An extension of this approach takes recourse to Umberto Eco's theory of the open art work.[24] This takes account of the fact that communication processes are not one-dimensional but productive on both sides, thus defining preaching as a fundamentally dialogical process (see Engemann, *Einführung in die Homile-tik*, 186–88).

Wilfried Engemann, following his principle of "tactical ambiguity" (199), draws methodological consequences from this fresh conceptual beginning for the sermon. He purposely employs the reception-aesthetically given (factual) ambiguity, that is, the possibility of interpreting that which one has heard in multiple ways, to communicate with his audience. Such an opening up for a dialog with the audience requires a clearly structured, generally intelligible presentation. This again presupposes attention to the expectations and lis-tening habits of those participating in the service. Experiments in so-called "alternative worship services" have shown the importance of the "connection

---

[23] See *PSt(S)* 2009/2010 Perikopenreihe II, 2nd semivol. (Freiburg, 2010), 4.

[24] A seminal text: Gerhard Martin, "Predigt als 'offenes Kunstwerk'? Zum Dialog zwischen Homiletik und Rezeptionsästhetik," *EvTh* 44 (1984), 46–58.

between sermon and liturgy," which facilitates listening and dialogical appropriation.[25] Empirical reception research in homiletics has produced interesting data in this respect, which however are only meaningful for specific regions (Germany: Schwier and Gall, *Predigt hören*).

Another methodically interesting approach comes from the movement of African American preaching, which Martin Nicol introduced into the German discussion using the metaphor of "preaching from within."[26] The attention is here focused on the presentation itself, and its design orients itself along the lines of cinematic suspense: by paying attention to "moves & structure,"[27] the sermon can be made more suspenseful.

Other forms of communication have sought alternatives to preaching from the pulpit that come closer to expressing the fundamental dialogicity of the communication of the gospel. In the 1960s and 1970s, so-called *Gesprächsgottesdienste* (dialogical worship) were tested in Germany. The goal was an open exchange between pastor and parish. This model however failed to gain long-term acceptance; probably because the necessary concentration and susceptibility for disturbances of speaking in a larger circle had been underestimated. In some places, talks prior to and after the sermon established themselves.

The form of the "cross examination" (*Kreuzverhör*) could break new ground: it complements the sermon—which is delivered from a bistro table—in the worship service model "GoSpecial," established in Niederhöchstadt (close to Frankfurt on the Main, Germany) in 1995:[28] during the singing of two songs, participants have the opportunity to write down questions for the preacher. These questions will then be sifted and sorted by a team and then read out. The preacher is then allocated a minute to answer the questions; time-out is indicated by a gong. In this model, preaching is doubly contextualized: the "cross examination" invites involvement and discussion, opposing paternalistic pastoral tutelage; the time limitation for the answers

---

[25] Lutz Friedrichs, "Anders predigen: Beobachtungen zur Predigt in alternativen Gottesdiensten," in *Normalfall Sonntagsgottesdienst? Gottesdienst und Sonntagskultur im Umbruch*, ed. Kristian Fechtner and Lutz Friedrichs (PTHe 87) (Stuttgart, 2008), 167–77, 167.

[26] Nicol, *Einander ins Bild setzen*, 55.

[27] Nicol, *Einander ins Bild setzen*, 109–10.

[28] See Fabian Vogt, "GoSpecial," in *Alternative Gottesdienste* (gemeinsam gottesdienst gestalten 7), ed. Lutz Friedrichs (Hannover, 2007), 82–96, 93–94.

reflects modern acceleration, opposing pastoral long-windedness. Method-ologically, the actors drawn on the stylistic devices used in television.

Summary

The essential foundation of Christian communication about God is the Bible. The fact that its narration refers to primary religious experience facilitates this communication. The scope of the communication about God is extended by the transformation of this experience into secondary religious concepts, particularly with regard to the historical actions of God and the ministry and destiny of Christ. The most remarkable aspect is the pluriformity of the meth-ods discussed, which provides for open-ended communication relating to spe-cific biographical and social situations. The future significance of preaching as a hitherto fundamental form of Protestant communication remains an open question: preaching oriented by obsolete ideas on communication as authori-tarian proclamation seems little suitable to further the communication of the gospel in a pluralistic society. On the other hand, besides Christian instruc-tion, the sermon is still the most familiar place for explicit reflection of the present from a biblical perspective. More recent homiletic approaches are try-ing to transform this concern into the communicative situation of a pluralistic society, by emphasizing, among other things, the authenticity expressed in a sermon and the scope for interpretation provided through tactical ambiguity. It remains to be seen in how far these approaches will actually manage to reform the practice of preaching and provide it with fresh relevance.

2. Celebrating Together: Communicating with God

Literature: Rainer Albertz, "Gebet II: Altes Testament," *TRE* 12 (1984), 34–42; Karl-Adolf Bauer, "'Da wurden ihre Augen geöffnet, und sie erkan-nten ihn' (Lukas 24:31a): Das Verhältnis von Sinngehalt und Feiergestalt im Heiligen Abendmahl," in *Thema: Gottesdienst* 29, ed. Beratungs- und Stud-ienstelle für den Gottesdienst der Evangelischen Kirche im Rheinland (Stutt-gart, 2009), 3–57; Rainer Flasche, "Gebet," *HrwG* 2 (1990), 456–68; Lutz Friedrichs, "Beten," in *Gott ins Spiel bringen: Handbuch zum Neuen Evange-lischen Pastorale*, ed. Klaus Eulenberger, Lutz Friedrichs, and Ulrike Wagner-Rau (Gütersloh, 2007), 185–92; Alfons Fürst, *Die Liturgie der Alten Kirche: Geschichte und Theologie* (Münster, 2008), 21–98; Manfred Josuttis, *Der Weg*

*in das Leben: Eine Einführung in den Gottesdienst auf verhaltenswissenschaft-
licher Grundlage* (Munich, 1991), 173–204; Manfred Josuttis and Gerhard
Marcel Martin, eds., *Das heilige Essen: Kulturwissenschaftliche Beiträge zum
Verständnis des Abendmahls* (Stuttgart, 1980); Bernhard Leube, "Singen," in
*Kirchenmusik als religiöse Praxis: Praktisch-theologisches Handbuch zur Kirch-
enmusik,* ed. Gotthard Fermor and Harald Schroeter-Wittke (Leipzig, ²2006
[2005]), 14–19

As much as the forms for the communication about God already transition
into a communication with God, this latter form has brought forth very specific methods, in Christianity as well as in other faith communities. The cultural context for this is provided by the search of many people for forms of
community. Praying is a communication in which people in concentrated form
express what moves them and enter into a dialog with God. While praying
may be susceptible to inner—also cognitive—struggles, the emotional, and
even ecstatic, sense of community with God and among the people prevails
in singing. The celebration of the Lord's Supper incorporates both forms: the
individual joins the meal community of Jesus and therefore enters into community with God; this in turn affects the community among the participants.

In these methods of communicating the gospel, major importance is
attached to the body. This is true not only of singing and eating and drinking together, but also for praying with its specific posture and gesture—all of
them contradicting the attested "excarnation" of Christian practice.

Praying

It is advisable to begin with general anthropological and culture-historical
considerations with regard to primary religious experience, since the motives
encountered here are the same that moved the people of whose experiences
the Bible reports. Furthermore, they opened up new perspectives.

Theologically, the Reformers generated important ideas that are worth
considering to this day. In practice, globalization poses new challenges. In
terms of Practical Theology, praying finds particular attention in catechetics
and religious pedagogy, and recently again also in pastoral care.

While the anthropological and culture-historical description of praying as the "central phenomenon of religion,"[29] as famously put forward by Friedrich Heiler, is based on a Christian idea of religion (for a critical assessment, see Flasche, "Gebet," 458–61), and some (so-called) religions and certain Buddhist traditions do not use this form of communication, the worldwide presence of prayer in highly diverse faith communities is beyond question.

Certainly, praying is connected with the prayer being heard or answered, however, this form of communication expresses basic human needs that cannot be one-dimensionally explained in utilitarian terms:[30] on the one hand, prayer reposes on the general neediness of every human being, which finds expression in desires and petitions; on the other hand, it expresses an individual's communion with another, of whom he or she expects good and with whom he or she wishes to make contact. Both of these things, petition and desire and communion with a much longed-for other, are deeply rooted in the human being, and their taking shape in prayer can take on a great variety of forms.

This general definition of prayer explains why disappointments cannot make it disappear. Furthermore, it draws attention to its fundamental dialogicity, which differentiates it from closely related forms like magic—which are clearly not dialogical.

The basic communicative situation of prayer is expressed in various faith groups by purification rites and/or dress regulations. As is generally the case for interlocutions, the praying person also wishes to approach the communication partner in an appropriate fashion.

From the culture-historical/anthropological perspective let us now turn to the role of prayer in the Bible. The Old Testament does not provide a generic term like "prayer" (Albertz, "Gebet II," 34); instead, we encounter a multiplicity of forms, all of which reflect the behaviors from the domain of primary religious experience outlined above. In practice, praying was not only a verbal act, but also accompanied by specific acts. Prayer was invariably occasioned by immediate joys and sorrows, eliciting either supplication or thanksgiving.

---

[29] Friedrich Heiler, *Das Gebet, eine religionsgeschichtliche und religionspsychologische Untersuchung* (Munich, 1918), 1.

[30] Compare Carl Heinz Ratschow, "Gebet I: Religionsgeschichtlich," *TRE* 12 (1984), 31–34.

Variously, as for instance in Jeremiah, this would include the lament (40–41). Sometimes prayer was intensified when God himself complained about Israel's unfaithfulness (see Jer 2:31-32 et al.; also see Albertz, "Gebet II," 41).

In the New Testament, praying stands in the tradition of the Hebrew Bible.[31] Supplication was the most important form for Jesus, which is in line with his message of the incipient kingdom of God. The address "abba" lend this form of prayer a particular degree of intimacy. The passion narratives give a dramatic account of Jesus struggle in prayer at Gethsemane, which ended in Jesus subordinating his urgent plea for being spared his destiny under the will of the Father (Mark 14:36). In this manner, the way in which a prayer could be answered came to be seen in a new light: the will of the petitioner is literally put into perspective, that is, seen in relationship to God's will. In Paul, the emphasis changed: thanksgiving prayer became more important, and petitionary prayer was for the most part turned into intercessory prayer. The New Testament thus accentuates the fundamental situation of praying as well as the communion with God slightly differently: thanksgiving and intercession become more important, the praying individual addresses the prayer to the beloved abba, faithfully complying with his will. All this extends the dialogical situation while at the same time focusing it: as in all communications, praying also is conditioned by the communication partner.

Moving now to the systematic determinants, the Middle Ages saw a major praying crisis, when Latin liturgical prayer was disconnected from the daily private praying of ordinary people. As can be illustrated by the acts of benediction, prayer was dominated by magical actions, that is, acts aiming at the direct manipulation of sense perception. This turned the liberating aspect of prayer as communication on its head. Punctilious recitation of Latin formulae replaced the open communication with God.

This situation was redressed by the Reformers, who emphasized the communicative character of prayer. Particularly intercessory prayers were soon worded in German. The extent of the Reformers' desire for comprehensibility is illustrated by the fact that Luther's *German Mass* allowed for the Lord's Prayer in paraphrase (WA 19,95). In the eyes of the Reformers, prayer as a communicative actualization of one's relationship with God was fundamental

[31] See Julie Kirchberg, "Theologie in der Anrede: Die jüdische Gebetstradition und ihre theologische Bedeutung," in *BETEN: Sprache des Glaubens—Seele des Gottesdienstes: Fundamentaltheologische und liturgiewissenschaftliche Aspekte* (PiLi 15), ed. Ulrich Willers (Tübingen, 2000), 243–56.

to Christian life. This is why Martin Luther added to his *Small Catechism* the morning and evening prayer: two prayer liturgies for regular practice in the home use (BSLK 521–22). The longest passage of John Calvin's *Institutio Christianae religionis* is dedicated to prayer (*Inst.* III: 20), developing a daily schedule oriented by prayer:

> [We should pray] when we rise in the morning, before we begin our day's work, then, when we sit down at table, further, after we have enjoyed God's blessing in the form of our meal, and finally, when we retire to bed. (*Inst.* III: 20, 50)

From an educational point of view, regular times for prayer, memorized prayers, and particularly the Lord's Prayer and certain psalms were deemed important.

Under Pietism, prayer became more individualized, a trend that continued during the Enlightenment, when prayer became more of a devotional exercise and its fundamentally communicative character lost its impact.[32] Furthermore, the question whether God answers prayers gained in prominence.

The phrase "interreligious prayer" draws attention to a new challenge presented by the growing numbers of Muslims in Christian cultures. The question is whether and perhaps how these groups can share in prayer during common celebrations in the public sphere. The communicative character of prayer provides differentiations that point beyond an either-or lacking in practical relevance. The "Liturgische Konferenz" has proposed the following practical implementation:

    I. Shared silence, or elements of celebration which facilitate contemplation and the inner listening to God.

    II. Approaching God in the mode of asking.

    III. Complaining before God in the face of a pressing situation.

    IV. Collective petition in the current shared situation.

    V. Intercessory prayers.

    VI. Grateful praising of God in virtue of his deeds in past and present.

---

[32] See, e.g., Johannes Spalding, "Von dem eigentlichen Werth äußerlicher Religionsgebräuche" (1785), *SpKA* I/6–1, 352–63, 358–60.

VII. Multireligious confession, in which the unifying and the divisive aspects are addressed in the perspective of hope (and not of differentiation alone).[33]

The first two forms are doubtless open for interreligious prayer, that is, a shared prayer. In specific situations, the third to fifth forms also offer themselves. The last two forms, however, lend themselves only to multireligious prayer, that is, a prayer shared by the members of one faith, at which the others are present, but in which they cannot share. The above arrangements, again, are suggestions from a Protestant-theological perspective, which in practice needs to be communicated to the members of the other faiths.

On the Roman Catholic side, the (first) Prayer for Peace in Assisi in 1986 constituted a much-noticed attempt at multireligious prayer.[34] Under a new pope, the separation, also spatially, from other faiths was reintroduced.[35] There are, in spite of such doctrinal restriction, contextually open-minded Catholic theologians who seek for an opening up toward the traditions and spiritual practices of others.[36]

Experience shows that interreligious prayer requires the ability to couch fundamental beliefs in communicable terms; elaborate theological terminology is here quite inappropriate.

Methodologically speaking, while prayer is a reflection of general human needs, praying, like any other form of communication, must however be learned. From an educational perspective, mimesis proves to be an important form of learning. A praying individual includes another, for instance his or her child, in his or her own praying. In this process, three things need to be given:

[33] Liturgische Konferenz, ed., *Mit Anderen Feiern—gemeinsam Gottes Nähe suchen: Eine Orientierungshilfe der Liturgischen Konferenz für christliche Gemeinden zur Gestaltung von religiösen Feiern mit Menschen, die keiner christlichen Kirche angehören* (Gütersloh, 2006), 59.

[34] See Gerda Riedl, *Modell Assisi: Christliches Gebet und interreligiöser Dialog in heilsgeschichtlichem Kontext* (TBT 88) (Berlin, 1998).

[35] See, for a critical view, Andreas Feldtkeller, "Assisi, auf die Melodie von 'Dominus Iesus' zu singen," *MdKI* 53 (2002/1), 1–2.

[36] See, as an example for (so-called) Hinduism, Sebastian Painadath, "Gebet und Meditation: Perspektiven eines indischen Theologen," in *BETEN: Sprache des Glaubens—Seele des Gottesdienstes: Fundamentaltheologische und liturgiewissenschaftliche Aspekte* (PiLi 15), ed. Ulrich Willers (Tübingen, 2000), 103–13.

the ability for appropriate speech, time for one another, and the opportunity provided thereby to open up to each other.[37]

For small children, the first encounter with praying is probably usually the passage from day to night, when they go to bed. In psychoanalytical terms, such prayer can be interpreted as a transitional object: in a precarious situation of transition it provides something familiar as a defense against anxiety.[38]

A special form of such a structuring of time by prayer established itself in monastic circles in the form of the liturgy of the hours (liturgia horarum). They organize the day and give form to the desire of living and structuring one's life guided by prayer—similar to the obligatory Muslim ritual prayer *salāt*. However, all efforts, such as those of the Reformers, to establish this form of piety outside the context of religious communities have proven unsuccessful.

Another form of mimetic learning for children is when they attend, together with their parents or other familiar persons, church service. The customary gestures during a Protestant service, like inclining the head, folding one's hands, and—perhaps—closing one's eyes, already signalize an unusual communication situation. Copying these gestures makes one enter the communicative space of prayer, before a single word is uttered. Framing the prayer by addressing God and expressing assent by the affirmative amen are further steps in its acquisition. And yet, already the address poses the important question of the content of prayer. To be able to answer it appropriately, cognitive knowledge is required. For instance, one does not, for pertinent reasons, pray for something that contradicts God's will. This is why instruction is so important.

As concerns learning within the church community, parish praxis offers diverse opportunities to participate in prayer. Rites of passage in particular are situations in which human wishes and the community come into contact with God. Therefore, they offer excellent opportunities for learning in the church community.

And finally, there is a growing interest in prayer in pastoral theory. Analogously to religious didactics, the reaction to one-sidedly dogmatic concepts had led to an overpsychologization, in which prayer was critically investigated with regard to possible suppression. However, already Joachim Scharfenberg

---

[37] See Hans-Jürgen Fraas, *Die Religiosität des Menschen: Ein Grundriß der Religionspsychologie* (Göttingen, 1990), 196–97.

[38] See Friedrich Grünewald, "Das Gebet als spezifisches Übergangsobjekt," *WzM* 34 (1982), 221–34.

alerted to the significance of prayer from a psychoanalytical perspective: for him, prayer is the "education of desire."[39] The aim of this "prayer school" can be found in Jesus' struggle at Gethsemane: clearly framing one's own desire and then trustfully putting it into the perspective of God's will.

A fresh impetus was provided by the orientation toward what has been called *Alltagsseelsorge* (everyday pastoral care),[40] for, in fact, prayer forms an important part of pastoral visits to the home. Prayer here opens up new perspectives (see Friedrichs, "Beten," 187): prayer allows the self to distance itself from itself—an important step particularly for narcissistic personalities. In this situation, canonical and free prayers each have their very own opportunities and limitations (see 189). Free prayers require great intimacy and express very specific needs. Canonical prayers allow the participants greater freedom of interpretation, but also of dissociation.

Finally, with regard to other forms of communication, we find in some Reformation writing, apart from the insights discussed above, a radical opening up of the notion of prayer toward all kinds of communication (see WA 10/I 1,435; *Inst.* III: 20, 50) in that there is a fluent passage from prayer to meditation, or singing, or listening to a story. This is based on the conclusion that the community with God supports the whole of an individual's life, which is expressed in different forms of communication. The more one's relationship to God becomes the central point of the communication, the more the boundaries between the single methods blur. From a theological perspective, this prohibits a legalistic insistence on a particular form of piety.

As silence is to speaking together, so is silent contemplation to prayer: a complementary form of communication. It can be seen as the accomplishment and foundation of prayer.

One very popular form today is meditation. With its various roots in the Ignatian meditation on Scripture passages, the multiply transformed Prayer of the Heart, and equally repeatedly modified Zen meditation, and by being fundamentally experience-based it provides access to transcendental experience for the interested seeker. Sitting, intensified observing, outward passivity

[39] Joachim Scharfenberg, *Einführung in die Pastoralpsychologie* (Göttingen, ²1990 [1985]), 108–10; see, for a theological specification, Michael Klessmann, "Das Gebet als Erziehung des Wunsches: Eine religions- und pastoralpsychologische Perspektive," *PTh* 94 (2005), 73–82.

[40] Hauschildt, *Alltagsseelsorge.*

with heightened inner attention, and repetition are the basic communicative acts common to all forms of meditation.[41]

Singing

The situation of singing in contemporary modern society is contradictory. On the one hand, liturgy and hymnology lecturer Bernhard Leube declares of congregational singing, "The natural tradition of singing has died, it needs to be revived" (Leube, "Singen," 18). On the other hand, cantor Christa Kirschbaum draws attention to a singing "boom" in many places.[42] Also, biblical-theologically its relevance imposes itself. And there is no doubt as to the importance of methodological considerations.

If we look at singing from an anthropological and culture-historical perspective, we first find that brain research has shown that singing is a form of expression in its own right that has not evolved from speaking: it has its own organic basis in the evolution-historically oldest part of the brain, the brain stem.[43] This explains why in some forms of mental illness, despite the loss of speech, the ability to sing remains. The oldest form of vocal utterance probably being the scream, Leube has, in evolutionary terms, referred to singing as "domesticated screaming" (14).

Singing has always been connected with movement, probably due to the vibrations produced by sounds.[44] Ethnological studies have drawn attention to the connection between singing and working (see Josuttis, *Der Weg in das Leben*, 175–76), the rhythm coordinating operations.

Overall, one can observe a great integrative potential of singing, up to the experience of mystical union (see 178), which explains the close connection between cult and singing or music.

---

[41] See Sabine Bayreuther, *Meditation: Konturen einer spirituellen Praxis in semiotischer Perspektive* (APrTh 43) (Leipzig, 2010).

[42] Christa Kirschbaum, "Singen in der Gemeinde als Bildungsarbeit," in *Kirchenmusik als religiöse Praxis: Praktisch-theologisches Handbuch zur Kirchenmusik*, ed. Gotthard Fermor and Harald Schroeter-Wittke (Leipzig, ²2006 [2005]), 199–205, 200.

[43] See Philipp Harnoncourt, "'So sie's nicht singen, so gleuben sie's nicht': Singen im Gottesdienst: Ausdruck des Glaubens oder liturgische Zumutung?," in *Liturgie und Dichtung*, vol. 2 (PiLi 2), ed. Hansjakob Becker and Reiner Kaczynski (St. Ottilien, 1983), 139–72, 142.

[44] See Philipp Harnoncourt, "Singen und Musizieren: 241 Terminologie und grundsätzliche Fragen," in *Gestalt des Gottesdienstes: Sprachliche und nichtsprachliche Ausdrucksformen*, ed. Rupert Berger et al. (GDK 3) (Regensburg, 1987), 132–38, 135.

With regard to singing and music making in the Bible, it is difficult to establish the actual practice of the times, since there are no written records of tonality. Singing was probably so much part of the culture that it did not warrant particular accounts or reflection.

It is rather incidentally that the Old Testament mentions the great power of singing and music: young David plays a string instrument to lift King Saul's gloom (1 Sam 16:14-23), and elsewhere we find reports of ecstatic phenomena triggered by music (1 Sam 10:5; 2 Kgs 3:15).

Of particular theological importance are the psalms, which are not only be found in the Psalter. From these, certain liturgical procedures can be reconstructed: The Doxology encompassed the whole of the Cosmos; in it, the Creation and all of God's saving deeds were affirmed. It expressed the community of the singers and of the one extolled (see Josuttis, *Der Weg in das Leben*, 187).

If we follow the equally sparse testimony of the New Testament, the young Christian community preserved this tradition. The singing of hymns was a natural part of Christian life (Col 3:14) and served to uplift the community (Eph 5:19-20).

Paul distinguished—in parallel with prayer—between two forms of psalm singing, one with "spirit" (Gr. *pneuma*) and one with "understanding" (Gr. *nous*) (1 Cor 14:15). The ecstatic and the intelligible stand side by side: this spells out a tension that permeates the whole of Christian history. The community with God, in which the singing congregation unites with God's heavenly choir of angels—as the eucharistic liturgy of the Orthodox Church and some Western liturgies maintain to this day—stands in tension to the worldly situation (not least in the parish).

The first thing to note when considering the systematic determinants of singing is that, throughout Christian history, the emotional approach to Christian experience induced by music was frequently—much like imagery—perceived as a threat. The ascetics of the early church criticized song for being at odds with the due fear of God (Josuttis, *Der Weg in das Leben*, 189). In large parts of the church instrumental music was prohibited: the instruments were too grim a reminder of the Christian persecution in the Roman circus, which was accompanied by sounds of the trumpet or organ. At the end of the eighth century, the organ, as an imperial attribute, slowly began to find its way into the churches. At the same time, particularly in the cathedrals, cantors began to assemble large choirs.

Congregational singing only witnessed a breakthrough during the Lutheran Reformation. While Zwingli resolutely opposed music and singing during service,[45] Calvin at least authorized monadic congregational singing as long as it used biblical wording (usually psalm singing). Luther, on the other hand, playing music since childhood, encouraged music making in all its forms.[46] To Luther the theologian, music was a creative gift of God. Congregational singing, sung by heart under the direction of the cantor, offered the barely literate parishioners the opportunity for active liturgical participation. At the same time, singing helped promulgate Lutheran doctrine.

The most important thing, however, was that beyond the doctrinal communication about God and word-based praying, in the singing congregation a communication form had returned to Christianity that primarily stimulated the emotions.

Yet once again control of the unleashed emotions dampened the Lutheran impetus—in the form of multiversed hymns in tandem with the introduction of the hymn book. In the long run, the formation of a tradition based on the success of church song led to a weakening of its impact. Luther's vivid exchange with the popular tunes that were sung everywhere gave way to self-referential church music. "Spiritual" and "secular" song were separated, and the creation-theological foundation of music was lost, or domesticated in the concept of the orders of creation.

One of the most important impetuses for contemporary church singing comes therefore from a cultural context in which, at a remove from such domestications, singing was an immediate expression of existential experience. In the Negro spiritual, the feeling of homelessness ("Sometimes I feel like a motherless child . . .") and bondage ("O freedom . . .") join hands with the Christian hope for liberation. Gesine Jost[47] has shown that the physical communication of a new beginning in slave singing corresponds, in a transformed manner, with the sense of life in contemporary adolescents. The growing German enthusiasm for the singing of spirituals and gospels in choirs and congregations is an eloquent testimony to this. The political dynamic of their origins, however, does usually not surface.

Now turning to methodology of singing, we can observe that today's church musicians increasingly attempt to relate liturgical singing to the rest

---

[45] See Kunz, *Gottesdienst evangelisch reformiert*, 125–35.

[46] See Christoph Krummacher, *Musik als praxis pietatis: Zum Selbstverständnis evangelischer Kirchenmusik* (VLH 27) (Göttingen, 1994), 14–33.

[47] Gesine Jost, *Negro Spirituals im evangelischen Religionsunterricht: Versuch einer didaktischen Verschränkung zweier Erfahrungshorizonte* (Theologie 48) (Münster, 2003).

of the culture, that is, to contextualize it. For instance, in observing the fan chants in sports arenas (see Leube, "Singen," 15), they find many behaviors reminiscent of Lutheran services during the Reformation, which however have disappeared due to multiple regimentations: the adaptation of tunes from popular culture and the responsive singing of repeating after the leader or leading group. In order to revive this connection, the education of church musicians needs to be improved, in particular with regard to pedagogical considerations.

As regards other forms of communication in Christian history, we variously find different but related forms. Paul's distinction between "spirit" and "understanding" (1 Cor 14:15) in psalm singing points to chanted glossolalia. We find this ecstatic form of expression to this day in Pentecostal communities, but also outside of Christianity. The attachment to language here in its unintelligibility clears the space for the—psychologically speaking—regressive, but for this very reason calming, action.

Apart from singing, instrumental music was already used in services in late antiquity. In many places, the organ has become the church instrument per se. The work of Johann Sebastian Bach (1685–1750) is generally considered to be the epitome and capstone of the productive period in service music prompted by the Reformation. His Passions, for example, were clearly composed for church service, but they reached far beyond common practice and thus marked the beginning of a development that emancipated itself from the service proper. Since then, music making in the context of the communication of the gospel has diversified considerably. From a reception-aesthetical point of view, it does not make any sense to distinguish—objectively, as it were—between church music, spiritual music, and secular music. Instead, the culture hermeneutical definition of the communication of the gospel suggests a principal openness for all musical genres and stiles.[48] The example of the cosmopolitan/German enthusiasm for Negro spirituals vividly illustrates the great potential of cross-cultural impulses. Similar tendencies can be observed for the music for rites of passage.[49]

---

[48] See Konrad Klek, "Gibt es einen Kirchenstil? Theologische und musikalische Argumente," in *Musikkultur im Gottesdienst: Herausforderungen und Perspektiven*, ed. Hanns Kerner (Leipzig, 2005), 43–72.

[49] See Stefan Reinke, *Musik im Kasualgottesdienst: Funktion und Bedeutung am Beispiel von Trauung und Bestattung* (Göttingen, 2010).

Finally, as mentioned above, we know from cultural history that singing and moving are closely connected. For some time now, due to cross-cultural encounters, dancing has entered the focus of liturgical attention. It is true that the church fathers rejected dancing during service; however, sacred dances can already be found in the Old Testament, performed by David (2 Sam 6:5) and Miriam (Exod 15:20), and invoked in the Psalter (Ps 149:3). For the Middle Ages, there are repeated reports of dances during church festivities in the face of official bans.[50] Only when the traditional fear of the body was slowly overcome, began dancing to be integrated into the communication of the gospel. From the theological side, it was Bombay-born Ronald Sequeira, who had earned his doctorate under Karl Rahner, who provided important impetus for the discussion.[51] Born and raised under the influence of Hindu dance practice, he drew attention to the significance of gestures and movement in the communication with God. Other important suggestions come from women's groups in the United States, who, through bodywork, are discovering the potential of dancing for the communication of the gospel.[52]

Celebrating the Lord's Supper

In the Lord's Supper we celebrate "Communion." From a dogmatic point of view, this celebration seems to be clearly defined as a sacrament, even though it might be accentuated varyingly in confessional and doctrinal statements. From a communication-theoretical point of view, the celebration as it was actually practiced took on rather different forms that had hardly anything in common:

First, it was subject to variable entry requirements: at the beginning, the risky confession to the Christian faith; later, authoritative enforcement.[53] Second, it was celebrated in all manner of places: first in private homes, then at the gravesites of martyrs, finally in representative basilicas. Third, times

---

[50] See Gabriele Koch, "Tanz als Gebet," in *BETEN: Sprache des Glaubens—Seele des Gottesdienstes: Fundamentaltheologische und liturgiewissenschaftliche Aspekte* (PiLi 15), ed. Ulrich Willers (Tübingen, 2000), 161–93, 169.

[51] Ronald Sequeira, *Klassische indische Tanzkunst und christliche Verkündigung: Eine vergleichende religionsgeschichtlich-religionsphilosophische Studie* (FThSt 109) (Freiburg, 1978).

[52] See Teresa Berger, *Liturgie und Tanz: Anthropologische Aspekte, historische Daten, theologische Perspektiven* (St. Ottilien, 1985).

[53] See Christel Köhle-Hezinger, "Abendmahl als Gesetz: Beiträge aus der Volkskunde," in Josuttis and Martin, *Das heilige Essen*, 69–81.

and frequency of participation varied: at the beginning, there was the regular congregation on Sundays, then the frequency increased to daily communions, which however did not include all members of the community, and later the frequency decreased again, which led to the postulation of the annual communion in the Fourth Council of the Lateran in 1215 (see Fürst, *Die Liturgie der Alten Kirche*, 42–43). Finally, the form of the celebration changed beyond recognition: first there was the full communal meal, aimed at satisfying the appetite, then a symbolically highly concentrated cultic meal during which for centuries most people received only a Communion wafer, if anything, but no wine. The church interior changed accordingly, the table being replaced by the altar (see 66).

In the face of these substantial changes in the form of the celebration it is important to recall the initial meaning of the Lord's Supper reflecting the basic Christian impulse. Obviously, cultural change and more significantly the changing shape of Christianity entailed profound transformations of the celebration. Both the opportunities for contextualization and the dangers of problematic adaptation need to be considered in this process.[54]

Finally, there is a practical problem. Only a minority of German Protestants fairly regularly partakes of the Lord's Supper. For many, their confirmation was the first and the last time they celebrated this sacrament.

The anthropological and culture-historical foundations of this form of communal celebration lie in the first place in the simple fact that eating and drinking are essential to life. Only for short periods can human beings liberate themselves from these needs. In hunger and thirst they over and again and inevitably experience the neediness of their existence. In a quite literal sense, eating and drinking are about life and death.

Communal meals stand right at the beginning of human culture. As ethnological studies have shown,[55] they united the participants in a special manner and created community beyond the mere intake of food. It stands to reason that conversation during the meal played a central role in this process. This also explains the strong connection between communal meal and memory, which can be observed throughout cultural history. Yet, memory not only focuses on the past, but equally orients the participants toward the future.

[54] For the following, see Christian Grethlein, *Abendmahl feiern in Geschichte, Gegenwart und Zukunft* (Leipzig, 2015).

[55] See Hans-Jürgen Greschat, "Essen und Trinken: Religionsphänomenologisch," in Josuttis and Martin, *Das heilige Essen*, 29–39, 32–33.

Historico-genetically, concrete connections between the culture and cult historical observations just outlined and the Holy Communion of the Lord's Supper cannot be made—or only indirectly. Hunger and thirst, community and memory however form important elements of primary religious experience without which the significance of the Lord's Supper cannot be understood.

Moving on to evidence from the Bible, we can first establish that the advent of God's reign in Jesus' appearance, ministry, and destiny is inseparably connected with communal meals. With this interpretation, Jesus stands in the Jewish tradition, which expected a sumptuous feast at the end of days (Isa 25:6; compare Luke 13:29). Jesus' last meal in the company of his disciples took on particular importance, although a comparison of the Gospels shows that the reports interpret this event differently. It is uncertain whether Jesus intended a repetition of this supper, however, it happened: believed to persist beyond his death, the community with Christ could be celebrated only mimetically.

Engaging with it in concrete ways, Paul elaborated the contentual profile of this supper. By metaphorizing the bread (1 Cor 10:16-17), he substantiated the especialness of the community of those sharing in the meal.[56] Common distinctions, as to religious, cultural, social, or sexual affiliation, became unimportant by comparison (see, e.g., Gal 3:28, referring to the baptism). Participants in the meal formed a "solidary group."[57] Theologically, this particular form of community was grounded in the fact that partakers believed it to be a communion with Christ, and therefore with God.

By attaching as much importance to the communion as he did, Paul opened the doors for a profound change of the Lord's Supper, namely the separation of the filling meal from the commemorative meal. In this manner, Paul marked out the central criterion of the supper's meaning and ceremonial form: the solidary community.

Moving on to the systematic determinants, one can observe that, on the basis of the New Testament, early Christian ceremonial practice, and the culture of the time, different interpretations of the meaning of the Lord's Supper emerged that in turn influenced the ceremonial form (for the difficulties with

[56] See Wick, *Die urchristlichen Gottesdienste*, 209.

[57] Christfried Böttrich, "Kinder bei Tische ... Abendmahl mit Kindern aus neutestamentlicher Sicht," *Christenlehre, Religionsunterricht, Praxis* 56 (2003), 9–12, 9.

sources, see Fürst, *Die Liturgie der Alten Kirche*, 10–12). In this process, the sacrifice of the mass was a Western development, later harshly criticized by the Reformers in the form of the Canon prayer. Here, the sacrificial action of the church—practiced to this day in parts of the Catholic Church—superseded the former orientation toward Jesus' ministry and destiny.

Historically grounded and, in terms of content, guided by the German Protestant service book, Karl-Adolf Bauer (b. 1937) construes the tense relationship between meaning and ceremonial form. First, he explains the discrepancy between the claim of the meal character and the actual practice of merely ingesting a wafer and taking a sip of wine by emphasizing that God's reign is only in the offing (Bauer, "'Da wurden ihre Augen geöffnet,'" 4). With regard to content, he underlines the early Christian connection between the Lord's Supper and diaconia (27–31). Finally, he illustrates at the example of the Doxology (*Sanctus*) that the Lord's Supper transcends both space and time (27–31).

This has far-reaching consequences for the celebrating community, as it comprises more people than merely those gathered around the Lord's table. Orthodox liturgy vividly enacts the cosmic dimension that is given by the exaltation of Christ and that negates the linear structure of time: those present as well as the deceased and those who come after us are united in Christ.

As a final point, the important connection between baptism and Holy Communion, which was of major importance to the early Christians and has been elucidated in ecumenical dialog, must be mentioned. As early as the beginning of the second century, the baptism was the only requirement for the communion (*Did.* 9:5). Both rites focus on Jesus Christ in their center: in the baptism, Christians celebrate God's acceptance of the individual, at the Lord's Supper the resulting community with him and the other people united in Christ.

As regards methodology, the first point that needs to be addressed is that the research into the reception of the Lord's Supper by those partaking in it is still in its infancy. Results from this research are necessary to begin thinking about questions of methodology. However, two important areas of focus are already crystallizing:[58] the atmosphere of the ceremony, which apparently is

---

[58] In this I follow Petra Zimmermann, "'Das gebrochene Brot verwandelt mein Leben': Abendmahl aus der Perspektive der Feiernden," *PTh* 93 (2004), 361–70.

much more readily appreciated than the spoken words, and the sense of community, which makes exclusions problematic.

The atmosphere of the celebration refers to its cultural contextualization, since participants tend to bring their general experience with celebrations to the ceremony and interpret their experience in the light of this context. This is particularly true of people who do not regularly attend the communion table and are therefore unfamiliar with church proceedings. It is precisely because many German Protestants abstain from Holy Communion that they must be invited in an appealing manner.

Another sensitive area regularly surfacing in surveys is the question of the community. The most important discussion in this context is concerned with admitting children (before confirmation) to Holy Communion. It should by now be clear for liturgy-historical, systematic, and not least (elementary) educational reasons[59] that the exclusion of children needs to be overcome. Children clearly belong to the solidary community of the Lord's Supper. In a society that largely excludes children, their inclusion questions customary practice from the point of view of the gospel. It provides celebratory practice with fresh impetus by emphasizing the meaning of the solidary group.

Taking the meaning of the Lord's Supper seriously changes its ceremonial form also in other ways. For instance, Andrea Bieler gives an eye-opening account of a brief but stirring extension of the Lord's Supper liturgy in American churches in the times of AIDS. In the Metropolitan Community Church in San Francisco, the pastor after the words of institution takes up the bread and speaks: "We are the body of Christ—and the body of Christ has AIDS."[60] In this community, which between 1982 and 1987 lost approximately five hundred of their members to AIDS, this small addition to the liturgy dramatically highlights what "solidary community" means for those united in Christ: it transcends current distinctions of the lifeworld and opens up new horizons of community—precisely that with God.

If we now take a look at other forms of communication in the context of the Lord's Supper, we find—in parallel with speaking and silence and praying and meditation—a complementary communication form closely related to

---

[59] See Christian Grethlein, "Abendmahl—mit Kindern?! Praktisch-theologische Überlegungen," *ZThK* 106 (2009), 345–70.

[60] Andrea Bieler, "'Und dann durchbricht jemand die absolute Quarantäne und segnet dich': Über die erzählte und die ritualisierte Leib-Gestalt von Krankheit," *ZNT* 14 (2011 H. 27), 57–66, 57.

communal eating and drinking, namely fasting. Culture-historically old, this voluntary abstinence from food has a community-building power, as can be observed during Ramadan in Muslim countries. In biblical times, fasting was a way of communicating with God (see, for specific fast days in the Old Testament, e.g., Lev 16:29-31; for penitential fasting, e.g., Jonah 3:5-8), as can also be seen in the ministry of Jesus (see, e.g., Matt 4:2). This practice was adopted in Christianity, and not only for the Lenten periods in preparation of the great festivities of Easter and Christmas. From the fourth century onward there are reports of so-called eucharistic sobriety.[61] This custom—albeit in vastly extenuated form—was included in the new Codex Iuris Canonici of 1983 (ca. 919: excluding water and medication, one must abstain from food and drink one hour before Communion). In the context with other forms of bodywork, the significance of fasting for one's conduct of life has in the last few years been rediscovered even outside of churches. Sobriety heightens awareness.

Summary

People communicate with God, not only in Christianity. This is why the forms of communication discussed here converge with practices of other faiths. The comparative task incurred by this fact has so far received only reluctant attention. Completing it requires interdisciplinary cooperation with theologians from other faith communities and can at this point only be described as urgent.

As regards content, the central issue is the capacity of the forms of communicating with God to—quite literally—relativize people's attitudes, that is, to bring them into relation with God. "Educating the desire" yields fresh cognitive insights, while singing caters to the affective side of communicating with God.

The manifold transformations of the ceremonial form of the Lord's Supper and the obvious tension between contemporary form and meaning mark important challenges for practical-theological work. The liturgy historically, systematically, and educationally meaningful inclusion of children in Holy Communion could provide an important impetus, if children are truly accepted as equal communicants. In a society that systematically excludes children, the countercultural dimension of the communication of the gospel

---

[61] See Hans Bernhard Meyer, *Eucharistie: Geschichte, Theologie, Pastoral* (GDK 4) (Regensburg, 1989), 231–32.

would thus be brought to bear. In addition, this would strengthen the important bond between family and church community.

3. Helping for Living: Communicating from God

Literature: Dorothea Greiner, *Segen und Segnen: Eine systematisch-theologische Grundlegung* (Stuttgart, ³2003 [1998]); Christian Grethlein, *Grundinformation Kasualien: Kommunikation des Evangeliums an Übergängen des Lebens* (Göttingen, 2007), 63–73, 101–52, 358–407; Ulrich Heckel, *Der Segen im Neuen Testament: Begriff, Formeln, Gesten* (WUNT 150) (Tübingen, 2002); Reinhard Meßner, *Einführung in die Liturgiewissenschaft* (Paderborn, 2001), 59–149; Anita Stauffer, ed., *Baptism, Rites of Passage, and Culture* (Lutheran World Federation Studies 1/1999) (Genf, 1998)

Theologically speaking, it is God's turning toward human beings that is the basis for all communication with him. Nonetheless, it requires human mediation. This poses a considerable communicative challenge.

One of the oldest forms of communicating from God is the blessing. This method, which is grounded in primary religious experience, can of course be found in the biblical texts, but only in the New Testament is it, with reference to Christ, theologically reformatted. To this day, the blessing is the culmination of the worship service and reaches even those that usually come little into contact with church practice.[62]

Similar things are true of healing. With regard to the vulnerability of human life, biblical texts tell of healings in the name of God. Healing was one of the marked characteristics of Jesus' ministry. However, does a culture of high-tech medicine still allow for "healings" in the tradition of Christus medicus, Christ the Physician? A brief glance at everyday life practices and the popularity of "popular religion" tells us that this question cannot be answered from a cognitive point of view alone. It concerns areas of being human that are simply not included in a techno-scientific worldview.

A unique profile is bestowed on the two forms of communication from God, blessing and healing, in the baptism. In the baptism Christians celebrate God's attention to each individual in hope of its unfailing presence throughout life and beyond death. By the initial act of water washing, the baptism

---

[62] See, for an impressive example, Scharfenberg, *Einführung in die Pastoralpsychologie*, 61.

is connected to primary religious experience; simultaneously, it is—at the secondary religious level—a mimesis of Jesus' destiny as initiated by his baptism by John.

Overall, the forms of communication considered in the following are uniquely compatible with the biographical work each individual in a society of options needs to undertake, since they express God's relationship to every single human being in a most tangible way.

Blessing

"Blessings" seem to enjoy a boom in modern societies. In the past fifteen years, the theological and popular literature on this topic has increased by leaps and bounds. The same is true of practical experiments inside and outside of the mainline churches. However, the origin of blessing reaches far back into history. Its biblical reception and transformation opens up a field in need of theological clarification. Superstition, in the sense of exclusively primary religious experience, and the forms of dogmatic reflection that exclusively (wish to) consider secondary religious experience, represent two misguided developments that impede the communication of the gospel. The much needed balance requires methodological rigor.

If we begin by first taking a look at the anthropological and culture-historical foundation, blessing patently refers to each individual's desire for welfare. It contrasts with the many imperilments, by deprivation or sickness, that threaten human existence. From a culture-historical perspective it is therefore understandable that blessing has for a long time been accompanied by its counterpart, the curse, that is, the negation of what blessing seeks.

Greeting and farewell are probably the social situations in which the blessing (and the curse) evolved as a form of communication (see Heckel, *Der Segen im Neuen Testament*, 19), as the farewells in many languages clearly indicate ("goodbye," "adieu," "adiós," etc.). Right from the beginning, blessing and curse are closely related to magic (see Greiner, *Segen und Segnen*, 132). Only the theologization of blessing has drawn a clear line of demarcation. Magical practice is not an open-ended form of communication like the blessing in its Christian sense. Magic aims at direct, usually material success, while the blessing is based on the trust in God's caring attention and dispenses with elaborate methodology and sophisticated esoteric knowledge (137). The Christian blessing is in line with the experience of prayer as a form of communicating with God, whose dialogicity expresses itself in an open-ended communication.

Turning to the biblical treatment of blessing, we find that the Old Testament still knew of the power of blessings and curses in a pretheological sense (see, e.g., Num 22–24). The original family context and the creaturely aspects are vividly illustrated in Isaac blessing his firstborn son (Gen 27).

When Israel had settled down, God's preserving activity within the creation came into view. The priestly account of the creation tells of the divine blessing that rests upon the fish, birds and people (Gen 1:22, 28). Later, the devout Israelites discovered the power of God's blessings in his historical action (e.g., Exod 23:25-27). In the effective history of blessing, the Aaronic Blessing (Num 6:22-27) assumed particular significance, in the main due to Luther's liturgical reception.[63]

> Enacted as an "audience" with God, as it were, the jussive or optative wording, expresses the blessing very well as a form that mediates between transcendence and immanence. In the blessing, God shows himself protective, merciful and pacifying. (Grethlein, *Grundinformation Kasualien*, 65)

As in Old Testament prophecy, blessing, albeit assumed practice, becomes less prominent in the New Testament. Only two personal blessings conveyed by Jesus are reported explicitly: the blessing of the children (Mark 10:16) and the valedictory blessing of his disciples (Luke 24:50). Other than these, Jesus of course bestowed benedictions typical for a devout Jew, by blessing bread and wine (e.g., Mark 6:41; 1 Cor 10:16).

In Paul and his school, the concept became theologically more elaborate, by relating it to Christ. Paul spoke of "the blessing of the gospel of Christ" (Rom 15:29), and finally Christ himself was understood as a "blessing" (Eph 1:3-14), relating back to the promise of blessing for Abraham (see Heckel, *Der Segen im Neuen Testament*, 238–41), which transcended the limitation to earthly matters hitherto inherent in blessing.

Let us now turn to the systematic determinants. Owing to the desire of each human being for welfare, the benediction is a particularly attractive and at the same time precarious form of the communication of the gospel. Its fundamentally catabatic structure, that is, being received from God,

---

[63] See Frieder Schulz, "Segnende Kirche und christlicher Glaube," *Gemeinsame Arbeitsstelle für gottesdienstliche Fragen* 28 (1997), 42–65, 47–48.

was throughout Christian history repeatedly in danger of being misused to manipulate God. Two particularly problematic tendencies can be observed:[64] The primary meaning of thanksgiving implied in the basic meaning of the Greek for the verb "to bless" (*eulogein*: literally, "to speak well [of]," meaning "to praise") already increasingly gave way to the plea in early Christianity. The defense against evil, ritualized in the form of the exorcism, became preeminently important. Moreover, the number of benedictions increased; those who bestowed the blessing, acting on the strength of their own authority, incorporated bits and pieces of other actions to increase its effective power.

The Reformers emphatically rejected these aberrations (e.g., WA 50,647), as they for instance materialized in the constant use of so-called holy water. This line of argument however made it difficult to capture the uniqueness of this form of communication. Consequently, Luther unceremoniously subsumed benedictions under the sermon (see, for a critical view, Greiner, *Segen und Segnen*, 211–49).

Only recently has the potential of blessing, in the tradition of the Reformation, begun to be (re)discovered. Female theologians arguing from a feminist perspective have warned against the danger of Docetism—similar to that of magic—in the communication of the gospel. Contrary to these forms, blessing implies "corporeality and sensory experience" (132). Blessing is a tender, motherly gesture (see 76), which gives expression to aspects hitherto neglected in the Christian understanding of God. Since receiving a blessing does not require any activity, it is a form of communication with a low threshold. Everybody can receive a blessing, independent of their age, level of education, or even involvement with the church.

As regards methodology, traditionally—and biblically grounded—personal blessing is conferred by a laying on of hands. This act expresses the individual's need of God's caring attention. The use of water or perhaps oil may also provide a pleasant stimulus. The sign of the cross relates the act of blessing to Jesus Christ. At the same time, it is of central importance that the blessing be performed as an expression of God's caring attention and not as a sacerdotal act. It may be a vital form of expression for the individual as a sensually perceptive being, but God's attention is quite independent of it.

---

[64] See, for the following, Christian Grethlein, "Benediktionen und Krankensalbung," in Schmidt-Lauber, Meyer-Blanck, and Bieritz, *Handbuch der Liturgik*, 551–74, 555–59.

The trust in God expressed in the jussive or optative moods ("The Lord bless . . .") and at the same time in recognition of his freedom suggests cautiousness. The act of blessing involves the gesture, and in personal blessings generally physical contact; the purpose of these forms of expression, however, is to express God's communication with individuals, and not to stimulate his actions. The christological, New Testament reserve with regard to the priesthood takes form in the act of blessing: a restriction of gestures of blessing to particular office holders is therefore misguided.

It follows from a christologically grounded understanding of the act that the blessing of objects only makes theological sense with regard to the specific use of these objects. A brief glance at the history of these kinds of blessing however reveals its problematic application—if one thinks of the blessing of weapons, or the inauguration of army barracks and the like. Quite obviously, it seems to be difficult to keep the balance between the necessary contextualization of the communication of the gospel and its imperative countercultural dimension. Both withdrawal from public life as well as uncritical affirmation of human productions need to be avoided.

The most essential criterion of distinction traditionally hearkens back to the exegesis of 1 Timothy 4:4: the question is whether the object to be blessed is a good gift of creation or can otherwise be received in thankfulness (Gr. *eucharistia*).

With regard to other forms of communication, the anointment is a form that is closely related to blessing. The historical reason for this is that oil was an important medicinal substance in antiquity (see Grethlein, *Grundinformation Kasualien*, 361). Today, its secular relevance is due to the widespread use of perfume. Anointing, the tactile contact with oil, is therefore at the physical level perceived as beneficial caring attention and supports the comforting and encouraging words of the blessing.

Another action closely related with blessing is to be standing. Standing up expresses "respect, attention, reverence," and has always been regarded as "a sign of the paschal existence of the redeemed."[65] By contrast, the—equally common—act of kneeling down while receiving the blessing is a gesture of receiving.

---

[65] Ronald Sequeira, "Gottesdienst als menschliche Ausdruckshandlung," in Berger et al., *Gestalt des Gottesdienstes*, 7–39, 32.

One thing that has almost completely disappeared from theological discussions of blessing is its complementary form, the curse. Everyday language, however, preserves the memory of the dark side of the benediction. Disasters and other forms of calamity, for instance, are often spoken about in terms of a curse that has fallen on people or things. The fact that dark side still preoccupies people, as fantasy literature, movies, and TV shows attest, needs to be borne in mind when wording the blessing.

Healing

Healing, as an ancient form of communication, forms a constitutive part of the communication of the gospel. The majority of Christian churches, including Protestant denominations, celebrates "healing rites" to this day (see Stauffer, *Baptism*, 93–150).

The anthropological and culture-historical roots of healing lie of course in the basic facts of health and sickness. The understanding of these facts is too a high degree culture-dependent. Differences express themselves primarily in the assumed causes for illness—which are decisive for the healing practices:

> Demons may be thought to cause disease; they again may be embodied in animals. Another cause for disease may be the wrath of the gods. This is connected with the idea of disease as a punishment, for which all kinds of offences or trespasses against the divine order can be the cause. A final form of interpreting sickness is as a time of trial and testing. (Grethlein, *Grundinformation Kasualien*, 360–61)

Healing procedures apply accordingly: demons are exorcized; the sick are absolved and thereby try to propitiate the gods; others see their lot as a trial to be endured.

To complete the picture, modern ideas of sickness and health need to be sketched in here. The definition of specific conditions rest on the scientific paradigm; accordingly, healing procedures (therapy) are based on technological applications. In contrast to earlier interpretations, the cosmological dimension is lacking, having fallen victim to the "disenchantment" described by Taylor. This techno-scientific understanding of sickness and health has however not gained general acceptance. Shamans and spiritual healers also practice in modern societies.

Looking at the biblical perspectives, one first of all does not find any clear-cut terminology for "sick" and "healthy." But we encounter people in a "state of weakness, of weariness and exhaustion, that is to say, a somehow broken vitality."[66] This was explained in terms of the patterns just described above (for the following, also see Grethlein, *Grundinformation Kasualien*, 361–62): sickness was God's punishment (Exod 9:14-15; Num 12:9-14; etc.), to which the afflicted reacted by undergoing rites of penance (e.g., Ps 38), and trusting in the help of God (Ps 103:2-5). Later texts, especially the Book of Job, expound the problems of the connection between deeds and consequences (e.g., Prov 3:7). Compared to the surrounding peoples, the Israelites display a marked restraint regarding common practices and also physicians. Appealing to Yahweh came first, the visit to the physician (see 2 Chr 16:12).

The New Testament of course tells of the many healings of Jesus (see Grethlein, *Grundinformation Kasualien*, 364). As shown, Jesus interpreted these actions as the coming of God's reign. This corresponded with the close relationship between his doing and the faith of the healed (see, e.g., Mark 5:34). Overall, Jesus' therapeutic interventions were overlaid by his message of the incipient kingdom of God. On closer analysis, Jesus' healing ministry does not display any consistent concept of disease and healing. One time, he assumes the relationship between sin and sickness (see, e.g., Mark 2:5), which he rejects on another occasion (John 9:2-3). Sickness, like God's relationship with each person, appears to be something that needs to be interpreted individually.

His disciples continued Jesus' healing ministry (1 Cor 12:9, 28, 30; Mark 6:12-13), which led to further interpretations of sickness. Paul, for instance, saw his own chronic affliction—after fruitless prayers for healing—as the will of God and a sign of his apostolate (2 Cor 12:7-8). The Anointing of the Sick in James 5:13-16 became particularly important in the reception history. At the center of this rite was the prayer of the eldest at the sickbed and the anointment of the invalid with oil. The possible connection of sickness and sin and the resulting necessity of forgiveness of sins are implied.

Let us now turn to the systematic determinants for this communication form. While the first Christians continued Jesus' healing ministry, they however spiritualized it and worshiped Christ as "medicus" in a soteriological sense.[67] Likewise, the Anointing of the Sick in James 5:13-16 was mod-

---

[66] Wolff, *Anthropologie des Alten Testaments*, 211.

[67] For the development of this motif, see Johannes Mette, *Heilung durch Gottesdienst? Ein liturgietheologischer Beitrag* (Studien zur Pastoralliturgie 24) (Regensburg, 2010), 200–208.

ified.[68] In keeping with the general tendency to clericalize ecclesial action, ritual action became bound to the priest. This changed the rite in a radical fashion: the Anointing of the Sick turned into the Last Rites, which were administered—as a common practice from the end of the eighth century onward—by the priest at the deathbed.

Martin Luther criticized this development as a misinterpretation of James 5:13-16 (WA 6,567–73). He also rejected the elevation of this action to a sacrament. In doing so, he however problematically pitted the Christian faith against the anointment. The criticism of the malpractice of the act eventually led to its discontinuation in Protestant churches. Second Vatican Council finally reversed the unbiblical conception of the Last Rite, and gave priority again to the Anointing of the Sick.

The Anglican Church and North American churches have for some time sought to establish a theologically responsible ritual treatment of sickness. The distinction between "cure" (to restore to health) and "healing" (to make sound or whole) has proven helpful in this regard.[69] This distinction makes for a meaningful cooperation with physicians. On the one hand, it helps specify what to expect of the healing rite: it is about God's relationship with the individual. The purpose of "healing" is to let the individual experience God's caring attention in a difficult situation. On the other hand, it helps prevent people from expecting too much of modern medicine. Modern medicine's reductionist focus on single parts of a person brings remarkable physical outcomes, but fails to fulfill the human desire for holistic care and attention. Especially the problem of mortality cannot be solved by medicine.

Considering methodological approaches, one can first observe that healing as a form of helping for living (in a sense that transcends the biological end) occurs in many different ways, which are reflected in hospital chaplaincy and in liturgics. The following four steps provide a meaningful setting for the Anointing of the Sick in a liturgical form:

I. Arrive, open up: feel, breathe, remain silent, sing, pray.
II. Hear that God does you good: address.

[68] See Reiner Kaczynski, "Feier der Krankensalbung," in *Sakramentliche Feiern* I/2 (GDK 7,2), ed. Reinhard Meßner and Reiner Kaczynski (Regensburg, 1992), 241–343, 258–304.
[69] Paul Nelson, "Healing Rites for Serious Chronic Illness in the North American Cultural Context," in Stauffer, *Baptism*, 93–104, 100.

III. Experience that God does you good: anointment.
IV. At the end, the pastor will show you out.[70]

Attention to atmosphere is crucial. Evening hours are particularly suitable: dimmed lights in the church are conducive to inner composure. The singing of Taizé and evening songs has also proven successful. A guided meditation helps to leave everyday concerns behind. The address should be brief, approximately a five-minute "sermonette." For the anointing, it is important to leave it up to the participants if and in what manner they wish to partake. The celebration ends with a travel blessing suggesting that everybody is one a life journey and that the celebration is a moment of rest.

In churches that have already been celebrating "healing rites" for some time, the baptism is often the central point of reference, the "baptismal community"[71] forming the social space for the celebration.

Finally, another important situation for the communication of the gospel in the mode of healing is pastoral care. The laying on of hands and anointing before major surgery, for example, are important ways of caregiving. They are manifestations of God's caring attention. On the whole, the following holds true: "Nobody has a claim to physical health. Healing in an evangelical sense can take on many different forms, right down to facilitating a passing away in comfort and confidence" (Grethlein, *Grundinformation Kasualien*, 387).

As regards further forms of communication, some of the forms that have emerged in Christian history are closely connected to healing. Some of the more important forms are doing penance, or confessing, and counseling. Guilt can encumber or even destroy lives. This is why asking and hoping for forgiveness is a concern that informs the Bible throughout (see, e.g., Ps 32:5; John 20:23; James 5:16), and which aims at healing the individual.

Reviewing Christian history and the diverse and variable developments of first penitence and then confession betray the difficulties they posed with regard to their concrete form. The early form of public penitence following the baptism, under strict requirements and resulting in admittance to the eucharistic community, was followed by phases of privatization and spiritualization, and finally juridification. The consequences arising from the latter, as for

[70] Waldemar Pisarski, *Gott tut gut: Salbungsgottesdienste: Grundlagen und Modelle* (Munich, 2000), 72.

[71] "Chicago Statement on Worship and Culture: Baptism und Rites of Life Passage," Stauffer, *Baptism*, 13–24, 20.

instance the dread of judgment, caused serious problems,[72] and it is precisely this development that incited the Reformers' protest.

The Reformers, however, did not succeed in giving penance a convincing form. The close connection of penance to the Holy Communion proved to be difficult for a strongly subjective piety. Consequently, Pietist theologians protested, among other things, against insufficient preparation, the absence of a confessional conversation, and the lack of church discipline. In the Reformed churches, individual confession—in spite of Calvin's enthusiastic endorsement—did not manage to gain acceptance; instead, the trend developed toward personal confession. This, however, could not adequately answer the need for a form of communication capable of addressing inconsistencies and problems surfacing in individual behavior.

In the meantime, this has been transformed under the pastoral-psychological paradigm of counseling. Yet it remains an open question whether this is an appropriate or adequate translation of the early Christian concept of penance and confession into contemporary culture. Be that as it may, the growing numbers of visitors to clerical counseling centers show that people are seeking help for living here.

Baptizing

Communicating from God finds particularly striking expression in the act of baptism. The individual is being baptized (passive mode); the succinct baptismal formula relates the water rite to the triune God. For early Christians, the baptism was the form of communication from which the "essence" of being a Christian was derived:[73] the baptism was the sign of Christianity and one of the most important events in the life of the community and of the individual. Yet, from the fourth century onward, a process of marginalization was underway, which even the Reformers were not able to stop. Only since being Christian is no longer a matter of course and church membership is declining, can a delay of this development be noticed.[74]

---

[72] For the following, see Lins, "Buße und Beichte," 326.

[73] See Alfons Fürst, *Die Liturgie der Alten Kirche: Geschichte und Theologie* (Münster, 2008), 100.

[74] For the following, see Christian Grethlein, *Taufpraxis in Geschichte, Gegenwart und Zukunft* (Leipzig, 2014).

The first thing to observe with regard to the anthropological and culture-historical foundations of this rite, is the central sensory role of water. Water elicits primary religious experience at many different levels: it is purifying and refreshing; as a fountain, it enables life; as the primal flood, it threatens life and brings destruction. To this day, many faith communities perform rites involving water. In myths, water plays a central role, generally in connection with the creation of the world.

In terms of ritual theory, baptism can be understood as an initiation rite (see Grethlein, *Grundinformation Kasualien*, 99–100). Referring to research from the field of religious studies, Reinhard Meßner distinguishes three types of initiation rites:

- age group initiation (primarily puberty rites of passage into adulthood);
- esoteric initiation (admission into an esoteric society);
- vocational initiation (as for instance that of a shaman; this type differs from the closely related second type above all in the central significance of the ecstatic moment). (Meßner, *Einführung in die Liturgiewissenschaft*, 60)

The baptism oscillates between the first two types. At its inception, the risky adoption into the Christian community, it became for many centuries a ritual following birth. Only the twentieth century witnessed a reversal of the trend. The change in baptismal age (see Grethlein, *Grundinformation Kasualien*, 121–23) opens the appreciation of the baptism again toward an "esoteric initiation."

From the biblical perspective, the first point to note is that the Christian rite of baptism emerged in the context of the Jewish Baptist movement, to which also John the Baptist belonged. While his baptizing Jesus is an important foundation, a direct historical link can however not be derived, since the meaning of the Christian baptism constitutes itself in relation to Jesus Christ and the initiation into a new community—two characteristics absent from John's baptism.

The oldest reports of baptisms can be found in the Acts of the Apostles. Baptisms took place in varying contexts. They were preceded by a convincing sermon (Acts 8:2), Scriptural study and interpretation (Acts 8:30-35), general hearsay (Acts 16:14), a reception of the Holy Spirit and glossolalia (Acts

10:44-46), or an audition followed by a healing (Acts 9:3-19). This pluriform practice corresponds with the pluriform interpretations of the baptism in connection with discrete theological concepts: it may be a forgiveness of sins (e.g., Acts 2:38), the reception of the Holy Spirit (e.g., Acts 2:38), the communion with Christ (Rom 6:3-10), adoption into a new community (1 Cor 12:13), justification and sanctification (1 Cor 6:11), filiation to Abraham (Gal 3:27-29), rebirth (Titus 3:5), or "circumcision" (Col 2:11). Already in the New Testament, the rite lent itself to many interpretations that were adapted according to biographical circumstance or situation.

A theologically far-reaching interpretation was bestowed on it in Romans 6, according to which the baptizands were crucified and buried together with Christ, their resurrection however lying in the future. The baptism is thus understood as a lifelong process that is only completed in death.

Let us now turn to the systematic determinants. While the baptism was practiced from the inception of Christianity, the procedure and the meaning of the water rite changed considerably. The *Apostolic Tradition* tells of a richly elaborate ritual. Over the course of the centuries, three problematic reductions occurred (see Grethlein, *Grundinformation Kasualien*, 110–13). The baptism lost its relationship to catechetical action, ethics, and the Lord's Supper. During the first centuries, several years of catechumenate prepared for the reception of the baptism. This practice for adults was abandoned when, in the fourth to fifth centuries, baptizing infants became the norm. In this manner, the baptism lost its catechetical (or pedagogical) context and was emptied of its content. As communities became larger, bishops were not able anymore to baptize children immediately after birth. In a time of high infant mortality, the parents nevertheless demanded that their newborns be baptized lest their souls be condemned. Local priests were therefore charged with administering the baptism. The bishop, however, reserved the right to the baptismal imposition of hands, which symbolized the gift of the Spirit. From this emerged, in a long process, the confirmation. Since the confirmation was administered by the bishop, it was soon held in higher esteem than the baptism, which was only conferred by the subordinate priest. The baptism's relationship with the gift of the Spirit and parenesis was thus lost. Eventually, at the end of the twelfth century, an increasing number of voices deemed the communion of the baptized, which was common practice, unnecessary. Under the influence of a cognitively narrowed understanding of their faith, the communion of infants seemed inadmissible. As a consequence, it was prohibited in the

West—while the liturgically conservative East practices it to this day. The West thus lost the relationship of baptism and the Lord's Supper, and the relationship between baptism and the community loosened.

The Reformers were unaware of these problematic developments. Luther, it is true, tried to strengthen the significance of the baptism as an act commanded by Christ and criticized the sacramentalization of the confirmation (see, e.g., WA 6:549–50). Not least, he rediscovered the pastoral power of the baptism,[75] and emphasized its lifelong process character (see, e.g., BSLK 516). All this notwithstanding, it did not engender any drastic changes in baptismal practice. The nominalist bent of Luther's theology stood in the way of an independent appreciation of the baptismal symbols (see Grethlein, *Grundinformation Kasualien*, 116).

The process of marginalizing the baptism continued through the ages of Pietism and the Enlightenment. The emphasis on a resolute and conscious faith opposed a liturgy that emphasized God's doing. The baptism degenerated into a family celebration in the context of birth.

Later criticism of infant baptism failed to acknowledge the celebratory form of the baptism. In his later work, Karl Barth attempted to change this rite that explicitly enacts the individual's passiveness toward God into an act of decision-making.[76] Only its decline in self-evidence brought the baptism and the question of appropriate practice into the focus of practical-theological reflection[77] and ecclesial praxis.

Considering methodological approaches, it stands to reason that the most fundamental challenge under contemporary circumstances is to recover the processual character of the baptism, that is, as an orientation encompassing the whole life of a Christian. The following suggestions might provide.

For one, the discipline of symbol didactics opens up a new avenue to the formal aspects of the baptism. This approach takes account of the baptism as a rite, and therefore as a form of communication, which is centered on the use of symbols. From an ecumenical perspective, the analysis of baptism as communication yields five basic symbols: the cross, water, names, laying on of hands,

---

[75] See Christian Grethlein, "Seelsorge im Kontext der Taufe," in *Handbuch der Seelsorge: Grundlagen und Profile*, ed. Wilfried Engemann (Leipzig, 2007), 411–27, 421–22.

[76] See Karl Barth, *Kirchliche Dogmatik* 4/4 (Zürich, 1967), 81.

[77] See Robert Leuenberger, *Taufe in der Krise* (Stuttgart, 1973); Christian Grethlein, *Taufpraxis heute: Praktisch-theologische Überlegungen zu einer theologisch verantworteten Gestaltung der Taufpraxis im Raum der EKD* (Gütersloh, 1988).

and the candle. These symbols are doubly suited for the communication of the gospel in the mode of the baptism: on the one hand, they are familiar from daily life, while on the other hand, by virtue of their ambivalence they open up an interpretive space that enables the individual to make their baptism their own. In Christian history, the rites of passage have established themselves as liturgies referring to primary religious experience; however, with regard to content, they are difficult to define. Firmly relating them to the lifelong process of the baptism helps to embed them in a meaningful context: school entry service, confirmation, marriage service, anointment of the sick, and funeral service then only mark different stops on the baptismal path (Grethlein, *Grundinformation Kasualien*, 390–407). Finally the Remembrance of Baptism plays a key role in adopting the baptism as a lifelong process.

With regard to other, closely related forms of communication, we already find a close relationship between baptism and exorcism in the *Apostolic Tradition*. In preparing for baptism, the baptizands renounce Satan. While presupposing a dualistic worldview whose biblical foundation is doubtful, this nevertheless expresses the principal endangerment of every human being. Pleas to God for liberation from evil during baptism are possible and meaningful:[78] trustingly, they bring the ambivalence of human life before God (see Matt 6:13). Accordingly, one finds in more recent baptismal agendas an—optional—renunciation of evil (abrenuntiatio diabolic),[79] which can be understood as a translation of early Christian exorcisms into a modern context.

Summary

The forms of communicating from God, due to their reference to the body and the senses, stand in close relationship to the common human practice of magic. From a communication-theoretical perspective, however, they can be clearly separated. While magic interventions aim at instrumentalizing God or divine powers to gain personal, generally material, benefit, the communication of the gospel is marked by dialogicity and open-endedness. The freedom of God remains untouched. Granting these assumptions, the appeal that blessing holds for many people awaits a constructive response. Equally, the

---

[78] See the interesting new interpretation of exorcism in Manfred Probst and Klemens Richter, *Exorzismus oder Liturgie zur Befreiung vom Bösen* (Münster, 2002), esp. 14–17.

[79] See, e.g., Kirchenkanzlei der Evangelischen Kirche der Union, ed., *Taufbuch: Agende für die Evangelische Kirche der Union*, vol. 2 (Berlin, 2000), 23.

manifest desideratum with regard to healing needs to be addressed in a resolute manner. The difference between "cure" and "healing" accurately defines the scope of the challenge: the techno-scientific reduction to "cure" inherent in modern medicine is, for the benefit of the people, in dire need of complementary "healing rites."

Finally, in the imitation of Jesus, the baptism celebrates God's caring for the individual. Through its symbols, it opens up a wide space for interpretation that needs to be ritualized and adapted to biographical and situational needs. Occasional services mark stations on the baptismal path and all forms of remembering the baptism help express the processual character of baptism. Again, the great relevance of the Christian family as ecclesia becomes apparent.

Summary of Part III

A Practical Theology centering on the communication of the gospel leads to an analysis of concrete methods. In this regard, the traditional practical-theological disciplines elaborate important insights that need to be developed communication-theoretically and with theological precision relating to the gospel.

The first striking observation is that the three elementary communication forms of telling, praying, and blessing show a remarkable continuity: they are quite evidently cross-cultural in their fundamental principles thereby providing the basis of the communication of the gospel and the dialog with other life and value orientations. It is a primary task of pastors and the church to provide support in the different social forms of telling biblical stories, praying, and blessing.

By contrast, the communication forms of preaching, celebrating the Lord's Supper, and baptizing have throughout Christian history been subject to various modifications and radical transformations: meaning and celebratory form were frequently in danger of being divorced. Today, sacralizations and exalted allocations of meaning, established only in dogmatic history, obscure the connection of these acts with daily life. The task here is to transform the significance of each of these acts into a form of celebration intelligible to all. In doing so, the contextual and the countercultural implications need to be balanced against each other.

The middle ground, as it were, is occupied by speaking with one another, singing, and healing: on the one hand, these forms are today cultivated in the specific areas of education, in (church) music, in the health care sector. For this reason they are methodologically sophisticated, but restricted to their respective domains. On the other hand, they are practiced in everyday life— generally unobserved, but extremely efficiently—first and foremost in (multi-local multigenerational) families. The crucial task here is to make professional knowledge available and productive for daily life, and, conversely, to incorporate people's needs into theory-driven praxis.

INDEX OF NAMES

SUBJECT INDEX